Other books by Dr. Wood

Principles of Critical Care. Eds J.B. Hall, G.A. Schmidt, and L.D.H. Wood. McGraw-Hill, New York 1992, 1998, 2005, 2012: pp 2304, 1767, 1778.

Principles of Critical Care: Companion Handbook. Eds J.B. Hall, G.A. Schmidt, and L.D.H. Wood. McGraw-Hill, New York 1993, 1999. pp 605, 1070.

Principles of Critical Care: Pre-Test Self Assessment and Review. Eds J.B. Hall, G.A. Schmidt, and L.D.H. Wood. McGraw-Hill, New York 1991, 1998: pp 230, 239.

SCIENCE, BELIEF, INTUITION:

Reflections of a Physician

L.D.H. WOOD, MD PhD

BALBOA.
PRESS

A DIVISION OF HAY HOUSE

Balboa Press books may be ordered through booksellers or by contacting:

Balboa Press
A Division of Hay House
1663 Liberty Drive
Bloomington, IN 47403
www.balboapress.com
1-(877) 407-4847

ISBN: 978-1-4525-4961-3 (e)
ISBN: 978-1-4525-4962-0 (sc)
ISBN: 978-1-4525-4963-7 (hc)

Library of Congress Control Number: 2012905704

Printed in the United States of America

Balboa Press rev. date: 04/11/2012

To
Liam Lionel Wood
my first grandchild

At the age of 2, he listened
as I whispered stories in his ear.
At 3 years old, he sat facing me in the blue chairs
and said "Let's discuss something".
At 4, he took his Grampa golfing
where he consistently hit the ball 100 yards and straight
and putted for par on many holes.
At 5, he read the _Chronicles of Narnia_ and
became a playful caring big brother for Ansel.
At 6 he read _The Hobbit_ and _Fellowship of the Ring,_
played in a Golf Tournament in Scotland
and excelled at Quiz Bowl at school.

For Liam is the promise of the future
who lives the interface of science and spirituality.

◇◇◇

Then Yahweh Himself passed by.
A strong and heavy wind was rending the mountains
and crushing rocks before the Lord—
but the Lord was not in the wind.
After the wind was an earthquake—
but the Lord was not in the earthquake.
After the earthquake was fire—
but the Lord was not in the fire.
After the fire was a tiny whispering sound
when he heard this, Elijah hid his face in his cloak.

NAB 1 Kings 19: 11-13

◇◇◇

CONTENTS

LIST OF ILLUSTRATIONS

Figure 1 – Science is Sometimes Misinterpreted
Figure 2 – Methods of Inquiry
Figure 3 – A gift From Elaine to Larry in 1980

LIST OF TABLES

Table 1: Sequential Steps of Science and Belief
Table 2: Limitations of Inquiry and Knowing
Table 3: Therapeutic Goals in AHRF
Table 4: Characteristics of the Still Small Voice
Table 5: Attributes of Methods of Inquiry
Table 6: Teaching Schedule
Table 7: Research Programs and Publications

LIST OF POEMS

Winter
Dining
Questions of a Mustard Seed
Six Years Later
Teaching

AUTHOR'S PREFACE

It was 10:30pm when my home phone rang. The Dean's message was terse: "Larry, the 30 year old daughter of a friend is moribund in the ICU of a nearby hospital. He asks that you see her." At her bedside an hour later, my examination confirmed her hyperactive circulation and low blood pressure (90/40) likely due to a serious infection (T = 39°C), complicated by excess liquid in her lungs with 4-quadrant air space filling on her chest x-ray, due in part to excess circulating volume as indicated by a pulmonary artery occlusion pressure (PAOP) of 24mm. hg. She was intubated and ventilated with 100% oxygen, positive end expiratory pressure (PEEP) of 20 cm H2O, and a tidal volume of 800 ml at 20 breaths/min. She was oliguric, comatose, and receiving a large intravenous dose of broad spectrum antibiotics.

As I examined her, I prayed silently "Lord, Agnes is dying, what can I do to help her get better?" Out of the noisy background of her ICU cubicle, through the bells and whistles of alarm systems and the chug-chug sound of her laboring ventilator came the still small voice *"less circulating volume, more dobutamine, less ventilation, less PEEP."*

Recognizing each as plausible interventions not tried together yet in her management, we began. First we cut the tidal volume in half to a volume more appropriate to her size and acute lung disease, and reduced the ventilator rate to 12 breaths per minute. Immediately, the auto-PEEP fell from 8 to zero cm H_2O and her blood pressure (BP) increased without much increase in $PaCO_2$. Then we removed 4 units of blood from her indwelling arterial line. As her BP decreased, we increased dobutamine from 2 to 12 microg/kg/min, and PAOP decreased to 4 cm H_2O. Her urine output increased to 80 ml/hour. Then we progressively decreased PEEP in small decrements to 8 centimeters H_2O overnight. By dawn, her cardiopulmonary status was nearly normal.

As I left to make ICU rounds at the University of Chicago, I prayed "Thank you Lord", still wondering whose voice I heard. So there I was, living the interface of science and belief.

TELLING THE STORY

Reflection on my life as a Physician revealed inclinations to spirituality and science. Spirituality is my awareness of a relationship with a personal higher power characterized by her loving acceptance and affirmation, and by my experiences of awe, wonder, delight and gratitude in our communication and in my interactions with all of creation. Science is the evidence-based generation of knowledge—the discipline that channeled my curiosity about how the world works. Together, science and spirituality were 2 lenses though which I came to know how the world operates. Science looked outward to describe the physical world around me, and spirituality looked inward for purpose and meaning. Given these different goals there could be no antagonism between them, and their considerable overlap often left me living their interface. Self reflection and review of this topic reveals that there are many more beliefs than scientific truths which help people navigate the vagaries of life. How I integrated my worldviews seen through each of these lenses informs many of the transactions in my life, making this book read like a memoir: a narrative of my life as it evolved around science and belief as methods of inquiry used to discover truth. For 30 years, I had kept a spiritual journal meant to keep track of happenings in my life, often expressed as conversations between me and the still small voice (see Chapter 6). At times of outstanding events, I wrote poems. I include five of those poems at appropriate places in this book to express the accompanying feelings and emotional intelligence revealed in the stories.

The story begins as I complete my medical internship in 1967 and assume a research position with the Canadian Armed Forces in Toronto. There I learned research techniques and philosophy before moving to McGill University as a PhD candidate. In 1972, I returned to Winnipeg to complete my residency in Internal Medicine and my Fellowship in Critical Care. Along the way, I lost my marriage, separated from my children and lived for 3 years with the Marianist religious community where I experienced a quantum leap forward in my psychospiritual journey. At a spiritual retreat in Pecos, NM in 1979 I met Elaine from Chicago, who brought me back to life and to the University of Chicago after a wonder filled courtship and sabbatical/wedding trip to Israel and New Zealand. At Chicago, I established a first rate academic Critical Care program with strong research, education and patient care components put in place between 1982 and 1987. My calling as a Medical educator grew rapidly, aided by my role in chairing a task force on review and revision of the medical school curriculum in 1994. This lead to my appointment as the Dean for Medical Education in 1996. During this time Elaine and I were engaged in spiritual growth through leadership of diverse programs in our parish, and then through a six week course in the school for charismatic spiritual directors back in Pecos, NM. I retired in 2003 to tend to a new diagnosis of Parkinson's Disease, moving back to Canada for the next phase of our life.

SCIENCE AND BELIEF–METHODS OF INQUIRY AND KNOWING

People are curious and like to know about their surroundings. Some even want to know how they know. More than ever before, we live in a scientific age where our understanding is gained by science, the evidence-based generation of knowledge. It defines a process—the Scientific Method—of observation, forming and testing hypotheses to explain phenomena and falsifying, confirming, or repeating experiments by independent reviewers. This method of inquiry confirms results or finds errors. It is slow and tedious because there are so many possible explanations to be excluded before a plausible statement of reality stands out. The Scientific Method has acquired a good reputation for finding truth, but it is sometimes given too much credit, leading to over interpretation of its findings and to being mimicked by belief. Not that science ever proves anything—it only falsifies. And science has nothing to say about many subjective issues of great interest. What the Scientific Method does best is help us avoid illusions stemming from projection of pre-conceived ideas, for people tend to see what they expect. Accordingly, we disprove hypotheses and reality or truth is what is left. Searchers who reflect on their beliefs find the majority have not been put to the test in large part because we do not have ways to measure beliefs, and so we cannot prove them false.

Not too long ago, the principles of science were not generally practiced, so another method of inquiry prevailed. Belief is a state or habit of mind in which trust or confidence is placed in some person or idea without convincing evidence. Compared to science, belief lacks a method to disprove it, for the substance of belief is subjective. God is a common focus of belief, but we have no "Godometer" and it is difficult to refute hypotheses built on the subjective. In their book, Andrew Newberg and Mark Waldman[1] outline contemporary understanding of brain function as serving two purposes: a) self preservation and maintenance, by describing what is out there and how to deal with it, and b) self transcendence, by which the brain changes as we undergo major changes from birth to death. In both functions, the brain acts to interpret or make sense of disparate data in our surroundings. If it has no experience with how they go together, the brain makes it up—a myth or a belief, often without supporting evidence or proof. And so the brain is a great myth-making machine. This can serve survival, but hardly contributes to new knowledge. Indeed one wonders how we ever got to know anything.

INTUITION AND THE STILL SMALL VOICE

In this book, I raise and discuss the possibility that proof of belief is the still small voice confirming or denying the questions we ask Her[1] about beliefs. Bill Hybels recently published a compilation of incidents by which his life was profoundly influenced by hearing and following the still small voice[2]. Citing characteristics of God's voice, he wrote as Pastor to his entire congregation of Willow Creek near Chicago one Friday afternoon requesting they write him about any spiritual experiences in which they believe God spoke to them. By the following Monday, his e-mail was flooded with over 500 replies! I told you that

---

[1] My belief system includes God's gender as both masculine and feminine, so I alternate randomly.

to tell you this—God's whisper is a common occurrence among believers, and it may constitute a proof of whatever belief is under scrutiny.

When the still small voice is heard, distinguishing it from intuition is difficult. Intuition is defined as a quick and ready insight, or the power of attaining knowledge without evident thought or inference. The most obvious distinctions between the still small voice and intuition are the words. Intuition is an awareness that comes wordlessly, while the insight provided by the still small voice is often captured by recalling the words heard. Beliefs ratified by intuition or the still small voice constitute a spiritual source of knowledge which may be a method of inquiry as effective as the scientific method. Furthermore, in any comparison with science, belief is more than a method of inquiry, for beliefs which seem true also build relationship with God, provide gifts more than expected, and pursue explanations of interior experiences more effectively.

Interface is defined as the process or place where independent and often-unrelated systems act on each other, for example, science and belief. As a man devoted to exploring the discipline of Medicine with the investigative tools of science, I often found myself living the interface of that science with my beliefs. When I purported to being instructed by a still small voice within, I sensed no conflict with my efforts to ensure objectivity in testing hypotheses. In fact, scientific revelation often caused me to give thanks and praise to the God of my beliefs. So science enhanced belief! On the other hand, when I was stuck in processing the results of an experiment and found myself seeking insight through prayer, the new interpretations of my data were easily attributed to my God. So belief enhances science!

I believe I am far from alone in noticing this interface, that a growing number of people are drawn to explain life or to understand it as living this interface of science and belief. Such company is the intended audience for this book, which attempts to define and reveal how I live this interface of science and belief. Growing interest in the relationship between science and spirituality is evident in the birth of relevant publications, such as _War of the Worldviews_[3], and _Principles of Neurotheology_[4]. Neurotheology is the discipline which studies correlations of neural phenomena with subjective experiences of spirituality, as well as hypotheses to explain these phenomena. This discipline offers promise to provide Neuroscientific explanations for spiritual experiences.

In my sub-specialty of Pulmonary and Critical Care Medicine, the prevalence of suffering and death in our patient population tends to bring spiritual concerns out into the open. My activities as a teacher in the School of Medicine and as Dean of Medical Education brought me in contact with diverse manifestations of spirituality and science. I believe there is a large interest in the medical community in how one lives the interface of science and belief. My transactions relating science and belief described in this book are a basis for discussion of living this interface, where I attempt to explain how science and belief work in the life of a Physician-Educator who believes a lot. I hope the reader will find part of themselves in my stories.

ACKNOWLEDGEMENTS

Many friends and colleagues contributed to this book.

First and foremost is the love of my life, Elaine, who consistently brought joy, delight, love and laughter as she read several times the details of this book, which she knew well. I valued especially her suggestions as to how to make the science more relevant and interesting to possible readers more focused on belief.

Then I am grateful to my daughter Catherine, who selflessly lent herself to the challenging task of transcribing this physician's handwriting—already obscured by the micrographia of my Parkinson's Disease. She performed this task admirably and without letting it interfere with her sense of writing for clarity, as she made innumerable suggestions to enliven my writing style and to clarify background material.

I am grateful too for the encouragement of my other adult children—John, Peter, Teresa and James and for input when my memory failed. Their return to relationship with me was a major source of joy for me, which drove me to write it down.

My friend and brother-in-law Jack Hansen served as a foil for my ideas, while reading several versions of this book, each time helping to clarify my communication. It was so helpful to have such a colleague share his medical background and his love of God freely in responding to my writing.

To that extraordinary group of Canadian scientists and mentors who showed me and their other protégés how to do it right while having fun: Charles Bryan, Peter Macklem, J. Milic-Emili, Nick Anthonisen and Reuben Cherniack.

And for reading and commenting on earlier versions of this work, I am grateful to my colleagues Jesse Hall, Greg Schmidt and Iasha Sznajder; having published so much together, a trust developed that created space for the constructive criticism we shared.

To my friends from our TGIF group Jan Deckenbach, Diane Durante, Jack Farry, Donna Harris and Lissa Romell, I acknowledge how our faith sharing and shared prayer made Eucharist come alive for me as we lived the interface of belief and science.

To my neighbours and new friends in Furry Creek—Anil and Veneeta Sethy, Paul Ryan and Martin Humphries for providing the community where these ideas were brought to fruition.

Last but certainly not least, I am grateful to the Lord of my life who first suggested this project, then stood by me when the going got tough and the benefits became obscure.

Lawrence DH Wood
Furry Creek, BC, Canada
2012

PART I

The Scientific Method and a Spiritual Source of Knowing

1

There Is Much Beneath the Surface

It was June 1966 when I graduated with my medical degree from the University of Manitoba in Winnipeg, Canada. Almost immediately, I began a rotating internship at St. Boniface Hospital in Winnipeg. The training there was provided by affable excellent clinicians, and proceeded very well, in part because I was industrious and diligent.

When I finished my internship in June of 1967, I was most fortunate in being assigned to the Canadian Forces Institute of Environmental Medicine (CFIEM), where a Physician-Scientist with MD PhD training published especially good work. Charles Bryan took me under his wing early in my time at Toronto, and taught me science with one-liners of philosophy and with active participation in our experiments. Always coming up with good ideas for study, he encouraged getting started—"Let's do a quick and dirty", or "if you need statistics, it can't be important".

"Larry," said he, "there is a hyperbaric chamber here which changes the density (ρ) of the air we breathe. And Jere Mead just published an analysis of factors governing maximum expiratory flow (Vmax) which predicts that Vmax will vary inversely with ρ. And we have a new wedge spirometer, which faithfully records flow and volume in the hyperbaric chamber unaffected by the gas ρ. I think this would be a great project for you to start on."

"Now, when you measure the Vmax at several gas densities in some volunteer divers, take some graph paper and plot Vmax versus ρ—if there is a linear relationship, write the equation and we will explain it. If it is not a linear relationship, get some semi-log paper and plot Vmax versus ρ—again, if it's a linear relationship, write the equation and we will explain it. If it is still not linear, get some log–log graph paper, plot Vmax versus ρ, and if that is linear, write the equation and we will explain it. I am going to the Yukon for 3 months to study altitude sickness, and when I return, we will discuss your progress."

He left. I began. The data was linear only on log–log paper. I learned that the slope of the line was the exponent n in the equation Vmax $\propto \rho^n$, that n was about -0.5 at all but the lowest lung volumes, and that these data showed that Vmax varied inversely as the square root of ρ.

I read Dr. Mead's paper, which predicted that relationship based on the dominant contribution of convective acceleration (Pca) to the expiratory pressure drop during maximum expiratory flow. Then I wrote the paper, which Charles read on his return. He got so excited, I thought he would have a seizure. He marched me down to the office of the Commanding Officer, Dr. Pete Kidd, barged in, and made me stand there while he explained the phenomenal job I had done! Then we three went to the Officer's Mess for a celebratory drink or two.

Do you think this was an enticing way to get introduced to science?!!

For the sake of brevity and continuity, I skipped over one small glitch in the progress of the story. It turns out that by Canadian Navy Regulations, not just anyone can enter a working hyperbaric chamber. The entry and use of the chamber is restricted to certified Navy Divers. When I heard this, I inquired what I needed to do to become qualified. "That is straightforward if not easy," explained Dr. Kidd, "you just need to pass the Navy Divers 3 week course in Halifax Harbour." The next course was scheduled in September of 1967, and Dr. Kidd said he would enroll me. And how should I prepare? Just be in very good physical condition and be able to swim the two miles across the harbour and back.

Well, I was in pretty good shape for running and lifting, but I wasn't a very good swimmer, and I didn't especially like the water. But learn to swim I did, with the help of a few lessons and daily swimming exercise at the pool on the Downsview Base where I worked. I was told that doing 30 laps of the 50 yard pool would predict that I could handle the course. So I aimed at that target. Before the course began, I had increased my swimming stamina from 10 laps to 30 laps. So off I went, confident I would be back in the hyperbaric chamber in 3 weeks.

I was billeted to stay on the HMCS Granby, the ship outfitted for diving training. Come day 1, we 30 matriculants of the course were awakened at 6AM, ran for half an hour, did calisthenics for another half hour, and then dressed hurriedly in our wet suits and dove off the ship to swim the harbour before breakfast.

Then we assembled at 9AM for classroom review of the learning materials for the course, and we received the course schedule. Monday through Friday inclusive, class time was from 9 to noon, and 1:30pm to 4:30pm with free time in the evenings except on several occasions when we had a night swim or a paper to write and submit. We worked through that day, and I believe we all slept well that night. I first noticed something was up on the morning run on Day 2, when the group seemed distinctly smaller. And after our morning swim, the changing room for doffing our wet suits was distinctly less crowded. At the first class, I counted only 18 students, and those present commented on the smaller group. Rumors of pulled muscles and swimming disqualifications circulated.

By the end of week 1, the class size was 10, and by the end of week 2, there were only 6 students left. New rumors circulated that we could not proceed with this course with fewer than 4. I called Commander Kidd to inform him of the course status and we discussed that I needed to pass the course to complete my experiments.

As luck would have it, the night swim consisted of manual sweeping of the bottom of HMCS Granby for "mines"—in fact, these were magnets we were tasked to find and remove while experienced diving instructors swam by us, removing our masks and goggles—2 more students left the course.

The remnant of 4 now faced a challenge—sea entry from the Granby deck wearing our scuba gear. Well instructed to point the flippers straight down and hold the top of the mask firmly as we hit the water, I stepped off the deck and hurtled 30 feet down, striking the sea surface with my flippers horizontal, driving both above my knees, while my mask was knocked off my nose and eyes. Somewhat surprised, even a bit stunned, I drifted downward to the sea floor about 30 feet deep, and my feet sank in the soft mud. Because I tended to float upward with the usual weights on my belt, I had worn 6 pounds extra to be slightly negatively buoyant.

I stayed put while trying to pry the ankle straps loose enough to slide my left flipper back in proper position—Ah, I was successful, and turned to my right flipper when I inhaled some sea water through my nose. I was breathing heavily from the exercise of righting my equipment, so I had difficulty replacing my mask and clearing it of water. Now I was worried for my safety, and I decided to strike out for the surface. Up I struggled, aided by only 1 flipper and impeded by my extra heavy weight belt. Breathing heavily, I was inhaling more sea water through my nose, so I chose to relax. Down I floated to the soft sea floor again. This time I reset my mask and cleared it and began to work on repositioning my right flipper when I realized I was in danger of losing control as I began to cough from the inhaled water. Quickly then—but I digress to make a point: There is a joke told to me by my golfing buddy Chris. "Do you know the feeling when you lean too far back on a four legged chair and lose your balance? I feel that way all the time." I told you that to tell you this—the anxiety I was feeling on the Harbour floor, short of breath, inhaling seawater, and uncertain how to fix the situation, was analogous to the fear I experienced many times before and after this diving incident as I took on challenges far beyond me and just like these previous brushes with death and failure, I felt helpless, hopeless and completely dependent on the Lord of my life to save me. But I do digress, so back to the harbour floor.—Quickly then, I doffed my weight belt and struck out for the surface, meeting a rescue diver about half way. Together we reached the surface and he helped me board the ship.

On the deck, still short of breath and coughing, I related the story to the instructor, who fitted me with a new weight belt and helped me reposition my right flipper. He asked me if I understood the problem I had in entering the water, and I told him how I would fix it. "Alright, lets do it right," he said as we walked to the edge of the deck and I leapt out from the ship, legs straight down, flippers vertical, right hand on the mask, left arm straight down. This time, I sliced through the surface cleanly and returned to the surface wearing both flippers and my mask before swimming back to the boarding point. The instructor met me with congratulations and helped me doff my flippers, mask and wet suit in exchange for some warm sweats. Then we boarded a van which whisked me to a nearby hospital. There, a chest x-ray was compatible with left lower lobe–lingula aspiration of sea water.

By morning I was back to normal and ready to join the only other diving candidate still in the course for our morning run. He didn't make it—pulled up lame with a charley-horse. I was alone! The instructor explained that the last 2 days could not be completed for only 1 candidate, and I explained in turn that my stopping 2 days short of certification would block my returning to the hyperbaric chamber to continue my research. Politely, I requested he call Commander Kidd. He did, and we finished the course together.

That study became my first of 167 publications, and nowhere in the manuscript is mentioned the challenge of qualifying to enter the chamber[1]. This kick-started a series of studies extending this work. In particular, Charlie and I performed exhausting bicycle exercise at the simulated depths of 100, 200 and 300 feet of sea water to demonstrate that dynamic airways compression limited exercise at depth[2]. Not only did Charlie applaud the experiment we designed to show this, but he also became an experimental subject. What a mentor! He provided challenge by setting tasks, unmasking assumptions, offering alternative perspectives, giving feedback and engaging in hypothetical thinking. He provided support, served as an advocate for my work, and helped structure next steps. And he supplied vision in new language and vocabulary of concepts, in supporting my plans and in mapping my development.

An important part of this mentoring was in connecting me with my next mentor and creating a space for me to link the initial research to a PhD program and laboratory at McGill University under the supervision of Dr. Peter Macklem.

Beyond the hyperbaric chamber, my new skill in SCUBA diving allowed for a fantastic undersea experience. I took our family for a winter vacation in Antigua. There, I went SCUBA diving in the pristine, warm water off the coastal reef. Compared to Halifax harbour, this was delightfully comfortable and remarkably colourful. The water was so clear it was like soaring through air with limitless visibility.

2

Try Another Way

In October 1970, the Prime Minister, Pierre Elliot Trudeau, sent the Canadian Armed Forces into the streets of Montreal to curb a potential insurrection. Having resigned my commission in the Armed Forces and left Toronto, I brought my family of 4 to Montreal where I was enrolled in a PhD program at McGill University and the Royal Victoria Hospital. As we strolled the empty streets of Hampstead near our rented home, a patrol car stopped us to suggest that we might be safer indoors until the military occupation had defined itself.

So home we went to the place we had rented from the Canadian poet, Irving Layton. I vividly recall first meeting him in the back yard of his home, sitting quietly under an immense apple tree. He was gracious in showing me through his home, and when I remarked on his large library, he cautioned, "Remember not to live vicariously". There was a human skull looking out from his mantle piece over the fireplace, and I asked him why. He explained that on a vacation in Greece, he was standing atop a hill gazing on the beautiful Mediterranean with its vast waterways between so many islands; when he looked down to see this skull doing the same. It moved him, so he brought it home and placed it on his mantle piece.

We rented his home, and I continued the research I began in Toronto. The work flowed smoothly with energetic input from me and several new research colleagues, Ludwig Engel from Australia, Harold Menkes from Philadelphia, and Bjorn Bake from Sweden. Brilliant, focused and fun, they all helped each other and the productivity was abundant. A fourth colleague, Brian Murphy, was an electronics engineer who helped all of us when we encountered obstacles to transducer function, the recording and processing of data, and providing electronic models for the mechanical physiology we were studying.

One evening when Brian was visiting our home, he suggested we pray together. In the course of our shared prayer, Brian broke out in tongues "an expression of the Spirit of God speaking through him", he explained. A short while later, we accompanied Brian to a meeting of his prayer group, where glossolalia was an integral part of their shared prayer. Subsequently, we observed other manifestations of God's spirit, as in prophecy, the interpretation of tongues, and healing. As part of joining this prayer group, I had the spiritual leaders lay their hands on me. Some nights later, I awoke from sleep, sat up in bed with my arms extended and hands open, and prayed in tongues for awhile. Glossolalia became a part of my prayer, and a change in my demeanor made me convinced that something was going on. For I could not stop smiling as an expression of the joy I felt. This actually became hurtful, as my smiling muscles became quite sore from this constant use. My experience of God's presence was powerful, and the charismatic movement with this gift of the spirit became part of my life.

Having completed and submitted for publication 2 complex studies, one with Ludwig[1] on the effects of gas ρ on airways resistance, and a second with Bjorn[2] on the effect of inspired flow rate on ventilation distribution, I began to collate this work with the Toronto studies and compile a review of the relevant literature for my PhD thesis. Inadvertently, I omitted a review of a parallel body of literature describing effects of gas ρ on airways resistance and Vmax. Reluctantly, I admitted my oversight to Peter Macklem, who immediately said "Ok, let's you do it".

I hadn't realized how brittle I was until then. This task was like the straw that broke the camel's back. Despite my best efforts I could not finish the thesis to a stage of being ready to defend it before I had to leave Montreal in early December of 1972. I had decided to complete my Internal Medicine residency and training in Critical Care, and had received a wonderful offer from Dr. Reuben Cherniack to complete this training in Winnipeg beginning January 1973 at what was essentially a Faculty salary. Our family of five (Catherine was born in Toronto in 1967, John was born in Toronto in 1969, and Peter in Montreal in

1972) spent much of the intervening month of December 1972 on a vacation/pilgrimage to Rome, Sienna, Assisi and Padua. The stresses of this extensive, expensive trip and the ensuing move poured oil on the fires consuming our marriage and gave our family a troubled return to Winnipeg. Despite both our families being there, there was no respite because Alicia refused to allow my parents to see their grandchildren, and she had little to do with her own parents, brother or sister.

Having agreed to start in Winnipeg before the PhD was done, I was torn between the heavy demands on an Internal Medicine resident, the luxury of time needed to think about the PhD thesis, and the challenges of raising 3 young children in an already strained marriage. Dr. Cherniack became aware of the stresses and how I seemed to be responding with the signs of clinical depression, so he recommended I see a psychiatrist, Dr. Harry Prosen. This helped but I remained sufficiently despondent that when I received an invitation from Peter Macklem to visit him in Montreal, I leapt at the chance. In fact, Peter had arranged for me to spend some restful time at the Benedictine Monastery in Oka, Quebec with counseling from Father Benedict Vanier.

Looking back, this had become the worst time of my life. I was carrying the heavy burden of great potential as a well-trained physician-scientist husband and father who had not achieved any of these yet. Sitting on the edge of success, all looked impossible to complete. I was so busy with my residency that I had no time for my children, and our marriage had grown loveless and resentful. All these and the requirement to finish writing the thesis before defending it made me feel incompetent, worthless, despondent and slow. It's hard to describe how such converging expectations act to aggravate each other, but it got very black inside. Searching for an escape so I didn't have to fix any of these challenges, suicide seemed a solution. I had access to a gun, so late one night at Peter's home, I decided to end it.

Suddenly, in the silence of my troubled heart came a still small voice offering an alternative:

> *"Larry, I know how you feel. You try so hard to succeed;*
> *yet your vision of the outcomes of each endeavor looks black/*

impossible, and fixing each seems beyond your control. So you need a way out of this ceaseless striving. Try Another Way! Choose life without your concerns by relinquishing them to my care and giving me your permission to look after them and you. Then watch what I do!"

So I did. I let go. With no responsibilities, my despondency lifted and I came back to life. I was given 2 months off from clinical training to tend to my PhD. My options became simpler—the literature review flowed, the thesis defense followed successfully, and my training in Critical Care got simpler when Dr. Cherniack shortened it and let me begin a Faculty position, not only in treating critically ill patients but in teaching how to do it. It turned out that I was good at both. The critical thinking required during my research training and the course work in advanced respiratory, cardiovascular and renal pathophysiology as part of my PhD program all helped prepare me for providing and teaching Critical Care. And the liberation from the thesis gave me a fresh approach to my new research projects as a Faculty member, which progressed rapidly and with great success.

How grateful I am for the insight from that still small voice enabling me to choose life by letting go!!

Yet as a scientist, how do I explain this life-saving, life-changing experience? First, there is the conviction I know that I know God spoke to me. To the extent that my awareness of God's words to me were acceptable evidence, I could phrase the hypothesis "God does not exist/speak to people" and use this evidence to reject these hypotheses. In fact, that is what I did to arrive at my own conclusions—God does exist/speak to me. Conceivably, this is the distinction between science and personal revelation—science demands objective evidence and reproducibility to protect ourselves from bias, whereas revelation relies on all we have—personal conviction of divine intervention. And that is meant to be—this message was for me, and others will not be convinced. On the contrary, when they hear of people conversing with beings not present, they seek other explanations, and well they should until they have their own spiritual experience.

3

My New Home

It was about 9PM on a cold November night in 1978 when the phone rang in my hospital office. In an angry firm voice, my wife said: *"Larry, I don't want you to come home—not tonight, not ever."*

Dumbfounded but not surprised, I told her that I cared for her and our five children, so I would comply tonight and call her tomorrow. I sat pondering our circumstances in quiet, and when the finality of her words set in, I gathered my tired self up to the Intensive Care Unit where I was the attending physician. On the way, I scanned the likely outcomes of each of the 14 patients I was caring for.

I chose to visit the patient with the poorest prognosis. Pulling up a chair at his bedside after I had announced my presence, I made eye contact while we discussed his ailments, his treatments, his family, his job, his hopes for the future while sharing with him my own. After about an hour, he dozed off and I went to a nearby hotel for the night. I believe this patient visit was an initial step in grieving my loss by reaching out to another in distress.

Next morning, I visited a Franciscan Friary where I had frequented Mass and Confession. There I contacted the Abbot who listened to my story of separation from my family and my concern that I find a place to reside where my grief could be nursed in a spiritual environment. He told me that his community did not take in strays, but he had an idea which might serve me, and asked if he might call me later after he had checked it out. True to his promise, he called to tell me that the Marianists in St. Boniface might have a place for me, and gave me the phone number of their Director, Fr. Ray Roussin.

I made an appointment, and after an extensive conversation, Ray said he would discuss my situation with the community, and get back to me. He called the next day and invited me to reside with his community. When I arrived at the Marianist residence he showed me to my room, in an elegant large home, and left me with a schedule of the activities of the members. Settling in, I found the single bed comfortable, the dresser space adequate, a functional desk and chair, and a short walk down the long corridor between other occupied rooms to the bathroom complete with shower facility.

The room itself was at the corner of the home on the third floor, where the cold November winds of Winnipeg were unobstructed as they lashed the window. Accordingly, the room became rather cold, especially at night when I returned from evening prayer in the chapel. I found an extra woolen blanket in the closet of my room, and managed to get some sleep between bouts of shivering. This went on for several nights while I was gaining my first impressions of the community—prayerful, pleasant but austere members of the Marianist order. As I came to know each, we conversed about many topics, including the circumstances in my life that brought me to their home.

Having decided that these Marianists must be tough to tolerate the cold conditions of their rooms at night, I did my best to emulate their tolerance, but I was not sleeping well in the shivering climate of my cold, cold room. At last, I mentioned to one of the community how impressed I was with the way the group tolerated the cold at night. Quizzically, he asked me to show him my room. Together we entered that chilled place. He walked straight to the radiator and turned it on.

Looking back, I realized that I tolerated the cold at night because I was too caught up with the emotional challenge of the loss of my family and the change in my lifestyle to mention it. Indeed, it seemed strangely consistent that my physical chill should match that of my soul. Now, if only someone would turn on the radiator of my heart.

BECOMING A WOUNDED HEALER

When I began living with the Marianists, we imagined a 3-day to 3-week stay. But living in this community revealed many pleasant supports I had not anticipated: regular scheduled morning and evening prayer, a bright and sunny sitting room where I had the opportunity for quiet reading and reflection during a temporary absence from my usual frenetic work activities, fine meals prepared by community members, and the sense of living in a holy place protected from the noise, hurry and crowds of the world. I remained in residence with the Marianists for 3 years.

During my time there, several scriptures came to my attention, and pondering their meaning for my life allowed me to let go of my anger and undergo a quantum change in my spiritual life. The Book of Job[A] introduced me to the just and righteous servant of God who was devastated by losses in his life. In conversing with God, Job seeks an explanation for his suffering. Instead of justifying his action before men, God speaks of his omniscience and almighty power. Content with this answer, Job recovers his attitude of humility and trust in God. And I, like Job, came to see that no purpose of God can be hindered, and now that I have seen God's power, I repent in dust and ashes for the lack of wholeness that contributed to my loss of my children, my home and my possessions.

And a companion piece informed my heart further—Psalm 51 tells of the sorrow and penitent demeanor of God's servant David for having stolen Bathsheba after sending her husband to certain death at the front lines of Israel's war. These words of the Psalmist convicted me and I cried "Have mercy on me, O God, in your compassion wipe out my offense. Give me back the joy of your salvation. O lord, open my lips and my mouth shall declare your praise. My sacrifice O God is a contrite spirit; a heart contrite and humbled O God you will not spurn."[B]

So, with Job and David, I let go of my ego, and ceased my pursuit of approbation. Having let go, I found myself freed from the past and unencumbered by the future. Instead, I was free for living the present, this moment alone with all my attentiveness. People came to me to tell me their stories, and I listened with my whole heart. Having accepted my losses and the suffering accompanying them, I found myself much more receptive to their suffering, and more able to understand empathically the nature of their pains—Mario, the cardiac surgeon

---

[A] *New American Bible (NAB)*: See Job; 38-42.

[B] NAB: Psalm 51; 3-4, 19

who had separated from his wife; Luis, the trauma surgeon, whose wife had left him without warning; Richard, the model, surrounded by beautiful women as he tried to find Jesus; and many more each day at the Marianists, at my office, in the hospital and in the community. Somehow, the pain of my suffering has made me able to heal my brothers and sisters with, at the least, an understanding heart, and somehow more with inspired advice. The wounded-healer[1] became my way, and it accompanied me back to the ICU where I was ready to dispense the same empathic listening for my very ill patients, and then for my students, Housestaff and Faculty colleagues.

The truth as I see it is that I could not have made this quantum shift in spirituality without experiencing the pain of loss. In a perverse way, I would do it again in order to grow. That is, I would choose to experience the loss of family and reputation if I knew the outcome would be conversion of my heart and deep relationship with God and His people. I am so grateful for God's loving care in supporting me through the pain until I could let go. The Marianists prayer rituals to start and end each day; their sunny bright blue library, so silent so replete with good inspired books to inform and lift my heart like _Reaching Out_[2] and _As Bread That is Broken_[3]; soul lifting music like John Michael Talbot's; fine food; and affable unpretentious company. Truly, I was blessed and could not have survived alone.

SEPARATING FROM MY CHILDREN

My choice to remain out of our family home and so apart from my 5 children in 1978 was painful for me. At the time, they were 11, 9, 6, 4, and 2 years old and so they had very different capacities for understanding their parent's differences. The alternative course of action for me was to continue the court proceedings pursuing my right to spend time with my children. In the best case, this would facilitate my interaction with each of them as they grew through their learning opportunities. But the behaviour of their mother was so resistant to my interaction with the kids that I foresaw prolonged turmoil to achieve limited and distracted access, a condition to which I did not want to contribute.

Throughout that time, I had made repeated overtures to their mother to visit with them. These were consistently resisted, with scheduling conflicts with any date I proposed, and when we arrived at a date and place for me to visit, a late cancellation occurred due to some kind of emergency. When the divorce decree clarified that I should have weekly visits with the children, if they were supervised by Father Baudry our parish pastor and good friend, then I needed to have him arrange visits with their mother at a time of availability for him and the children. When he encountered the same resistance from their mother, he became exasperated and wrote to the judge that he was no longer available to facilitate my meeting with the children.

All the while, I was regularly and often in prayer for them and for our potential meeting. As time went on, it became clear that I was not going to see them unless and until their mother changed her point of view. And all evidence pointed to the opposite, that she grew even more convinced that it was not good for the children to see me.

I resigned myself to God's will as it was unfolding before me—that I was not going to see my children again until they chose to see me at some age of independent decision making. And I then gave up my futile and exasperating attempts to negotiate a meeting with them. I broke down in the grief of letting them go, and when I collected myself, it was with the resolve that I was now awaiting the decision of the children to see me—an outcome which was unlikely to happen for years. I further resolved to write each of them regularly to keep them informed of my loving concern for their wellbeing, including the availability of support for their education. Absenting myself from the home, living with a religious community, cutting back on my work, and dropping the Parish commitments were all appropriate self-care, if not survival tactics, for me. This was a big step. It was one thing to respond to a wake-up call to spend more time with my children, for that could be fixed with better time management and resetting my priorities. But it was a larger change to live elsewhere and have no access to my children. It is difficult for me to describe the pain associated with my grieving from my lost children. It was a physical discomfort like a rake scraping the inside of my thorax. When it was triggered, it lasted hours. It came down on me with finality one grey afternoon while I was praying in my room—invisible forces from within drove me from my knees to the floor, prostrate with outstretched arms and open hands. Helpless, I cried out to God: *"All right, all right, all right, all right—your way, Lord, not mine. Lead me."*

And so it continued, this non-involvement with each of them. How I conducted myself throughout that time helped me recover and heal the scars, which I subsequently labeled as abandonment and humiliation. Little did I know I would be much assisted in this healing by Elaine's loving heart, which prepared me for the reunions as they came, one by one, back into relationship.

SEASONS OF THE HEART

Every place on this planet has its unique wonders. The province of Manitoba, Canada is in the center of the country. Far North, it is relatively cold, with long winters and short summers. Hills and trees are rare, and one can see a long way from any point on the prairie. While I lived with the Marianist community, I encountered several of this region's wonders, which I embraced with the awe and gratitude I have come to recognize as my characteristic response.

WINTER

When I heard about the impending solar eclipse, I wanted to see it. It was February 26th, 1979 when the weather was oppressively cold. Day time temperatures were regularly—30°F, but the skies were cloudless, deep blue, and the flat farmland where I went to observe the eclipse was covered evenly with pure white snow several feet deep. I dressed warmly and stayed in my little Toyota with the engine and heater running as I awaited the event. Not another living being could be seen in any direction. As the appointed time approached, I got out of the car and walked from the plowed icy road across a shallow snowy ditch onto the farmer's field, gloved and scarved with a woolen toque tucked under the fur collar of my parka.

Then it began, imperceptibly at first as a small shadow moved across the face of the sun. In the distance, I heard roosters crowing and dogs howling a mournful tune. It got colder and darker as the sun disappeared. For a moment all was still, not completely dark but like the late edge of dusk. Suddenly, from the trailing corner of the shadow across the sun, burst a brilliant point of light which grew in seconds until it looked like a shiny diamond on a dark ring. Now the light began to bathe the arena in which this wonder was displayed. Across the snowy fields began to move shadowy lines as if blown by a wind that wasn't there. Larger and faster they swept as this second dawn broke into brilliant light.

I think I held my breath while all this went on, and when I took a breath, I heard myself say, "Lord, look what you have done", and I fell to my knees in awe. Even in the icy chill of a lonely broken heart, wonders abound. Look out and behold, for they are the way to new life.

SPRING

Sometimes, Spring came early in Manitoba. Or at least came quickly after the cold cold winter, so the contrast surprised even the locals. Sitting in the Marianists living room after breakfast on a early April morning, I read the startling weather forecast—high today 90°F. The sky was bright blue and on the outdoor porch, I felt a warm breeze. "Beach", I heard my body cry. Moments later I was packing a duffle bag with a change of clothes, a beach towel, and a manuscript I was writing. Into my Toyota I climbed, pulled out of the driveway and made a bee-line for the nearest beach on the east side of Lake Winnipeg.

Grand Beach was just that. Forty-five miles north of Winnipeg, a small town was the access to an immense sand dune running about 5 miles along the lake. After parking the car, I got out into the hot air—I'm sure the temperature had reached its predicted high—and walked toward the massive dunes separating me from the water I couldn't yet see about 100 yards away. As I walked, I noticed a distinctly cooler breeze coming at me over the dunes. The closer I got the cooler got the breeze, though the ground level temperature was sweltering. At last I climbed over the dunes, and there it was.

A completely frozen Lake Winnipeg!! Incredulous, I checked the air temperature again and found it hot as ever behind the dune, but on the lake side, the cool breeze made me uncomfortably cold. Putting down my beach equipment, I walked to the edge of the ice and cautiously stepped on it—it did not give way, and I could have walked on it. Instead I returned to the other side of the dunes, found a comfortable soft smooth sandy spot, spread my towel, and began a peaceful afternoon of tanning and writing to my heart's content in tropical weather by the frozen lake. The icy chill of a heart frozen by too much pain is not far removed from the heart warmed into new life by a change in the surroundings.

SUMMER

Peter Breen—a research fellow working in my program—and I visited Paul Schumacker in San Diego in February; a treat and an escape from the frigid Winnipeg winter. We planned to conduct some complex experiments to determine how increased pulmonary blood flow interfered with oxygen exchange in the edematous lung. We hypothesized that increased blood flow would decrease the time it took for the red blood cell to traverse the O_2 exchanging interface between lung air spaces and blood vessels. Paul Schumacker, a postdoctoral research fellow, and his research supervisor, Peter Wagner, were world experts in the only technique (Multiple Inert Gas Elimination Technique—MIGET) we knew which could distinguish incomplete diffusion of O_2 from increased intrapulmonary shunt. By May of that year, we knew that MIGET had excluded the incomplete diffusion mechanism[4], so we wanted to test another hypothesis: conceivably, increased blood flow raised the microvascular pressure in the edematous lung, and so increased the pulmonary edema and the O_2 exchange defect (Q_S/Q_T).

Paul came to Winnipeg in mid-June to join Peter and me in this complex experiment. Each day began early with setting up and calibrating the measuring devices, and then baseline measurements were obtained before an acute lung injury was produced. Then 5 sets of measurements were obtained as the edema developed and Q_S/Q_T increased. It turned out that there was not much further edema developed between 2 and 3 hours, facilitating an intervention at 2.5 hours which produced a large increase in blood flow and Q_S/Q_T. Yet the edema measured at 2.5 hours did not change, disproving our hypothesis[5]. Now this day's experiment was over, except for the re-calibration of the measuring devices and cleaning the lab for the next day's experiment.

Late in the day as it was, we walked out of the laboratory into the warm sweet air of a summer evening in Winnipeg. Paul eagerly accepted our invitation to take a 45-minute ride to see Grand Beach. Busily chatting all the way, we arrived and took a walk along the sandy shore of Lake Winnipeg without footwear and with our legs wading in the calm warm water. We had walked a long way in the evening sun when I asked Paul what time it was. Glancing at his watch, he replied "10:45pm, no—it can't be. Can it be so bright at 10:45. What time do you have?"

The sun sets late during summer in the North. And it is good for Winnipeg residents to have wonders to show to San Diego residents. We enjoyed the walk back to the car even more, especially Paul, who was enthralled at the long day we had.

The opposite of this experience occurred when another American friend visited Winnipeg in the middle of Winter. As we walked to the hospital parking lot at 3:30pm, it was dark. I stepped in front of her to pull a plug connecting a power source in the parking lot fence to my car. Puzzled, she asked about it, and was surprised to hear that the plug powered an engine block heater to keep the cold weather from freezing the engine to prevent ignition. But her surprise got a lot greater when we got in, started the car, and I took an ice scraper to clear the inside of the windows.

Yes, there are wonders in every climate!

AUTUMN

As summer wanes in Manitoba, residents value the last lingering days of warm weather. And the beach becomes even more alluring. All Spring and Summer, I had begun to enjoy the peace and tranquility of Grand Beach. Essentially, I had moved my office to the sand dunes lining the lake. There, I had identified a large tree with abundant leafy branches, under which I spread my beach blanket and towel, made a sand chair at the start of each visit, opened my briefcase containing several manuscripts I was writing, and went to work in the shade. After a suitable stretch of writing, I would close up temporarily and go for a refreshing walk or swim.

In my musings under the tree, I recognized the mechanisms whereby the life-saving value of positive end-expiratory pressure (PEEP) saved many patients who were dying in our ICU following acute lung injury. The work on this manuscript discovered[6] that PEEP redistributed edema out of the flooded air spaces into the lung interstitial space to improve lung oxygen exchange and reduce that Q_s/Q_t. So I named the tree under which these deliberations proceeded "The PEEP Tree". Nostalgia brings me back there from time to time, for the environment for creativity surrounding the PEEP tree is among the finest in Academic Medicine. I have looked at several positions in Academic Pulmonary and Critical Care Medicine before and after this story. As part of my decision-making I always discuss office space and location, but never did I try to negotiate for a PEEP tree. On the other hand, having a job with the flexibility to work under the PEEP tree is an essential item in job satisfaction.

Being present to these seasonal wonders made the darkest times tolerable, even exciting, for each provided a broader perspective, and was an invitation out of the darkness of the involuted self and into the interesting world outside. These stimulated my curiosity and increased my sense of awe and wonder at the marvels of this world.

Winter

It snowed last night.

This morning came down white and heavy and wet.
Beautiful, its true.
But looking out my garret window
I only see a season past

like too many others
yet this time it feels more like
my motivation and enthusiasm fell
with the leaves

so now my bare soul is covered
with the icy chill of an exterior
fashioned by too many pains
While inside, fat and forty indolence

decays without hope.

Dining

I woke from an afternoon nap
taken to escape my deadlines
to the smell of home cooking.

Dimly recalling commitment to diet,
I tried to remember why life was so grey
but anticipation of eating got in the way.

Broken vows and lost children,
missed deadlines and sore joints,
even the distance between me and God

all seemed
less important
as I showered for DINNER!

Five succulent chicken pieces later,
my sorrows are not less,
they are just harder to ponder

because they are covered with lard,
and slip away when my fat brain
tries to punish itself by grasping them.

4

Elaine

MEETING

It was Friday evening in the Benedictine Chapel near Pecos, NM in October of 1979. Quiet guitar strumming led the songs between the sharing of stories by the participants. The retreat on Inner Healing began last Sunday evening, and now 5 days later the healings were told.

She stood to speak, tears in her voice. Beautiful face, slender body, she cried softly "I gave up on finding the man in my life, but the Lord put him in the space I made." Later, she spoke of bargaining silently when she walked into the chapel to find me and 3 others praying—"if Larry were alone, I would speak." The 3 women I was with left the chapel once she had made her bargain. As she spoke, Abbott David looked to me as if to invite my comfort for her tears before he went to her, somehow knowing more than I did.

As she left the chapel, she paused at the aisle where I stood with open arms to welcome her home. "Its you", Elaine sighed as she melted in my embrace.

We spent several hours in secluded conversation while the retreatants partied next door. She told of parents, nieces, siblings, colleagues, Chicago and I listened with my heart. Before we ended our evening, I invited her to join me at the altar.

There, we committed our new relationship to our God, asking only that he make of it and us whatever He wanted. At breakfast, I learned Elaine had decided to stay another day and walk the Pecos hills with me. As we set out on a clear, cool bright morning, the Monastery dog, a Golden Labrador Retriever who liked to play, accompanied us. High up the hillside, we sat together in the warm sun to rest and take each other in. When some dirt fell on my jeans, she brushed it off. Enjoying her touch, I spread a handful across my lap and waited while she brushed it away, smiling knowingly at the tension we were creating.

"Would you like to try something different?" I asked her softly. She replied with trust "Ok". So I whipped out my rosary, on which we prayed together for awhile, committing to whatever God had in mind by bringing us together.

So committed, we renewed our walk in the sunshine. I took off my shirt for coolness. Later she confessed that she fell in love with my back as she walked behind me. Coming upon a mountain stream, we took off our shoes and bathed our tired feet before returning to the Abbey for dinner.

That day had flown by, so already it was bedtime when we arrived at her room. Our senses were alive when I kissed her—a long and gentle kiss to commemorate our exotic day together. She slipped between the sheets and welcomed the covers lifted to her shoulders. Smiling softly, she watched as I walked toward the door.

The next morning, we attended the Monastery's Sunday liturgy together, ate breakfast, and boarded the bus to the airport, engaged all the while in conversation. I traveled to a scientific meeting in New Orleans while Elaine went home to Chicago, but not before we agreed to meet again at the O'Hare airport on my way back to Winnipeg. Having learned that the next day was Elaine's birthday, I sent her flowers, and called her to talk that night.

As I left my arrivals lounge at O'Hare, I walked through the airport corridor hoping she would be there. Sure enough, as I approached our planned meeting place, there she was! We loaded my luggage into her car on a brilliant autumn day, and Elaine drove us to the Morton Arboretum, where we spent the day enjoying the fall colours and getting to know each other better for the rest of our lives.

HEALING

It was May of 1980, and the Annual Meeting of the American Thoracic Society (ATS) was held in San Diego. Elaine, from Chicago, took some time off to meet me there which gave her the opportunity to meet my work colleagues from Winnipeg. On a warm evening, the Winnipeg group had a dinner celebration at the side of an outdoor pool. Our Section Chief led us down the garden path to our tables arm in arm with a drop-dead gorgeous brunette with an engaging smile and a quick wit. "Dazzling", said my friend to me, "Elaine is dazzling".

The next day, Elaine and I took a ride north along Highway 1 to the beach in front of the Hearst Mansion. As we strolled the beach, a baby seal emerged from the water, barking at us like a puppy. Elaine squealed in delight at being so close to this cute creature, until momma seal emerged from the water to bring her baby back.

That night I told Elaine about my bothersome peripheral poly-arthritis that was stiffening my fingers and caused fluid to collect in my knee joint and pain in my left shoulder.

She responded compassionately, and asked if she might pray for me. Of course, I said yes, and she laid her hands on my left shoulder, praying *"Lord, please heal my Baby Seal"*.

Immediately, there spread heat from her hands like a warm liquid running down my left arm into my fingers, and across my back and down my right arm to my fingers, until all 10 digits burned with the heat. The stiffness disappeared and has never returned, the knee fluid went away, and the shoulder pain ceased.

Then and there, we joined hands in the thanksgiving prayer that had become part of our lives since we met in Pecos.

Given the theme of this book, I am compelled to express my opinion about the origin of this Healing. I have not the slightest doubt that the Lord of my life used Elaine's love to heal my arthritis. I know that I know God healed me. Further, I do not believe this healing can convince any thinking persons that God exists or that God heals. This is my healing, and so my conviction. Others can be attracted or repelled, and offer alternative explanations—the power of love, the mind-body connection that lets placebo effects heal. And they should consider alternatives until they have their own personal experience of God, healing or otherwise. Even then, my belief and theirs does not prove that God exists, for there is no measure of God here—we do not have a "Godometer"—so from a scientific point of view, God cannot be disproven. Of course, that does not say God does not exist.

So I have a choice. It seems like my healing transcends all my understanding of how it can occur, so it is not unreasonable for me to invoke divine intervention. To the extent God did it, it is the polite behaviour for me to feel grateful and to express my gratitude to Her. Suspending my search for scientific proof seems like a good idea given my improved health. It is an even better idea given my prior faith experiences, so I have no trouble dealing with God as if She exists. Among other things, this sets me free to converse with God and to hear His still small voice. How else can God communicate with His children? Besides, everything for which I do have scientific proof is so complex and beautiful that it draws out of me wonder and praise. So I get it both ways: my skepticism can't disprove God in scientific terms because I don't have a "Godometer"; and whenever I can prove anything scientific, the result causes me to praise God.

REJOICING IN THE WONDERS OF OUR LOVE

One might imagine that courtship would be difficult with Elaine in Chicago and me in Winnipeg. But 2 circumstances favored our finding time together. First was the Air Canada non-stop flight between our cities, and I became a frequent flyer while Elaine also visited Winnipeg to meet my family on several occasions. Second, we both had jobs with considerable travel, so with a bit of planning, we could meet in other cities. Elaine was a Systems Engineer with Data 100 who did a lot of teaching to customers acquiring new computer programs. I attended several scientific medical conferences each year to present or support the presentation of our research work, and I usually had 2-3 site visits/ year to review research programs or grant applications. Accordingly, our long distance relationship aided rather than hindered our intimacy, especially because our travel together was often exotic and characterized by a mutual sense of awe and wonder at what was unfolding for us.

An example—I was invited to speak at a Canadian Critical Care Conference in Banff, Alberta during the warm summer month of June. Elaine had a teaching engagement in New York City which ended the day before my conference started. Expecting to be denied, she inquired whether her round trip business airfare could have a stop in Calgary on her way home from New York to Chicago. The answer was yes, a surprise to anyone familiar with the geographic location of those 3 cities. So I picked her up in our rented car at the Calgary Airport, she attended my presentation at the conference, and we enjoyed together a famous barbeque that evening. We spent the next day in the beautiful mountains surrounding our accommodations at the Banff Springs Hotel, before we drove north towards Jasper. Along the way we stopped several times to take pictures of the bighorn sheep and grizzly bears scattered about the foothills and mountainside, and to walk on the Athabasca Ice Fields where we learned more about glaciers than we knew before.

Our friend Gordon Ford from Calgary had recommended that we stay the night at Tekarra Lodge on the outskirts of Jasper. So we checked in about 7pm to a cozy log cabin with a natural fireplace, and learned that the restaurant was open until quite late for dinner. Quickly changing into hiking gear, we set out for an evening walk in the woods. And walk we did—for 3 hours through magnificent silver birch trees which seemed to reflect an ethereal light from the setting sun. Encountering deer, rabbits and other wildlife, we hardly noticed the time, as we were lost in nature and each other. When we returned hungry to the restaurant about 10pm, the sun had not yet descended below the horizon. We were treated to an exquisite meal in rustic ambiance before a log fireplace. Lost in the romance of this environment and each other, we relished sleeping together more than ever before. Funny, but we said that a lot to each other, especially after every trip.

After breakfast the next morning, we checked out to drive back the highway to Lake Moraine. We stopped to take in the emerald green waters made so by the glacier's crushing of rocks into fine silt, or moraine. It was a warm pleasant morning to walk and talk by the lake, so we decided to extend our day by driving to Lake Louise. This gorgeous lake was on the route to the Calgary Airport where we planned to have Elaine fly back to Chicago while I drove west through the Rockies to Vancouver to attend and present some of our research at a satellite meeting of the Canadian Critical Care Society. At a roadside restaurant, I picked up a roasted chicken and a loaf of bread for our lunch, and we rented a canoe to paddle around Lake Louise.

I said it was gorgeous, but I can't say it enough! Looking across the lake from the shore near Chateau Lake Louise, this pristine blue lake extended to the snow capped mountains on the other side, making a breathtaking sight. Captivated by the beauty, we embarked in our canoe and paddled toward the center of the lake. There in the noonday sun on the tranquil water in our canoe for two, we enjoyed our picnic of roast chicken and French bread.

Of course, we missed Elaine's flight. In fact, the writing was on the wall early enough that instead of proceeding east from Lake Louise to the airport, we drove west through the Rocky Mountains, enjoying the awesome sights of snowy, craggy mountains and abundant wildlife. Stopping for yet another enchanted evening in Kelowna on Okanagan Lake, we enjoyed each other's company even more because our plans had us a thousand miles apart that night. Again, sleeping together was more wondrous than ever before, including last night. It just couldn't get any better, but it did!!

The next morning, we set out for Vancouver after learning the availability of a timely flight to Chicago the following day. Arriving early, we set out on foot to explore Stanley Park and to walk its seawall. Elaine had not seen Vancouver before, and I think her love affair with the Pacific Northwest began then and there. Twenty years later, we found ourselves back in that region where I was speaking at a Canadian Critical Care Conference in Whistler. Having heard there was a challenging but beautiful golf course in Furry Creek about an hour's drive south, I arranged to play, while Elaine and Catherine contacted a real-estate agent to show them some homes in the small community of Furry Creek.

As I golfed the course, I marveled at the drop dead gorgeous scenery extending from the fairway down to the tranquil waters of Howe Sound across to the Tantalus Mountains still capped with snow. Elaine and Catherine were waiting for me at the 18th green. As I came to meet them, Elaine blurted out "I found it!!". And that was it! I visited the home she found and within 5 months we had bought it to move into our beach home in the mountains the next summer of 2004.

But I digress. Back in Vancouver in 1980, Elaine and I enjoyed a fine meal and a good night's rest in our spacious hotel room overlooking the city from the 30th floor. Then Elaine missed her flight to Chicago—no, just kidding. The next morning, we went early to the airport, where Elaine's round trip ticket from Chicago to New York City with a stopover in Calgary now had a second stopover in Vancouver for a modest fee. So Elaine was back to work the next day after a whirlwind extension of her business trip by four days.

I told you that to tell you this—this trip was one of many, and each was filled with surprises and delights. We were awestruck as they happened, and remain amazed even today by our courtship. The remnants of my recollection of my first marriage faded, and I could not wait to declare my commitment to Elaine. We were married on November 7th, 1981 and true to our blessed pattern, left for a 7-month honeymoon in Israel and New Zealand to enjoy more wonders of our World.

WEDDING

In the beginning, it was a maze. As of September 1981, the pieces consisted of four overlapping goals, each fraught with uncertainty: marriage, sabbatical, post-sabbatical employment and immigration.

Elaine and I were committed to marry. We had each applied for annulments, gone through the interview process, and we awaited the decision. No decision could be made until our divorces were final. Elaine's had been final for some time, but the Decree Nisi for my divorce had not been received. So we proceeded as if it would arrive, and as if our annulments would be granted. Our discussion with the pastor of Elaine's parish in Chicago scheduled our wedding for November 7, 1981. We proceeded with his permission to ask our 2 favorite priests to concelebrate our wedding mass. Fr. Dan O'Connell was Elaine's spiritual advisor and friend at St. Louis University; Fr. Ray Roussin was the Director of the Marianist Community in Canada where I lived for the last 3 years. Our plans were like a house of cards which could collapse if my first marriage was not annulled. We waited to see the outcome.

Still employed by the University of Manitoba, I had planned a complicated sabbatical leave in Haifa, Israel for November through February, followed immediately by the second half of this study leave in Auckland New Zealand. Considerable bureaucratic organization was already in place enabling my salary and it's disposition in my bank account, our health insurance, immigration visas, accommodations, travel arrangements and the curriculum for the new courses I would teach in both countries. And Elaine had arranged a leave of absence from her employment at AT&T, as well as terminating her apartment lease. So it would be good for us to bring our plans to completion.

A potential glitch was my intention not to return to Manitoba after my sabbatical, for I had severed my ties with the ICU and Department of Medicine while seeking new employment in Chicago after the sabbatical. So during the 3 months preceding our wedding and travel, I had looked carefully at positions in Academic Pulmonary and Critical Care Medicine offered in Chicago at Northwestern and Loyola Universities and at two other excellent programs at the University of Michigan and at the University of Colorado in Denver. Beyond their excellence, these two programs outside Chicago had the advantage of short direct air flights to help Elaine keep in touch with her family.

One further uncertainty introduced by the hurried plans was how I could complete the immigration process for any of these positions in the United States as a Canadian citizen, especially one living in Israel, New Zealand, or in transit between. The successful immigration process usually has a simpler construct requiring the applicant to remain in the USA after his initial interview for up to 6 months.

Filled with the overlapping uncertainties in all 4 areas, we fell back from our planning to pray and to wait. Finding the words for our prayer was not difficult they just seemed impossible. So we voiced our wishes as simply as we were able: "Lord, let us marry, and enjoy our wedding trip on Sabbatical and find future employment close to Elaine's family."

Our discomfort in waiting for God's answer was analogous to sitting astride a picket fence, being so uncomfortable as to want off on either side, but sitting in the pain to listen for the still small voice providing an answer. In short order, my divorce was finalized, my marriage was annulled, we were married in the church of our upbringing. We traveled to Israel and New Zealand to complete my sabbatical. During this dramatic interval, I was offered a position at the University of Chicago. It was far better than the others, so during our travel from Haifa to Auckland, we stopped in Chicago to accept that position, which was to begin in July 1982. And my immigration to the USA was facilitated to allow me to complete my sabbatical in New Zealand!!

What a joyous outcome! And I didn't even know what an extraordinary environment was provided by the University of Chicago for the development and implementation of my academic instincts. That nurturing environment began with a new Chairman of Medicine, Dr. Arthur Rubenstein, who actually read my publications and discussed them at my interview. His interest was enhanced by an opportunity to fill a gap in his Department, which had no meaningful Critical Care, but was embarking on building a 6-story Critical Care tower to house such a program. Unbeknownst to me he presided over an Internal Medicine Housestaff Program, which was among those with the highest quality in the nation, and his Department provided teaching to Medical Students at the prestigious Pritzker School of Medicine, features which made the best use of my teaching abilities.

It was possible for me to describe the transitions above as an orderly, planned implementation of marriage, sabbatical, and new job at Chicago by a thoughtful, intelligent person. In fact, I just wrote it this way. But that story is misleading, for it overlooks the sense of mystery and gratitude I experienced in the process. Whistling through the graveyard at night to hide from the likely emergence of failure at many steps along the way was more like the truth. And a true recollection needs to include the joyful response when heartfelt prayers are answered in the most unexpected and blest way to solve problems far beyond my ability. Such outcomes create an active receptivity and humility which builds relationship with God.

Each of these 4 transitions to new life can be viewed in the context of Science versus Belief. People of science often express awe at the complex and intricate workings of the world they investigate. And those devoted to understanding psychospiritual growth and development are often drawn to the methods of science to expand their tools of study. Not infrequently, there seems to be conflict between the revelations of these two viewpoints—science and spirituality. But many scientists understand the limits of their discipline in seeking truth as defined by those mechanisms or realities that can't be falsified or disproven. To be scientific requires that a hypothesis has essential elements that can be measured. In this sense, beliefs are not scientific because they cannot be objectively measured. For example, if one is interested in the belief that God exists or God is responsible for creation, these beliefs cannot be disproven with out a reliable "Godometer". Given such, failure to detect God's presence would disprove Her existence in the circumstance under study. But without a God-ometer, no scientific conclusion is possible. Accordingly, beliefs are not scientific but they exist fully in man's consciousness right beside the truths of science.

Questions of a Mustard Seed

Now that it is over
how do I recall the value of the pain it took
to be lifted out of the slimy stagnant well
dug by years of frightened response to lack of love?

How shall I inform my forgetful heart that saw—
let alone the hearts of others that didn't—
about the path to healing and resurrection
from heaving sobs in anguished rejection
by my woman and children while driving from them
to my new home with the brothers

without hope or plan
sitting in the pain
shouting in anger and fear and desperation
screaming in guilt and shame and desolation
without even a hint of belief
that my cry went beyond the car

To peace and thanksgiving
to joy and anticipation of the next good things
the Lord will offer for my surprise and delight
and my journey to Him?

How do I ensure
that I will grow in wonder and wisdom
from experiencing in my pain
how all things came together for my good
when the hurt brought helplessness enough
to liberate me from saving myself
by understanding and doing—

Instead, to seek Jesus and no other?
In the fears that arise from my lack of wholeness
how do I keep from forgetting again,
sliding back down the slippery walls of the well of reliance on my efforts
to consider and solve tomorrow's problems

Turning my joyful journey to the kingdom of my heart
into a fretful risky venture
fraught with frightful giants
who surely will deprive me of my joy?

How long must He be with me
before I learn to relax and enjoy
the garden of delights set before me
as a gift to a child-prince from his Father-King

That I might celebrate, rejoice and give thanks always
that by a loving laughing appreciation of His life in me
others will see the path through no effort or design of mine
but through mere living the affirmation He gives me daily.

5

Our Wedding Trip

Two years after our meeting in Pecos, we were married in the sunny bright chapel of St. Julianna's parish in Chicago. The joyful liturgy of the Eucharist was concelebrated by Fr. Ray Roussin S.M from Winnipeg, and Fr. Dan O'Connell S.J. from St. Louis. A small group of musicians from our prayer group made beautiful music. Our parents were in the front row, near Elaine's brother Bill, her sisters Georgia and Maddie and their husbands Jack and Bob. And on the other side were my siblings Vic, Betty and Howie and their spouses, Brother Richard from the Marianists, Charles Bryan and Peter Breen. Dazzling Elaine was lead down the aisle by her seven nieces as bridesmaids.

At the end of the ceremony, Elaine and I walked down the aisle to *"And the Father will Dance"* feeling God's joy in our committed love, and made our way with the entourage to the new Hamilton Hotel in Itasca, Illinois where we had a warm wedding meal accompanied by soft piano music. Adjourning to the Bridal Suite, we bounced on our wedding bed with Elaine's nieces. Then we tucked them in to our bridal bed with Bob & Maddie's oversight, and spent the night in the nearby extra room to celebrate our day.

ISRAEL

Several days later, and despite the protests of our families that it was too dangerous, we boarded El Al at O'Hare and flew to Tel Aviv. We were met and warmly greeted by Drs. Uri Taitleman and Fabio Zweibel, who drove us to the home of their chief, Simon Burzstein who himself was on sabbatical in Brussels. We settled in his home on the high plains of Haifa not too far from the Catholic Cathedral, Stella Maris where we often attended morning mass. From there, I would drive Simon's car to the Rambam Medical Centre each Tuesday, Wednesday and Thursday mornings to make Teaching rounds in the ICU, and to give seminars on the Pathophysiology of Critical Illness each afternoon.

Early on, we met Iasha and Elena Sznajder who welcomed us with Peter Breen to their home on a nearby kibbutz. In turn, they introduced us to another Critical Care fellow, Dr. Zohair Bshouty—he was the fellow who taped my seminars and lent them to Elaine to transcribe—who soon invited us to dinner at his family's home. In the midst of this socializing, we spent parts of the long weekend (Friday to Monday inclusive) with our new friends from the ICU attending staff and their wives, Uri and Daniela, Fabio and Cybelle, Iasha and Elena, and Meshke Michelson. Meshke was an intensivist trained in Scotland who often had thoughtful comments to make on Rounds or in the seminars. They were always greeted by Uri's response "I am sorry, Michaleson, but . . . ." Uri and Daniella often had us to dinner in their home, when Uri would give us a well prepared cocktail, saying he was an alcoholist—a specialist in alcoholic drinks—to be distinguished from an alcoholic who drank too much. And Fabio, so proud of his country, took us on road trips to the Lebanon border to show us where last night's shells fell, and had us get out of his car to walk until he had to warn us not to step off the road where land mines were planted.

One sunny midday, Uri and Fabio drove us to a Druze village and led us into a large reception room where a circle of Arabic men were awaiting our company. When Elaine and I were seated, many veiled women servants brought abundant succulent food to spread in front of us, and then rejoined the group in the kitchen. Elaine was the only woman present, and had the attention of all the servants from behind the walls to the kitchen. We were so well treated!

One other weekend, Elaine and I flew to Eilat and rented a car to drive down to the coast of the Red Sea and to visit Beersheva. All the tourists on the beach at Eilat were bare breasted, but Elaine preferred a quieter beach down the coast to doff her clothes and bathe in the Red Sea. Just as she entered, a jeep carrying six soldiers came rocketing towards us. Elaine called "what shall I do"? I replied "smile" as the jeep roared past.

These and other early anecdotes of our marriage may not differ from those of many readers. But they gave us a profound sense of wonder about how we were so very well looked after. Looking back from this time in Israel, we saw a continuum of treats from our courtship. Indeed we marveled at our God's generosity, and we began to wonder what return we could make.

After 8 weeks of teaching and traveling, we prepared to board El Al again, this time headed back to Chicago on the weekend before the Israeli troops invaded Lebanon. Back in Chicago, I visited Dr. Rubenstein's office to make our final agreement for my job offer. Among other errands, Dr. Rubenstein asked me to see Harvey Stein at the University's Immigration Office: a stern Stein reviewed my documents and said

"You may have a problem. You wish to become a resident alien while you are here in Chicago. Usually, our US Immigration Office will stamp your passport "unable to leave US pending receipt of Resident Alien Status". Yet you also want to leave for New Zealand in several days. You must do the following. Go down to the US Immigration Office to process your documents. If the agent stamps your passport "Unable to leave US", leave his office and call me directly. Then wait until the agent calls you back in to his office."

We did all he said, and when the sullen Immigration Agent called us back into his office to change our Passport to "Resident Alien. Able to travel out of the US", he said to us "I don't know how you did this, but you tell whomever did it that if they ever do it again, I will retaliate. We left, and several days later, boarded a plane for Auckland.

THE LAND DOWN UNDER

Elaine and I flew from Chicago to Los Angeles to Auckland in February of 1982. We were met by our professional host and hostess Ed and Barbara Harris, who took us to their home for tea and conversation. We so much enjoyed their charm and quiet elegance, and spent many hours with them during the next 10 weeks. A bit later that day of arrival, Ed drove us to Green Lane Hospital, and helped us settle in a cozy guest apartment in their Nurses' Residence. Once unpacked, we went for a walk on the green hills of the Hospital property—sprinkled with white-fleeced sheep—where subsequently we ran nearly every day.

After a good night's rest, Elaine set up our home away from home by shopping at the nearby centre—baby back rack of lamb was my favourite—while I visited Ed in his Pulmonary Physiology Lab and met his staff and colleagues. Together we mapped out the plan pre-arranged for my visit. Each Tuesday, Wednesday and Thursday morning, I made rounds with the famous team of cardiovascular surgeons lead by Sir Brian Barrett-Boyes, learning the principles of cardio-vascular surgery and especially of heart transplant which they pioneered and the peri-operative care that I sought to learn. On appointed mornings on that schedule, I joined Ed's Physiology team in the operating room to observe the working relationship the 2 teams were cultivating.

After lunch, we adjourned to the Conference Room where I conducted interactive seminars on Cardiovascular-Pulmonary Pathophysiology in the Critically Ill patient. I taught a slightly revised version of the Pathophysiology of Critical Illness recently completed in Haifa. And I spent part of my preparation time crafting the illustrations, legends and narrative that I would subsequently use in the first part of _Principles of Critical Care_ entitled _The Pathophysiology of Critical Illness_[1]. As judged from their feedback, the learning was useful to them, and the two teams helped me hone my teaching and writing, especially of cardiovascular physiology.

These 30 days of teaching covered the curriculum I had intended, leaving plenty of time for Elaine and me to visit this beautiful country each Friday through Monday inclusive. One long weekend we visited the deer farm of Barbara's brother, Bruce. Their property line ended at a long Cliffside overlook of the Tasmanian Sea. We were treated royally by Bruce and his family to fine Kiwi food and interesting conversation. So we were happy to be able to reciprocate the next summer when Bruce visited Chicago and enjoyed a Cubs ball game and many of the sights of Chicago with us.

On another weekend, we visited the Kauri forests of the North Island, taking in these magnificent old and gigantic trees. Then we attended a Maori feast and enjoyed excellent food, music and dance of the indigenous people. And on yet another North Island trip we enjoyed the Seven Mile Beach. All these travels were interspersed with the hospitality of Ed's friends and colleagues who frequently had us to dinner.

Then there was our South Island trip. I took 2 weeks off from my teaching routine so Elaine and I could fly to Christchurch and rent a car to tour the South Island. What magnificent terrain, with mountains, plains and fjords!! Near Queenstown, Elaine and I found ourselves high above the city on a mountain road surrounded by a herd of mountain goats. Elaine got out of the car to take their pictures and feed them, but quickly retreated back inside our car. As the goats clambered on top of our car roof, we drove off!!

In Queenstown, we embarked on one of many boats carrying tourists down the fjords to the open sea, passing close by hundreds of seals on the rocks and in the water. It was back in Queenstown when we inadvertently lost each other in the crowds and shops of the city. After several hours we reconnected, but it took several more hours to forgive each other. The mountainous terrain west of Queenstown came back to us 20 years later as we watched the Lord of the Rings trilogy and reminisced.

Back in Auckland, we took advantage of an inexpensive side trip to one of the South Pacific islands, New Caledonia. A French territory, the cultural mix of the Islanders with French traditions was a marvel to enjoy, perhaps second only to the extraordinary beaches where Elaine's second experience of topless sun bathing was complicated by a painful sunburn.

On returning to Auckland, we said our goodbyes to the Harrises and their friends, and flew to Sydney, Australia. At the Agricultural and Immigration station in the airport, a burly Australian agent gruffly asked us "where are you arriving from". I replied "from Auckland New Zealand". "And how long were you there?". "Ten weeks", I replied. "Hmph", he exclaimed, that's a bloody long time to be in New Zealand" as he stamped our passport for embarking to Australia.

While in Sydney, we visited my friend Ludwig Engel, who had done his PhD at the same time and with the same supervisor as I had at McGill in Montreal. Ludwig entertained us at a dinner party at his home, where other Australian friends from Montreal met Elaine, and we renewed acquaintances and traded stories. Paul Despas, David Lindsey and Norbert Berend were there with their families. When Ludwig asked his 8 year old daughter Jacqueline to ask the other children to assemble for dinner, "OK kids", she hollered, "go for it!!". And we all had a hearty laugh. Ludwig seemed proud to show me his laboratory and the hospital where he had his clinic and admitted his patients. And just like many times before, he gave me a lucid, enthusiastic explanation of his current research ideas and projects. I so regret his acquiring multiple myeloma, leading to his premature death.

As I write and reread this description, it sounds like an idyllic travelogue. And that is part of how it felt, but there was also the contribution this environment made for the growing intimacy of our relationship as we enjoyed together quiet interludes in these spectacular travels.

While in Australia, we took another side trip to Heron Island on the Great Barrier Reef. There, we could walk the reef at low tide to see the most marvelous array of living sea shells next to gorgeous sand beaches. And each evening after dinner was a slide presentation by one of the Sea Park Rangers on a different topic of reef life. This quiet gave us opportunity to reflect on the wonders of our meeting, how rich and many were the blessings we received, pressed down and flowing over into an attitude of gratitude that was hard to dismiss.

CHICAGO AT LAST

Flying home to North America brought us first to Los Angeles where we visited our friend Howard Goldberg. Howard is one of the two smartest people I have met in this interesting life. The other was Ludwig Engel, so it was an extraordinary coincidence that I met them both within days of each other on our way home. I was pleasantly surprised to notice how well I got along with each of them, for their demeanor and way of being with people tended to irritate whomever else they met. It wasn't that we didn't disagree, or even argue vehemently about many issues, for we did. If I understood our comradeship at all, it was because I often found them right and told them so. Accordingly, I learned more from Ludwig and Howard than from any other acquaintances, and for that gift I am grateful.

On the long flight from Sydney to LA, Elaine and I discussed the type of accommodation we would like in Chicago, for we had no experience before of living in our own home together. The upshot of this long conversation was the following dream we imagined for ourselves: location, in Hyde Park so I could walk to and from work across the campus in less than 20 minutes; décor, fully wooded with beams on the high ceilings and walls; spacious, with four bedrooms one devoted to us, a guest room in case our children or others came to visit, a home office for the 2 of us, and a quiet room for shared prayer with music including Elaine's guitar; a bright spacious dining room contiguous with a well equipped kitchen on one side and a bright airy living room on the other having a large natural wood burning fireplace; and 3 bathrooms, each with toilet, sink and shower. Ideally, these facilities would be housed in an elegant apartment building or a stand-alone home.

On arrival in Chicago, we settled in a downtown hotel near Hyde Park and the University of Chicago, and contacted a University Real Estate Agent. She picked us up to hear about our housing desires, and before we finished our description, she invited us to join her to look at an apartment we might like. It matched absolutely every feature we had imagined!! "We will take it" we said. "You can't have it", she replied. "It was rented earlier today, but I showed it to you anyway to get a concrete idea of what you were looking for."

Crestfallen, we looked at four or five other places, then took a 13th story tenement apartment in a slum-like setting for a short term accommodation until we could find something better. We looked at another listing in Mayor Washington's building, but the man who opened the door wearing a dirty t-shirt and talking on the phone invited us in to look around saying, "Don't leave before I tell you how I handle the cockroaches." Elaine replied, "I know, you put leashes on them", and we left. One dreary hot morning, our tenement phone rang and the familiar voice of our real estate agent said "Do you remember that first apartment I showed you? The people who took it found a home in the suburbs they want to buy, so that apartment is back on the market—would you like to see it again?"

See it?!! We'll take it, and we moved in to make it our home in August 1982, living there for 22 years until I retired. It was as perfect as we had imagined it.

6

Science, Belief and the Still Small Voice

The intuitive mind is a sacred gift
The rational mind is a faithful servant
We honour the servant
And have forgotten the gift.
~ A. EINSTEIN

So far in this book, I alluded to how the scientific method was used to answer several pathophysiological questions, and how my belief was associated with preventing my suicide and healing my arthritis. In the Preface, I told how Agnes' recovery seemed associated with both belief and science. Such incidents occur throughout the rest of the book, revealing my living the interface of science and belief. This chapter discusses the contributions of science and belief to gaining new knowledge.

As a prominent philosopher of science, Karl Popper thought that truth is revealed by determining what is left after all erroneous explanations are falsified[1,2]. This can be a slow and tedious process when there are many hypotheses to be tested and falsified. This makes truth an elusive concept, and science never proves anything; it only fails to falsify the existing mechanisms. The pursuit of truth is even more limited without accurate and reproducible measurement tools, such as MIGET in the first study, or double-indicator thermal dilution measurements of extra vascular thermal volume (ETV or edema) in the second study in Chapter 3. How then can we ever arrive at truth concerning questions of belief when we have no objective measures? So the search is on for an objective measure of God's existence in healing or conversation with Her people, or perhaps for a new paradigm as to what constitutes evidence sufficient to falsify hypotheses about belief such as *"God does not exist"* or *"God does not converse with His people"*.

SEQUENTIAL STEPS OF SCIENCE AND BELIEF

Science is the evidence-based generation of knowledge. The scientific method was developed to reject erroneous hypotheses because people observe what they expect[3]. Table 1 organizes the sequential steps for science (left column). Step 1 provides the background to the question from observation and experience, and Step 2 proposes an explanation—a hypothesis usually expressed in the negative—the null hypothesis (H_O), meaning that any difference observed between groups being studied is not due to one of the groups having been affected by the intervention being studied. Step 3 makes a prediction from the H_O, and Step 4 performs experiments to disprove the prediction[1,2] and so falsify the H_O. Living in an age when most new knowledge is generated by the scientific method makes most think there is no other way, but science has limitations. When followed rigorously, the scientific method is tedious and slow, it handles subjective hypotheses of great importance poorly, and the requisite controls make some experiments so cumbersome that the question under study is obscured.

Table 1:
Sequential Steps for Science and Belief

Steps	Scientific Method	Steps	Belief
1	Characterization from experience and observation	1	Noticing co-variables not seen together before.
2	Hypothesis; a proposed explanation	2	Develop a myth to explain and cope with the phenomenon
3	Deduction: prediction from the null hypothesis (H_O)	3	Expect to see the myth, as developed above, again
4	Test and experiment to falsify H_O	4	Confirmed/denied by still small voice or intuition

Not too long ago, scientific principles were not known or practiced, so another method of inquiry prevailed. Belief is a habit or state of mind which places trust in an idea or person without convincing evidence. Although many trace their system of beliefs to their mother's knee, modern neuroscience ascribes to the brain a function to help the organism cope with it's environment[4]. *Table 1* (right column) is my attempt to organize the corresponding steps for belief to those of the scientific method. When the brain notices disparate objects not seen together before (see Step 1, right column in *Table 1*), it makes up a myth—a belief to explain the phenomenon (Step 2). Beliefs are often subjective and not measureable, such as God or spiritual issues, so Step 3 expects to see it again as originally developed. Because it cannot be measured, and falsified, there is no corresponding disproof of Step 4 for belief, unless a credible witness can verify the belief. Then we can choose among the innumerable beliefs the explanation most likely to verify the phenomenon, generating an intuitive source of knowledge for those Physician-Scientists who seek it. I propose that belief most resembles science when the still small voice is heard to verify that belief. Many look down on such beliefs as a method of inquiry because they are strongly personal, cannot be externally verified, are not subject to falsification and can arise from preconceived ideas (*see Table 2, right column*). Yet it is compatible with science to keep an open mind about explanations that have not been falsified.

Interface is the site or process where two independent systems act on each other, such as science and belief as different methods of inquiry. Many transactions in my life are living this interface where I feel, think and work toward processing the integrated systems with ceaseless striving to understand or with active receptivity for revelation.

THE SCIENTIFIC METHOD AND ITS LIMITATIONS

For all its contributions, the scientific method has provided enough incomplete or erroneous explanations of reality to make us wary (*see Table 2, left column*). Many ascribe the birth of science to the publication by Issac Newton in 1687 of <u>The Mathematical Principles of Natural Philosophy</u>. For about 250 years thereafter, scientists probed nature with this ingenious theory or way of thinking to reveal more and more discoveries of how nature works. But in the last century, science revealed the world of sub-atomic physics which moved by different forces not explained by Newtonian laws, in a world of sub atomic particles requiring a different set of laws describing "quantum physics". When Einstein's general theory of relativity provided concrete explanation of Newton's physics, it was expected that general relativity would be compatible with quantum physics. Not so! Despite one hundred years of focused research, we haven't yet developed a unified theory to explain both classical and quantum physics. Though we may just be slow, the possibility arises that the scientific method is wrong[5,6].

Table 2:
Limitations of Inquiry and Knowing

Scientific Method	Spiritual Sources of Knowing
Newton's "Laws of Motion" do not explain Quantum Physics—no unified theory	Strongly personal
Darwin's "survival of the fittest" does not account for environmental influences on heredity by Lamarck	No external checks
Crick's "Primacy of DNA" excludes epigenetics—wrong	No measurements
Human Genome Project (HGP) predicted 120,000 genes but found only 25,000; only 300 genes differed between mouse and man	Cant' be falsified
misinterpretation of any step leads to the wrong conclusion	May arise from preconceived ideas
Belief can masquerade as Science	Requires verification by the still small voice
Controls can obscure the question	other voices intrude
Slow, tedious due to many erroneous hypotheses	

Similarly, formulation of the Laws of heredity of the species by Charles Darwin emphasizes "survival of the fittest" to account for the range of creatures in the world. Recently the data and interpretations of heredity put forward 50 years earlier by Lamarck demonstrated beyond a doubt that development of new structure and function is promoted by the environment of the species. Accordingly, Darwin's theory is now questioned as incomplete or even wrong and has been altered while we went looking for a more comprehensive theory[5,6].

The co-discoverer of the double-helix, Francis Crick, insisted that all reproduction was explained by the arrangement and duplication of four nucleic acids. This dictum excluded, even ridiculed, scientists presenting data suggesting influence on the expression of the nucleic acids by cell membranes, cytoplasmic substances, and extra cellular influences. The new science of epigenetics is reversing the Crick dictum and its interpretation to explain these extra-nuclear effects[5].

The completion of the Human Genome Project was accompanied by several startling revelations. The human genetic makeup had 75% fewer genes (25,000) than was predicted (120,000) from the theory "one protein, one gene". So current scientists are left wondering how the limited numbers of genes can produce so many proteins. Even more startling, the human gene makeup differs from that of the mouse by only 300 genes—where in the world came the influences to cause size and shape differences of the species so dramatically[5,6]?

I cited these 4 important theories with demonstrated error so that we all, scientists and believers alike, may retain skepticism about scientific evidence and its interpretation. Non-scientists need not feel triumphant about these shortfalls of science, for it is a strength of the scientific method to make itself vulnerable to criticism by obtaining accurate, reproducible data and interpreting these data in clear, unequivocal language. This scientific candor helps the scientific community revise erroneous theories as the most rapid approach to new knowledge. When we consider the limitations of belief, we do not compare errors for they are hard to detect in the softer language of belief. Instead, we look for outcomes of belief which, if true, provide enhancement of understanding sprinkled around the surface of science. In this sense, there is no war of worldviews for these two modes of inquiry are not competing for the same prize[7]. Instead, they arrive at the truth from different points of view: science looks outward to describe accurately how the world works, while belief looks inward with consciousness to find meaning and purpose. Choosing to see these processes as antagonistic perpetuates the human trait of arguing about which approach is best, whereas more knowledge is achieved when the participants admit that each has something to offer the other in the search for knowledge[7].

Every working scientist can look to their own research programs and find examples of the science process gone awry for one or more reasons. Let me illustrate other limits on science with several examples from my own research program.

1. A common limit on science is that the underlying mechanism may be misinterpreted, so care must be taken to question each step of the scientific method. An example with clinical implications was illustrated by the observation that O_2 consumption measured by the Fick technique ($VO_2F = CO\ (CaO_2\text{-}CvO_2)$) increased in septic patients when O_2 delivery ($DO_2 = CO \times CaO_2$) was increased[8,9] (*see Figure 1*). This observation could indicate that metabolism at lower values of DO2 was anaerobic. However, plotting calculated variables having shared parameters (viz CO, CaO_2) with measurement error produces just such a correlation in the absence of anaerobic metabolism. This was confirmed in the same studies[8,9] by measuring VO_2G ($VE \times (FIO_2 - FEO_2)$), a variable which showed no correlation with DO_2. Unfortunately, earlier studies concluded erroneously that metabolism was anaerobic which led to maximizing DO_2 when the patient didn't need more O_2, so volume loading and high levels of dobutamine aggravated pulmonary edema and arrhythmias.

Figure 1 – Science is Sometimes Misinterpreted

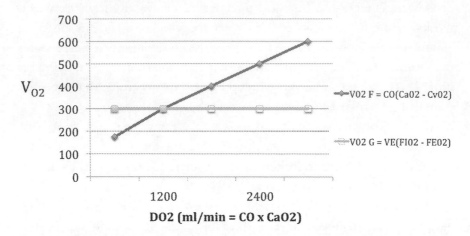

DO2 (ml/min = CO x CaO2)

Figure Legend: Schematic illustration of the relationships between mean DO_2 (abscissa) and two simultaneous measures of mean VO_2 (VO_2F equals diamond-indicated line, and VO_2G equals square-indicated line) in 10 patients in Reference 8. VO_2G does not increase with DO_2, indicating no anaerobic metabolism and so no benefit from maximizing cardiac output. But VO_2F increases with DO_2 due to coupling of shared measures having experimental error (CO, CAO_2).

To convince yourself, consider the data point $DO_2 = 1200$ml/min, $VO_2F = 300$ml/min, derived from cardiac output = 6 l/min. Now repeat these measures assuming no change in the patient status, but allowing experimental error to give cardiac output = 8 l/min; the new DO_2 is 1600 ml/min, the new VO_2 is 400 ml/min, and these coordinates lie on a positive relationship between VO_2F and DO_2, a spurious correlation due to the measurement error of cardiac output, but having nothing to do with anaerobic metabolism.

    2. Sometimes it is difficult to distinguish science from belief in revealing truth. In 2006, a multi-centre clinical study of fluid management strategies in 1000 patients with ALI demonstrated that conservative fluids were associated with fewer ventilator days without adverse cardio vascular effects compared to patients with liberal fluid

management[10]. Twenty-five years earlier, we had demonstrated in canine models of AHRF that reduction of PAOP by 5 mmhg 1 hour after ALI reduced edema accumulation by 50% during the next 4 hours[11,12]. In the intervening quarter century, considerable debate was waged between proponents of these strategies. I thought our results and the management goal arising—seek the lowest PAOP providing adequate CO and DO_2—were good science, and I used that goal in all my patients with AHRF (*see Table 3*), while others were worried about causing inadequate cardiac output, so they ensured enough positive fluid balance to maintain or even maximize CO and DO_2. Accordingly, I was delighted that the clinical study confirmed our approach, but asked myself, "was this science or belief?" It was indeed scientifically sound treatment for canine models of AHRF, but it was my belief that these canine

Table 3:
Therapeutic Goals in AHRF

	1980	2005

1	Seek Least PAOP/CVP
	- Adequate CO
	- Absent Pre-Renal oliguria
	- Absent Lactic Acidosis
	    J. Clin.Investig. 67:1981[11]
		Conservative fluid management
		- $\downarrow$ Ventilator Time
		- $\downarrow$ ICU Time
		- Without $\uparrow$ organ dysfunction
		    N.Engl.J.Med. 354:2006[10]

2	Seek least PEEP
	- 90% Saturation
	- Adequate Hemoglobin
	- Non-Toxic F_{I02}
	    J. Appl. Physiol. 57:1984[15]
		Higher PEEP not better than
		lower PEEP in ARDS
		    N.Engl.J.Med. 351:2004[18]

3	Seek least VT
	- Absent Acidosis
	    Am. Rev. Resp.Dis. 142:1990[16]
		Low VT (6 ml/kg)
		- $\downarrow$ Mortality
		- $\downarrow$Time on ventilator
		- $\downarrow$ Time in ICU
		    N.Engl.J.Med. 342:2000[17]

results would occur in patients that drove me to treat them with this regime while awaiting the clinical trial results. Perhaps we were lucky, perhaps intuition counts, or perhaps studying an appropriate animal model can provide direction long before the clinical trial can be organized and implemented. The lesson from these studies is that solid science in animal models led to treatment goals for the models, but extension of those goals to treat patients in the ICU is a belief until the clinical study demonstrates its utility in patients, no matter how long it takes.

Yet, clinical intuition should play a role until controlled clinical studies are performed. In the case reports and textbook guidelines describing treatment goals in AHRF[13,14,15] we used the least PEEP achieving its goals (*see Table 3*) and coupled that with the least tidal volume preventing unacceptable acidosis[13,14,16]. As indicated in Table 3, the therapeutic goals were supported by subsequent multi center clinical trials[17,18], conducted 25 years later, while all our patients were being ventilated with smaller VT and goal directed PEEP during that quarter century. This practice of ventilating patients with ALI with small VT was based on the intuition that if our patient's lungs were 80% flooded[15], we better give smaller VT or we will injure the aerated units further.

How many other standards of Critical Care cause similar damage until disproven?

3. This study illustrates another limit on Science[10]. The first protocol intervention occurred on average 43 hours after admission to the ICU. Thereafter, conservative fluid management was associated with a return to spontaneous breathing in 5 days by 255/500 patients, but only 200/500 patients receiving liberal fluids resumed spontaneous breathing. Accordingly, 55 patients were spared ventilator therapy by conservative fluid balance in the first 5 days, and no further difference was seen between groups after 5 days. It seems that most of the benefit of conservative fluid management occurs soon after ALI, and this study nearly missed and almost certainly underestimated it, by taking so long to get started.

So many controlled variables take time to organize[10]. This early therapeutic effect was evident in our canine studies when the reduction in PAOP was effected 1 hour after the injury, and promptly stopped further edema accumulation and its effect to increase Q_S/Q_T and reduce lung compliance further[11,12]. In a retrospective study of 40 patients with ARDS[19], the PAOP was already reduced 24 hours after admission, so one might expect a greater beneficial effect of conservative fluids than was observed in the multi-centre trial. Indeed, we reported an increase in survival from 29% to 75% in the low PAOP group[19]. It seems possible to obscure therapeutic effects by delaying the intervention until all the controls are in place. One cannot help but think it wise to lighten up on the controls in large clinical studies when intuition focuses on the important variable; otherwise you might end up with a very well conducted scientific study that concludes erroneously that the intervention had no effect on outcome. In the guise of critical thinking and right reason, the scientific method may cause us to falsify effective treatment.

4. Another question we attempted to answer was: How does increased pulmonary blood flow (Q_L) cause increased shunt (Q_S/Q_T) in pulmonary edema? For efficiency, we formulated two hypotheses which we could test in one canine study.

H_Oa: incomplete diffusion of oxygen between inspired gas and pulmonary blood contributes to Q_S/Q_T in pulmonary edema, and this diffusion defect gets worse when Q_L increases because the transit time for lung O_2 exchange shortens;

H_Ob: increased Q_L distributes preferentially to edematous lung regions.

To test H_Oa, we used the multiple inert gas elimination technique (MIGET) in both lower lobes and the whole lung before and after increasing QL suddenly and reversibly from 3.0 to 5.5 lpm by opening 2 systemic a-v fistulas. Unilobar acute lung injury (ALI) was produced by oleic acid injected into the left lower lobar pulmonary artery. MIGET demonstrated no diffusion defect for O_2 at either Q_L, so we rejected H_Oa.[20] And the lobar distribution of Q_L measured by differentially labeled radio active microspheres did not change when Q_L increased, so we rejected H_Ob,[20] and formulated another hypothesis.

H_Oc: increased Q_L increases edema to increase Q_S/Q_T. The key additional measurement needed to test H_Oc was an in-vivo reproducible accurate double indicator dilution estimate of extra vascular thermal volume (ETV) which uses heat as the diffusible indicator. When Q_L was increased from 5.0 to 6.9 lpm by opening a-v fistulas, Q_S/Q_T rose from 30 to 38%, but ETV did not change (7.8 to 7.4 ml/g dry lung). So we rejected[21] H_Oc and formulated a fourth H_O.

H_Od: increased Q_L raises mixed venous PO_2 (PVO_2), which blocks hypoxic pulmonary vasoconstriction (HPV) to send a greater proportion of increased QL to intralobar edematous regions to increase Q_S/Q_T. To test H_Od, we used an isolated blood perfused edematous canine lower lobe. When lobar blood flow increased with no change in PVO_2, Q_S/Q_T did not change. But when PVO_2 was increased using an oxygenator with no change in flow, Q_S/Q_T increased. At last, we found an hypothesis we could not falsify, so we concluded that Q_S/Q_T is increased by increased Q_L when the greater PVO_2 blocks HPV to increase blood flow to edematous intra lobar lung regions [22].

Pheewf!! That was a lot of work, and the scientific method was slow and tedious despite creative experimentation with optimal measuring devices, in part because there are so many erroneous hypotheses that need to be falsified before the truth becomes evident.

THE STILL SMALL VOICE VERIFIES BELIEF

My brief description in the Preface of Agnes' complex case probably makes sense to many readers, but I venture to guess that many more are confused or skeptical about the still small voice. For me, there was this background. Some 35 years ago on a spiritual retreat, I was instructed on the use of a spiritual journal[23]. Each entry began with a letter from me to the Lord of my life, describing my concerns and considerations for that day. But the second part of this experience seemed unusual—I write the Lord's response. The retreat directors, Matthew and Dennis Linn, outlined the characteristics of the response as: affirming, with a vocabulary of words and concepts not recognizable as mine, but compatible with my nature, usually of scriptural origin, and almost always surprising (*see Table 4, left column*). About that same time, I read two books recording the conversations with God by two listeners[24,25]. Immersed in reading the daily entries, I became habituated to these conversations as a prayer. When I found another compilation[26] of God's conversations 20 years later, they seemed perfectly natural.

Table 4:
Characteristics of the Still Small Voice

Linn's Attributes	Hybel's Filters
1. Scriptural	1. Scriptural
2. Consistently Affirming	2. Compatible with God's Character
3. Vocabulary of concepts/ words not easily recognized as one's own	3. Wise, simple, elegant choice of words
4. Surprised by novelty and fit of answers to questions	4. Direction of message compatible with character of listener

An interesting corroboration was published last year[27] in which author Bill Hybels describes how his life was favorably influenced by hearing and following the still small voice. Wishing to guide his readers on who was speaking, Hybels offered several filters to ensure it was God's voice. They matched the Linns' guidelines (*see Table 4, right column*). Then he told of writing his parishioners to solicit from those who had such experiences descriptions of God's conversation. Over one weekend he received 500 replies each describing messages of affirmation, admonition or calls to action. He concluded that we have a communicating God, and hearing His voice is a common experience, at least within Hybels' Parish. So I wonder how common it is among my colleagues in Critical Care. Again, I invite you to find in your own experiences any similar occurrences as a basis for exploring further this topic.

My experience with spiritual journaling over the intervening years was repeated, consistently affirming, scriptural, surprising. I recently scanned my ten 3-ring binders in which I had collected those conversations, and selected 10 consecutive conversational exchanges. I compiled these with other stories told in this chapter to get some feedback from some twenty friends. One reply was especially helpful:

"I was totally stunned by your story of "the still small voice". I have a HUGE problem with people who believe they communicate directly with God, and I have an even greater problem with those who try to justify it with such lightweight and 'shaky' logic. If I didn't know you better, I would say the person who wrote that was delusional, dysfunctional or just plain crazy."

In my view, this response articulated well several problems with living the interface of science and belief. First, "if not delusional, dysfunctional or just plain crazy", what am I? My best explanation is that I am a man living the interface of science and belief, taking the evidence of each seriously. This allows me to experience the joy and awe of discovery through science and the gratitude and blessing of conversation with God through belief. Second, what would we accept as evidence for God's existence or willingness to communicate? Classical arguments about God's existence convince believers and cause non-believers to look for more convincing evidence.

Listening for and hearing the still small voice is a complex human endeavor. It requires some or all of the following: belief that God can and will speak to me; a quiet spirit free from noise, hurry and crowds; a desire to know God's answers to my questions, or God's preference among courses of action in front of me; and a willingness to obey the instructions after putting the conversation to the test. Meeting all these criteria does not ensure hearing the still small voice, which is a mystery and a gift. Ceaseless striving for discovering alternative explanations for intuition or the still small voice can squelch these subtle movements of the spirit. Alternatively, cultivating these aptitudes for active receptivity is an all-consuming spiritual practice that can interfere with the search for more convincing evidence. So my approach is to go with the flow of the still small voice, choosing to listen rather than search.

MYSTICAL EXPERIENCES CONVINCE THE PARTICIPANT

After years of such spiritual journaling, I developed an ear for the still small voice, and the more I listened, the more I heard. If I were able to use the scientific method to test my belief that God exists and speaks to his people, I would phrase the null hypothesis "God does not exist/speak to His people". Then I would examine each of the entries in my spiritual journal for God's conversational attributes, and finding multiple responses to my inquiries, I would reject the hypothesis and conclude the opposite—God does exist and speaks to his people. I compiled ten such examples which falsified this H_O, provided my subjective evaluation is allowed as evidence. And there is the risk, for as convinced as I am by my subjective evidence, I do understand why the scientific method cannot accept it for lack of objective evidence and reproducibility in the observers. This does not weaken my belief that God spoke to me; indeed, my faith is enhanced and my enthusiasm to hear His word is heightened. Yet I do not expect others to be convinced by my subjective evidence—they must have their own spiritual experience before they become convinced.

Two other events add to my conviction that god intervened favorably in my life. In chapter 2, I told the story of the converging stresses I experienced in trying to complete and defend my PhD thesis while engaged in an arduous Critical Care fellowship training program. In the darkness of clinical depression, I considered suicide when the still small voice intervened "Try another way, chose life without your concerns by relinquishing them to my care and giving me your permission to look after them and you. Then watch what I do." In short order, I was given leave of absence from my Fellowship to complete and defend my thesis. When I returned with my PhD, I was informed by my Department Chair that my clinical training was complete and would I accept a Faculty position caring for critically ill patients and teaching Trainees how to do it while establishing a research program?

The other intervention occurred early in my relationship with Elaine when I told her about the progressive peripheral polyarthritis which I had suffered for the previous year. She listened empathically as I finished the story, and then asked if she could pray for me (see *Chapter 4*). "Of course", I answered, so she laid her hands on my left shoulder, praying. Immediately, I experienced warmth spreading from my left shoulder down my left arm and across my shoulders to my right arm, warming all my joints from shoulder to wrist and the metacarpal joints of each finger. This feeling lasted a few minutes, when the stiffness, pain and fluid in the joints disappeared and never returned. I know that I know God used Elaine's love to heal me, and I expect that this spiritual experience will have no effect on the belief of any others who hear this story—it is my spiritual experience, done for me alone, so anyone hearing this story is unlikely to be convinced—and any of my friends who wish to tap in to the spiritual experience need to have their own. It seems one cannot accept God's healing presence vicariously; one needs their own spiritual experience.

So belief becomes a personal choice to act on subjective perception of God's presence. It seems like my healing and my learning transcend all my understanding of how it can occur, so it is not unreasonable for me to invoke divine intervention. To the extent God did it, it is the polite behaviour for me to feel grateful and to express my gratitude to Her. Suspending my search for scientific proof seems like a good idea given my improved health. It is an even better idea given my prior faith experiences, so I have no trouble dealing with God as if She exists. This sets me free to converse with God and to hear Her still small voice. How else can God communicate with Her children? Besides, everything for which I do have scientific proof is so complex and beautiful that it draws out of me wonder and praise, so I get it both ways: my skepticism can't disprove God in scientific terms because I don't have a "Godometer"; and whenever I can prove anything scientific, the result causes me to praise God.

NEUROSCIENCES, QUANTUM PHYSICS AND MYSTICAL EXPERIENCE

In his discussion of the physiology of spirituality, Andrew Newberg outlines his attempt to elucidate the underpinnings of the spiritual experience using Single Photon Emission Computed Tomography (SPECT). During spiritual experiences in seasoned meditators, he discovered a neural pathway for spiritual experiences which differs from that used in day-to-day processing of materialistic observation. In particular, both parts of the autonomic nervous system were activated (sympathetic and parasympathetic outputs are almost always antagonistic), and there was a thalamic mediated shift in activation of self-orientation associated areas toward attention-associated areas within frontal lobes. These spiritual pathways help the brain in interpreting concepts like worship, love, prayer and altruism; and are used to process spiritual experiences, like those accompanying meditation, glossolalia and yoga[28].

Conceivably, this is how we are wired for spiritual experience. Yet he is quick to point out that the use of neural spiritual pathways does not prove the existence of God nor Her participation in conversation with, or healing of, Her children[C]. The "report back" of mystical or spiritual experience "feels real" to the reporter. To understand better, Dr. Newberg invites us to compare perceptions in the awake state with those in the dream state where those in the dream do not "feel real". This may seem flimsy evidence to validate spiritual experiences; certainly it is much more subjective than is allowed by the scientific method.

Epistemology alerts us to other ways of knowing. One such is the New Archaic based on performative spiritual practices which bind together fragmentary subjective experiences into one subjective sensation. Considerable neuroscience observation parallels this behavioral binding—there are 17 distinct brain areas in both hemispheres and at all levels responsible for religious, spiritual and mystical experiences (RSMEs) when they are integrated, yet during everyday activities each acts separately[29]. This brain activity underlies RSMEs as another form of belief.

A new discipline, Neurotheology, studies correlations of neural phenomena with subjective experiences of spirituality as well as hypotheses to explain this phenomena. The principles of Neurotheology are described in a new book by Andrew Newberg in which 54 principles are discussed as the foundation for this discipline[30].

Bruce Lipton is a cell biologist whose research focused on the cell membrane. He describes a spiritual awakening while contemplating the beauty and elegance of the membrane's mechanics:

"the fact that scientific principles lead me, a non-seeker, to a spiritual insight is appropriate because the latest discoveries in physics and cell

---

[C] My belief system includes God's gender as both masculine and feminine, so I alternate randomly.

research are forging new links between the worlds of science and spirit".[6]

One such link is our growing understanding of fields, the non-material region of influence which surrounds the energy of a system such as a magnetic field. Matter is energy bound within a field. And a field of compassion surrounds the physician and patient during the healing process to provide a space for the still small voice to speak and be heard[31].

In his classic series of lectures in 1902, William James cited numerous accounts of persons who had mystical experiences[32], often with profound and life-changing effects. He concluded that the beneficial effects of these experiences could not be discounted, yet he highlighted that these experiences were personal, could not be externally validated, and were limited to a select group of persons. Can others tap into this spiritual knowledge? Speaking from an extraordinary background as a healer, Caroline Myss says:

> "medical intuition can help Physicians to understand the human body to be both a physical system and an energy system, who have a spiritual context for the human experience, to identify the energy state of a physical illness and heal the underlying cause as well as the symptoms."[33]

An extraordinary interview tells about the power of myth[34]. A key concept is how myth exposes and explains the mysteries of life, most often inner mysteries through introspection. The far-fetched mechanisms said to underlie these mysteries lead many scientists to skepticism and disbelief. But these same scientists need to recall that many hypotheses to explain reality were equally outrageous before being put to the test without being falsified. Accordingly, it is not scientific to reject beliefs before they are falsified.

Taken together, theses eight observations link modern neurosciences with belief, inviting greater attention to a spiritual source of knowing. Accordingly, a demeanor of humility and docility seems to me a fruitful soil to grow understanding, for we have just begun to understand the meaning of belief.

A clarification of my meaning seems necessary. Standing at Agnes' bedside examining her and praying for help, I heard the still small voice. Yet it was not clear to me whether intuition intervened at that moment, or whether these circumstances facilitated the coalescence of brain activity set up and stored in neural circuits during 30 years steeped in the care of such patients and the 20 studies I published about acute lung injury to produce correct clinical judgement. Either way, I acknowledge being used to help Agnes. Furthermore, I have no doubt that what one hears is influenced by how deeply one is immersed in the psychospiritual drama of the patient and her illness. I believe that hearing and acting on this voice is every person's challenge, not confined to Physicians and Patients. I invite the reader to search for such occurrences in their own lives, for here lives the person—fully alive in balancing science and belief to seek truth and be helpful. This is living the interface of science and belief, standing in the uncertainty trying to discern the integration of acquired knowledge most helpful to a patient.

SUMMARY—SCIENCE AND BELIEF ARE COMPLEMENTARY

We have been discussing two modes of inquiry, Science and Belief (*see Figure 2*). With ceaseless striving scientists develop H_Os which might explain phenomena and use the scientific method to falsify these H_Os, such that truth consists of H_Os which could not be rejected. Clockwise rotation from the interface of science and belief depicts the start (and end) of our understanding when we began reading this chapter.

But I introduced the notion that belief and its interface with science can be processed with active receptivity to develop innumerable myths to explain reality. Then the still small voice or intuition serves as the hammer to nail down the myth which best explains the phenomena under study, verifying it as truth to contribute to our new knowledge as depicted—by counterclockwise rotation from the interface—in the right side of Figure 2. When intuition verifies a myth, it creates a spiritual source of knowing, akin to the scientific method. Accordingly, science and belief are complementary methods of inquiry and knowing, each providing limited understanding, but together increasing the probability of knowing.

Figure 2 – Methods of Inquiry

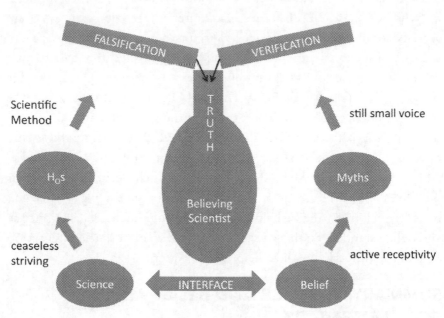

Figure 2: Schema depicting the methods of inquiry and their interface. Science goes clockwise toward falsification, and those H$_O$s not disproven pour into the chamber of Truth; belief moves counter-clockwise from the interface through innumerable myths until the most benevolent and the true myth is verified by the still small voice and enters the chamber of Truth.

Table 5 compares the attributes of these methods of inquiry. The scientific method protects us from bias and erroneous H$_O$s using intellectual disciplines of statistics and logic, while the still small voice requires faith to verify beliefs. Science is objective and measured, but belief is subjective and often not measured. Accordingly, science cannot process phenomena of great importance, but belief can process interior mysteries with active imagination ratified by the still small voice. Science is tedious and slow and too many controls can distort the study, while belief proceeds at a furious pace when the believer is affirmed, presenting innumerable myths for the still small voice to choose from. And even when the chosen belief is wrong, the process of communication builds relationship between the believer and the still small voice.

Table 5:
Attributes of the Methods of Inquiry

Science	Belief Verified
The scientific method	Spiritual source of knowledge
Formulate null Hypotheses (H_O)	Makes up a stories—myths
Falsifies H_O	Sorts, chooses most benevolent myth
Truth is what can't be falsified	Truth is verified by the still small voice
Objective, Measurable, Calibrated	Subjective, no measures but belief
Can't handle the subjective	Can process subjective mysteries with active imagination ratified by the still small voice
Slow, tedious to rule out H_Os	Imprecise innumerable myths
Excess controls distort the study	Intuition simplifies the study
Conclusion: Science and Belief are complementary	

As often, Albert Einstein has a last word. Consider one meaning of his opening verse: acknowledging the rational mind as a faithful servant of the scientific method deserving honour, we risk unbalanced comparison when we forget the sacred gift of intuition expressed as belief verified by the still small voice.

PART II

Return of the Children

Six Years Later

I miss you today. Not often,
but today there crept an inner sadness
from beneath the residue of completed grants—
a feeling dark and empty
emerged in the wake of passing accomplishment
and struck my satisfied heart.

It snuck up on me while I planned to work at home
but I cleaned my dresser instead
—there you were
three years old in a red coat and white scarf
to match the snowman we built
Then five with John on a beautiful Banff mountain
and last—yes, last—about eleven
with all of your family—

Mother, three brothers and sister
looking composed, content at all ages.
Squirming James—just two—
made me cry like the baby he was.
And impish Teresa kept me flowing
with her happy face.
Over Peter and John
I wept on for my mistakes.

But you I missed.
As the daughter of the man for all seasons—
leaving him to his self-inflicted solitude
after losing to him her loving battle of wits—
was missed by Thomas; deeply soberly, calmly,
missed.

7

The Courage To Be First

I became separated from my children in 1978. Then, they ranged in age from 11 to 2 years old. In the ensuing 6 years, I had gained considerable new life while living with the Marianists and then in my marriage to Elaine. We often prayed for the children, and I wrote to each as they grew older, aware that their mother would likely not allow the mail through.

Then came a breakthrough! Fr Ray Baudry, who had been my parish priest in Winnipeg and was the court appointed mediator of my visits with the children, visited me and Elaine in Chicago. He said that Catherine was well, but that she had received none of my previous letters. He thought she would appreciate hearing from me! She was no longer living at home (at 15!) and supported herself financially by working part time after school and during the summers. Since grade 9, Catherine had received bursary support from her private Catholic school based on her grades, which, in combination with the money earned during her summer jobs, allowed her to continue her education at St. Mary's Academy. I was impressed with her industry, and was clear that she must want to attend that school!

So it was that Catherine received a letter that I wrote to her for her 16th birthday, sent in care of the Principal of her high school, Sr. Susan Wikeem. Catherine was invited to Sr. Susan's office and advised of the arrival of my letter. Sr. Susan offered that if Catherine wanted my letter it was there on her desk, and further offered that Catherine could have use of her office to read the letter at her leisure if she chose. So supported, Catherine received my letter, and we began a letter-writing relationship which lasted two full years and led to her visit in September of 1985, just prior to her 18th birthday.

The years of letter writing helped to solidify a new ground for relationship between father and daughter, and introduced Elaine and Catherine to one another. In her letters, Catherine conveyed that our connection through communication was helpful/vital to her at this time in her life.

Over those 2 years, I learned that her Granny—with whom Catherine had always been close—had allowed Catherine to live with her in her small one bedroom apartment. Given her situation, Catherine had accepted my offer to legally sever the child-support payment intended for her from the monetary contributions I had been sending to her mother, and to send it directly to Catherine as of her 16th birthday. She reported that this was helpful, as she was able to manage her finances without having to work so many hours and this benefited her school work.

I was encouraged as to Catherine's wellbeing despite the acrimony with her mother and the separation from her siblings because of the lively written descriptions of her engagements with scholastics, extracurricular activities including Drama Club, Student Council and her selection as Editor of her high school newspaper. It appeared that her physical and emotional wellbeing benefited from her close relationship with both her Granny and with her aunt/friend Marianne. Her social, intellectual and spiritual development were reflected in her academic pursuits and her community of friends both at school—and then at her job. I read on through the years as she graduated from high school and moved into her own small apartment with help from her Granny who co-signed the lease. I wanted to meet her, but I didn't want to push.

It so happened that Catherine had a friend who attended a school at which Brother Richard—a member of the Marianist community with whom I had lived for 3 years—taught. One night, that friend (Michael) excitedly and carefully told Catherine that Brother Richard had taken several students on a school trip during which they had a stop-over in Chicago and had stayed overnight with a 'Larry and Elaine Wood'. Michael related that he had approached Brother Richard and the two of them had sorted out that indeed these same hosts were Catherine's father and his wife. Michael encouraged Catherine to meet with Brother Richard: "Talk to him, Catherine. You've been doing so great on your own for so long, but what if this guy and his wife—who everyone says are so fantastic—just want the opportunity to love you? You owe it to yourself and to them to check it out." So a meeting was arranged with Brother Richard, and Catherine was able to assure herself that visiting me would be safe and even life-giving.

Brother Richard and I later discussed the feasibility of a visit by Catherine to Chicago. He explained that since Elaine and I had each other to discuss the visit as it proceeded, he thought she should bring a friend to support her. I wrote to Catherine inviting her to visit, and offering the opportunity for her to bring a friend.

So while I was out jogging, Elaine answered the phone in the late summer of 1985. The voice on the other end of the phone inquired, "Hello, is Larry there please?" "No, he's out right now," Elaine replied, "may I take a message?" There was a pause, and then "Elaine? It's Catherine."

"CATHERINE!!" squealed Elaine in her characteristic playful outgoing voice and excited demeanor. They talked for a few minutes, and Catherine told Elaine that she was calling to accept my offer that she visit, "and Garth agreed to come with me". When I got home to hear Elaine's story, I was excited that I was going to have a visit from my 17-year-old daughter. And I was doubly excited that Elaine had taken the call, for I did not trust myself with the news that my 17-year-old daughter was bringing Garth. Who was he—she must have written about him—wasn't he her grad date? Are they romantically involved? Do they need separate bedrooms? Elaine calmed me by telling me that Catherine said Garth was a good friend who volunteered to keep her company while she met her Dad again. And he was just that—a mature young man who took his role seriously, and also looked forward to seeing Chicago.

Catherine and I had a lot to discuss. We always conversed well. Back when she was 3 years old, we were waiting for the luggage in a Caribbean airport. I was explaining the luggage transfer system, and she was asking me questions about it when the attendant interrupted to say "Can she understand all that?" to which Catherine replied, "of course I can he's my dad! I understand most of it, and I can ask about the rest." So we picked up where we left off! Over the 2 weeks of her inaugural visit to our home in Chicago, we gave each other updates on the missing 6 years of our relationship—at home, out driving, at Cubs, Bulls and White Sox games, while enjoying the Art Institute of Chicago and Theatre performances and while walking the shore of Lake Michigan. She met Elaine's large family, and tentatively began new friendships with the older nieces. Her appreciation for the size of my "new" family and the love that was evident between me and them grew. She told me of her love for her own sister and brothers, and how sad she was that her mother would not let her see them. Her mother believed that Catherine was not good, even threatening to obtain a restraining order if Catherine called, visited or tried to communicate. In the quiet of her heart, Catherine worried about her siblings. Simultaneously, she sought a balanced life.

You had to be there as Catherine and Garth experienced Elaine and me! Our memories of recent distance were informed by the marvel that we were together after all these years.

Our relationship with Catherine flourished, and we enjoyed many visits, vacations and adventures over the years that followed. Catherine moved from Winnipeg to Calgary to be a fulltime, live-in Nanny for 3 young children whose mother had died suddenly. She also engaged in independent travel, moved to Ontario and completed her University degree in Communications (with Honours) and followed that later with a Graduate Certificate in Executive Coaching from Royal Roads University in Victoria, BC. She was reunited with all of her once-estranged siblings, and enjoyed successes in her career life. She fell in love in St. Catharines, moved to Montreal then Vancouver, discovered self-expression in the world of entrepreneurship, and married Nicole in a created ceremony on a West Coast beach.

Catherine's communication skills, business acumen, and a desire and competency to help others fulfill their dreams brought her to a career as a Certified Executive Coach (CEC) in Vancouver, BC. A member of the International Coach Federation, she was awarded their Professional Certified Coach (PCC) designation in the Spring of 2010. She has been a practicing Coach since 2000, founded her own Coaching business in 2006, and incorporated in 2008.

In her spare time, Catherine enjoys kayaking, cycling, walking on the oceanfront a few blocks from her home, and spending time with family and friends. We are blessed to spend time with her and her spouse Nicole. I am especially grateful for Catherine's loving transcription of this book. I frequently ran into roadblocks on the way to finishing this book, so I appreciated Catherine's ingenuity in helping us find a way past. In particular was the new world of acquiring a Literary Agent, preparing a Book Proposal after the book was completed, and working with the Agent to get a Publisher to accept and promote the book. Her companionship in the decision to Self-Publish helped to move both energy and action forward. Smaller victories Catherine brought to my book writing were the multiple correspondences concerning 10 invitations to write and speak about aspects of the book in its diverse format, including Journal Editorials, Medical Conferences, Podcasts, and acceptance speeches at receptions for awards given to me. These activities continued the depth of communications begun in the Caribbean luggage room.

8

The Joy of Being Loved

It was during conversations with Catherine that I learned that John was not living at home, but in an adolescent half-way house because he had had trouble with the law, and his mother felt she could not discipline him to control his behaviour.

I was livid—my not-yet-15-year-old son in a half-way home to control his behaviour while I was excluded from his care because his mother judged that I was not good for him!! I also learned that the monetary contributions I was sending to his mother were not going to John at all.

Immediately, I made contact with the Provincial Child Care Services Department to indicate my desire to care for John. In due course, they responded to say it might be possible for John to visit us in Chicago, provided their counterpart organization could interview us and visit our home to assure them the environment was healthy for John. In the meantime, having returned to Winnipeg from her inaugural visit to Chicago, Catherine met with John to tell him of her visit with us. And she proposed to him (and us) that she would love to accompany him on his first visit. She encouraged him to write us a letter, and perhaps send us a current photo of himself. She also told him that his dad was looking forward to meeting him and to helping if John would let him. For his part, John endured his mother's dismay and reluctance to have him visit his father; she released him to the care of the social system and his social worker approved the plan for John to visit with me in Chicago. On our end, we met with Childcare Services in Chicago who approved a visit for John (now a ward of the Manitoba Court) to our home in Chicago in April of 1986.

We were ecstatic!! And sensitive to the troubling encounter John had endured. Catherine arrived a day or so before John, and the three of us eagerly awaited John's arrival at the O'Hare Airport. John was all of 6 feet tall, a bit porky at 210 lbs, with shoulder length curly hair and an easy-going disposition. Catherine's presence during the first week of John's inaugural visit was helpful to her brother while he reacquainted himself with his old man—whom he had last seen when he was 9 years old—and my wife Elaine. Overall, we had a marvelous visit which included spending time with Elaine's large family—her 2 sisters and brother and their families which included Elaine's 7 nieces and a nephew.

During his visit, we planned to attend a Van Halen concert at the Rosemount Horizon in Chicago. On the day of the concert, we three got into our car—Elaine driving, John in the front passenger seat and me in the back—and set out. We had traveled less that a block when John pulled out a Mickey of whiskey from his pocket and took a swig. Dumbfounded I asked Elaine to pull over and stop, while I interrogated John. "What do you think your doing?" He replied "getting ready for the concert." I then lectured him succinctly. "You are not at the legal age to drink alcohol. And open bottles of any liquor are illegal in the car. If you are going to live with us, you are going to follow the rules." We proceeded to the concert, where John lost himself in the pot-filled audience, and we who had not been alerted to the noise problem, lost a modicum of hearing.

John had to return to his Group Home in Winnipeg per prior agreement, but in a few months he received permission to move permanently to live with us in Chicago. Shortly after arriving, we met with Mr. McConnehae, the principal of the Lab School, a prestigious high school on the University of Chicago campus across the street from our apartment. It was established that John could return to school there in grade 11, and he did so in September 1986. A gregarious youth, John fit in well in the classroom where he excelled, and on the varsity soccer, baseball and track-and-field (shotput) teams, because he played those sports well. He took his Scholastic Aptitude Test (SAT) and scored well to set himself up for admission to a good University.

It happened that I was scheduled to speak at a Critical Care conference in Australia in the autumn of 1986, and Elaine's expenses were paid to join me. We discussed options with Mr. McConnehae, who urged us to take John with—"he will learn much more on such a trip with you than he would learn if he stayed home". Then we contacted Catherine to invite her to join us. We four had a splendid trip to Sydney, stopping on the way for about a week in each of Fiji and Tasmania. After visiting Sydney briefly, Elaine flew home with John so that he didn't miss too much school, while Catherine and I proceeded to several interesting side-trips and speaking engagements for me in Sydney, Perth and Adelaide. In each site, we encountered friends and professional colleagues of mine who were most hospitable to each of us, so we had a marvelous time, and got to know each other a lot better.

Elaine was an integral part of welcoming John (and Catherine) into our home and our lives, and making us a family. But she was about to experience the death of her mother (May 1987) and father (September 1987). When her mom was hospitalized with pneumonia, we brought her dad to live with us during his radiotherapy for prostate cancer. He did well for several months after Elaine's mom died, but he deteriorated in the fall while John was living with us and attending grade 12. John and Poppo got along well, and John was with Elaine when her dad breathed his last on a sunny Saturday morning; I was out of Chicago speaking at a conference when Elaine called to say her dad died, so I hurried home.

Elaine was so busy arranging her dad's funeral and serving as executer of his will that my next trip snuck up on us. For I was scheduled to give several talks at a large gas exchange conference in Barcelona in mid-October. In the midst of Elaine's grief, we decided she should come with, and we made arrangements for John to stay with our friends in Hyde Park, Barbara and Jesse Hall.

So we took off for a 3 week trip to Barcelona, and stayed for a week in the Benedictine Monastery at Montserrat just north of Barcelona in Spain. This was a quiet time for Elaine to process the death of her 2 parents, with whom she was very close—rest, choral music, fun food, and beautiful Montserrat surroundings blessed our time there. Before we left Spain, we visited friends in Mallorca.

On our return home, we found John depressed. This condition worsened until he felt unable to go to his classes, and he became quite insolent toward Elaine. We sought help for him, and a professional offered the following as the psychodynamics of his condition: John felt excluded from his birth mother, who would not correspond or speak with him by telephone, so he was taking it out on Elaine. John and I made a futile interview trip to some top west coast engineering schools of his choice—Harvey Mudd and Claremont Colleges—but John was in no condition to interview well, and our time together was not helpful for his depression. Finally it grew so uncomfortable for Elaine in her own home that I met with John to discuss his departure. We agreed that if he maintained a civil behaviour toward Elaine, he could stay until his graduation. He did, and in mid-June, John left our Chicago home for Winnipeg, having applied to several good colleges before he left.

And immediately he improved! We got reports of his making breakfast for his host family, getting and working at a well paying job, and having warm encounters with my parents, his grandparents. Then came the good news of his being accepted at Trinity University in San Antonio, Texas. John flew from Winnipeg to San Antonio by way of Chicago, where he stayed with us for a few days to gather his requisite belongings and then John and I traveled together to register at Trinity. Then, during his first year, Elaine and I attended parents week-end to meet his friends, see his classrooms, watch him play lacrosse, and generally enjoy his University surroundings.

John made a powerful difference for at-risk youth while volunteering with the Upward Bound Program in San Antonio, and growing it into the Youth Empowerment Services (YES) for which he served as Chair; YES flourished and became the reputed Higgs Carter King Charter School. Beyond graduating in Engineering, John is a Certified Professional Engineer (PE), a Certified Commissioning Professional (CCP) and a LEED Accredited Professional (Leader in Energy and Environmental Design). John worked for 5 years with Sun Energy Systems building solar energy collectors and designing, installing and maintaining solar thermal systems. He also worked with Jade Mountain as the Appropriate Technology Access Facilitator where he designed, installed and facilitated access to renewable energy, water conservation, water purification, energy efficient appliances, lighting, and other appropriate technologies for sustainable living. He currently serves as the Commissioning Professional on the Building Commissioning Projects for Architectural Engineering Corporation in Boulder.

After Trinity, John also earned his black-belt in Tae Kwan Do, and he learned to play golf. On a summer visit to Chicago, he got me back on the golf course for my first game in 30 years. This kick-started my game during the next 20 years, as he lowered his handicap to 5.5. But the golf highlight for me occurred during the last two summers when a 3rd golfer joined our game—John's brilliant 5-year old son Liam—who already has a wonderful swing and hits the ball every time up to 100 yards straight down the middle. We are so blessed to have John back in our lives, together with his wife Kirsten—a former Engineering classmate—and our grandson Liam, who has recently become the big brother to our 2nd grandson, Ansel. John has become a loving, caring father for his two boys. We have seen him more with Liam over the last 6 years, but we notice the same affection and quality time devoted to Ansel during his first year of life. John's reading quality books to Liam facilitates Liam's prolific reading habit; sharing building and construction games give Liam confidence in expressing himself with creativity; and quality play time with diverse sports has encouraged Liam's development in soccer, baseball and lacrosse—and above all in golf, where Liam recently won his first US Kids Golf Tournament. I am very proud of John's parenting.

9

Longing For Home

Catherine and John came back into meaningful relationships with us in 1983 and 1986 respectively. Several years passed, while we learned that Teresa had left her mother's home at the age of 16 to live with her good friend's family. She applied successfully for a scholarship to take her Grade 11 in Évreux, France, returning to Grade 12 to her friend's family in Winnipeg. After graduating, she returned to live with her host family in Évreux for another year.

We took the opportunity to visit Catherine at her University town of St. Catharines, Ontario in 1992, during a time when we knew Teresa was visiting her sister. This was a reunion for the sisters who had not seen one another since Catherine had left home—9 years. Not wanting to impose ourselves on Teresa, we left it up to Catherine to discern whether Teresa was open to meeting us. I recall vividly wasting time bowling with Elaine as the time for meeting Teresa passed without a call. We later learned that Teresa told Catherine that she was not ready, for she had not received or not read our letters.

Catherine told us that the experience of letting Teresa know that we were at the bowling alley awaiting a chance to meet her but not wanting to pressure her was intense. The sisters drove to the bowling alley, but Teresa chose in the last moments to not go in. Honouring her sister's timid and racing heart, Catherine had to drive out of the parking lot, hoping that we would not be too upset. Teresa was leaving the next day, and we were slated to visit with Catherine. Although this was an enjoyable visit, there was a shadow, as we had missed Teresa, and the pain of separation was present. Yet we were grateful that our daughters had spent this time together.

When Teresa was back in Évreux, she made a plan to manage a first phone call with me including hooking up a tape recorder to the phone. Surprised that our voice mail was activated, and disappointed that her tape recorder plan was not going to work, she abruptly left her name and phone number. Let Teresa recall in her own words what happened when Elaine returned her call: "I kinda gulped and picked up the phone and said hello. All I heard was "Teerreeeesssaaaa!" in that super-excited Elaine squeal. In that instant all my concerns and fears dissolved. When his gentle voice came on the phone, I already knew that I loved him and I loved the woman who loved him. That is how I remember meeting my dad."

Shortly thereafter, Teresa wrote us to describe her life circumstances and willingness to meet us; she included some photos of herself. We wrote back in August 1992 with an invitation for her to join us during the Christmas holiday season. Our Christmastime together with Catherine, John, Teresa and Elaine's family was yet again a wonderful reunion and a rich process of getting to know each other.

We continued to correspond during the next year, and arranged to spend Christmas 1993 with Catherine at her University home. Teresa flew from her Évreux home to Toronto to join us for our second Christmas together. We had many conversations to update each other about happenings since last Christmas, to talk more about our lengthy separation, and to discuss future plans while we visited Catherine's campus at Brock University. Teresa brought with her some academic records to discuss the possibility of studying law in Paris. And I had brought the application for admission to the College of the University of Chicago.

On the last day of her visit, Teresa and I reviewed the Chicago application, and found that she had all the requisite records with her to complete the application, with the exception of several essays, which she needed to submit. When Teresa saw the deadline for receipt of the application was in early January, she realized that she would have to complete the essays and mail the application that very day if she were to begin University in the fall of 1994. So she did it! And she was accepted!!

Looking back, I see how this remarkable cascade of events plucked Teresa out of a leisurely plan for post-high school hiatus in education in Évreux, and kick started her study at one of the finest Colleges in the world. And we who lived on the campus of the University of Chicago got to see a lot more of her during the next four years. A mature student with excellent grades, Teresa applied for a position as Resident Assistant (RA), and was accepted during her second year. This was unusual, for almost all RAs are in their junior or senior years. She often spoke enthusiastically about her counseling and mentoring roles with her cadre of freshmen protégés, and she was proud of the team work she helped facilitate in that group.

Accordingly, it was a great loss when two of the freshmen students in another group suicided in the Spring of Teresa's sophomore year. Her grieving took a toll, and Teresa elected to study abroad for her third year, returning to her roots in Western Canada at British Columbia's Simon Fraser University. There she performed well academically, and regained her poise and confidence. She returned to Chicago for her Senior Year, graduating with honours and a major in Philosophy in the Spring of 1998.

Throughout these 4 years, Teresa participated in quality scientific research with my colleague, Dr. Paul Schumacker. She developed a respect for the research process, and contributed significantly to a paper published with Paul in the Journal of Biological Biochemistry. And I had the pleasure of Teresa's participation in a Spring Elective course during her Senior Year, "Spirituality and Healing in Medicine". An avid learner always well prepared to discuss the topic of each session, Teresa chose to write an essay required of students seeking a Letter grade for this course. She wrote a splendid exposition entitled "Listening to the Heart", in which she compared and contrasted two patient interviews to illustrate the values of empathetic listening by physicians to their patients. She came to several Medical School Curriculum Review Committee meetings with me, where she was quick to pick up on the strengths and weaknesses of this forum.

Several years later, Teresa applied to Medical School at the University of British Columbia, and was admitted in 2002 after completing a postbaccalaureate pre-medical course to prepare for the Medical Sciences. She graduated in 2006 with her M.D., and was chosen by her class to be Valedictorian. During Medical School she spent away rotations in Zimbabwe, Africa and in Vanuatu, South Pacific. Subsequently she completed her Residency in Family Medicine; shortly after she enjoyed a 6-month vacation in New Zealand and Hawaii, one month for every year of training in Medicine. Since her return, she has practiced Medicine in the Yukon to connect with her younger brother James who worked there, and then in diverse medically underserved regions of BC. She married Alfie and they bought a condo in Squamish BC, a short drive from their parents' homes.

Beyond her career in Medicine, Teresa cultivated talents as a Spoken Word/ Slam Poet, and she has published several poems. Before entering Medicine, she developed a seminar series on sexuality, which she presented to diverse audiences to great approval. She continued to develop her ideas through Medical School and Residency, and is planning to integrate couple's therapy into her Family Practice. Intensely interested in how women are mistreated by the current practice of Medicine, Teresa is constantly searching for ways to make medical care more effective and more sensitive to women's issues. To achieve this end, she has seriously considered entering the political arena. It is a source of pride for me to see how she does all things well. We are so lucky to have her back in our life—the 13-year absence that once seemed interminable is now followed by 17 years of renewed relationship.

An unexpected joy comes to me in our relationship—Teresa's enthusiasm for sharing stories about her patients, their diagnosis and treatment. I am glad she entered Medicine, for I enjoy listening to her think through complex presentations of her patients. And it satisfies me to notice that I rarely have anything to add except to affirm her plan. A unique strength of her practice is her ability to listen empathically to her patients. As a result, she shares frequently about the nuanced process of getting to the bottom of the patient's real problem—that which lies below their entrance complaint. My experiences with many Medical Students helps me distinguish the true healers in the medical profession.

Paternal bias aside, Teresa is a Healer as well as a doctor. Indeed, her healing approach often wins over supporting staff of the clinics where she works so she is getting to make the systematic changes in women's care as she intends.

10

Building Community

When I left his family, sweet baby James was a toddler and while we were apart, he had grown through grade school and graduated from St. Paul's High school. By then, he and his brother Peter were my only children living at their mother's house. I heard from his other siblings that James was a good football player—a running back with his High School team and with the Juvenile team in the community league. With his childhood friend Ryley, he embarked on a long road trip from Winnipeg to St. Catharines' to reacquaint himself with Catherine (whom he had not seen in over 9 years) while Teresa was also visiting with her. While there, James sought opinions from his sisters about visiting us in Chicago. Hearing nothing but favorable reports, and struggling to find a path after high school, he wrote and phoned us to plan a holiday visit in December 1994.

He arrived on November 22nd! I was surprised to see the 2 year old toddler I remembered as I last saw him—now grown at 18 years old to 6 ft 1" and 190 lbs. He had graduated from St. Paul's High School several months earlier, and wrote before he came about his goals for the near future: to visit us for several months; to travel to San Antonio Texas to become re-acquainted with John; while there get a "Texas" job, preferably working with horses; and once he had saved enough money, to travel to Europe and meet/stay with some of the family friends with whom his siblings had visited. This plan was a distillation of many more possibilities he considered during the 2 months he stayed with us in Chicago. If there was one glitch in his plan, it was that he was also seeking financial independence, and he could not see how to achieve it while conducting his 4-point plan.

So we helped him by offering travel and living expenses, arguing that these funds replaced those he did not get while he lived with his mother. His presence warmed our hearts, for he was a bright, articulate, gregarious young man who said he enjoyed his time with us. He fit well with Elaine's family of nieces, and Elaine was her hospitable self in making James comfortable while he was getting to know me. Looking for someone to lead him forward, he said he enjoyed the many hours of discussions we had about his future.

When he left Chicago for San Antonio, he seemed much more clear in his plans for the near future, which were quite similar to the ideas he arrived with. What had changed for him was the new confidence he acquired in these plans. To our surprise and delight, he got a job working with horses shortly after meeting John. They hit it off well together, and James spent another 3 months there. While in Texas, James contacted his sister Teresa, and when he left Texas 3 months later for Chicago, they arranged a trip to Myrtle Beach, a reunion trip for 2 good friends who had grown up together until Teresa left home when James was 13 years old.

During that time, he contacted several of the family friends in Marburg, Germany and Évreux, France to set up a travel itinerary for Western Europe. He traveled for 5 months on his own and with friends from Winnipeg before working for 3 months in Scotland in various tourist jobs, earning spending money and extra funds to stay longer. James returned home to Chicago in November 1995 with great travel stories complete with illustrative maps and timetables from his 7-month tour.

Once back in North America, James relocated to the West Coast of Canada. There he enrolled in the University of Victoria in the winter of 1996, and he graduated with a BA and Major in Anthropology in 2003, together with a Certificate in Community Economic Development from Simon Fraser University. While enrolled in academic programs, James gained valuable practical experience in Community Economic Development working with several non-governmental agencies (NGOs). In 1999, he worked with the Victoria International Development Education Association (VIDEA) for 8 months on a project aiming to mitigate poverty and health concerns in rural Mexico. While living in Cuernavaca, James learned first hand the dilemmas and successes of economic development. He then worked on a volunteer NGO project in Vanuatu in the South Pacific, focusing on sustainable development in the sectors of Forestry, Health and Nutrition and community capacity-building.

While completing his degree in Vancouver, he established the Critical Thoughts Network, a Participation Action Research Network dedicated to addressing community needs and finding practical solutions to mutual problems. Among other projects, this group, aided by his work with Oxfam and his recent enrollment in a Master's program at Simon Fraser University (SFU), organized an Ethical Purchasing and Fair Trade Conference in Vancouver in May 2004 that lead to the adoption of ethical purchasing policies by the City of Vancouver and by Simon Fraser University. James learned about leadership and management of organizational change—bringing together key players on all sides and listening to all opinions helps to break down barriers to large initiatives.

I believe these lessons became important to him when completing his Master's Degree (MA). It turned out that his Master's Program addressed a topic which was not the strength of the Faculty at SFU, though James had himself conducted considerable preliminary research addressing Ethical Purchasing Policies using an incorporated group of colleagues, and the Critical Thoughts Network Association. When it came to assemble and write his thesis, James found himself without clear direction, so he turned to me for guidance in the new year of 2006.

When I read the first version of his thesis, I found the data gathering he had done was extensive, quite enough for a Master's Degree. This was contrary to the direction he had received from his advisors who were seeking more experimental work. This saved a lot of time, which he devoted to data analysis. Within 6 months he had reorganized his thoughts in an excellent 100 page thesis, which he successfully defended in the summer of 2006. It was a special joy for me to see his progress as a scholar, to read his thoughtful thesis, and to attend his successful thesis defense, where if I did not know him, I could easily mistake the casual excellence of his remarks as coming from one of his panel of examiners.

A particular source of my joy came from the following anecdote. After 5 months of hard work, James gave me a current version of his thesis which I thought was complete and should be submitted. But he told me there was a problem with it—the principle investigating tool he had used to analyze the topic of his thesis was not adequately described. In fact as I re-read it, the tool was hardly mentioned, and could be missed by the most discerning reader. I told James that I did not think including a description of Action Research would change the results or their significance, and he should not take on a re-write at this late date. He politely disagreed, saying that omission of this tool would change the understanding of the process by which his results were obtained, and that was important to him. Accordingly, he wrote pieces about Action Research in consecutive sections of his thesis—Rational of the project, Methodology, and Results, which clearly augmented the quality of his thesis. And he added a final section to his discussion showing how Action Research is a model for future studies of related issues to the one he studied, *"Corporate Social Responsibility: Examining the Impacts of Ethical Purchasing Policies on Canadian Public Institutions"*.

I was proud of his independent thought!

> "Let not your students be to you as the moon
> whose light is but a reflection,
> but let them be as the stars
> whose brilliance shows forth of their own nature."[D]

Since receiving his MA in 2006, James has applied the concepts of Community-Building in the Far North. In Old Crow in the Yukon, James was hired as Program Manager & Instructor by Yukon College (Alice Frost Community Campus) which involved responsibility to meet and network with the Vuntut Gwitch'in First Nation's Chief & Council and Directors to assess educational wants and needs. He worked to promote community-building by having community members

---

[D] From the poem, *The Teacher*, by Pamela Yearsley

teach each other their special skills. The following year, he was hired by the Vuntut Gwitch'in Government (VGG) as Director of Health & Social Department. James was responsible for all Health & Social programs & services in the areas of social assistance, family and child welfare, addictions and personal counseling, home care for Elders & clients with disabilities, community wellness and justice. Following that contract, James was hired by the Yukon Government as an Economic Development Advisor. Shortly thereafter he returned to the Yukon College as the Program Manager—this time in Dawson City (Tr'odek Hatr'unohtan Zho Community Campus), where again he used his community development skills to encourage more innovative College courses. He was an active member on many College committees, including one with substantial financing to rebuild the physical structure for this campus, which had been needed by the community for some time.

Through his many travels, James sought to keep in touch with his family—with his mom, siblings, his friends, and with Elaine and me. He is currently in Boulder, Colorado living with his talented and sensitive friend Anne; very close to John, Kirsten and Liam to reconnect with them; enthusiastically celebrating the birth of his second nephew, Ansel! James is now working with the Sustainability Office of Boulder County, towards a county-wide Integrated Sustainability Plan. James continues to burst with enthusiastic passion for new ways of advancing social, economic and environmental sustainability and he is taking a shot at it.

11

Leadership and Qi

John and Kirsten were engaged to be married in Boulder, Colorado in the summer of 1999. A cause for great joy, it presented us with an opportunity to address a division in the family, for until that event, Elaine and I had nothing to do with Alicia. Just how were we all to be together in celebration?

At that time, Elaine was enrolled in a Landmark Education course, the Self Expression and Leadership Program (SELP) which included a major project. Elaine chose as her project to put on a dinner party before the wedding to enhance family relationships. Out of this experience, Elaine called Alicia, and they had a pleasant 60 minute conversation which ended with Alicia thanking Elaine for giving her the confidence to attend the wedding. Our other adult children—Catherine, Peter, Teresa and James—were dumbfounded, for they all were aware of the acrimony in our relationship with Alicia. When they asked how the telephone call came about, Elaine said simply "I made it my project during my SELP at Landmark." When the kids heard this, they wanted to take the course; and all 4 of them did eventually enroll in Landmark Education programs, with 3 of them completing the initial course less than a week before John's wedding.

Elaine's project was to plan and implement a get-to-know the family dinner at a fine restaurant in Boulder—fittingly called John's Restaurant—on the day before the rehearsal dinner. Twelve were invited: Elaine and me and the 5 kids—4 with their dates, and Alicia. They all came. That night, there were several strained and strange encounters of long separated family members—for Alicia had not spoken with Catherine or me for almost 20 years, nor had Peter seen me, Catherine or John for about the same period. Nevertheless, the dinner proceeded amicably and its purpose was achieved—when we all met again the next night at the rehearsal dinner, we not only knew each other but there was a continuity and flow to the celebration which would not have happened without Elaine's project.

It was at Elaine's dinner that I met Peter for the first time since he was 7 years old—he was 27 years old now. It was an unusual greeting—I approached Peter with my hand extended, shook his hand and said "Hi Peter, I'm your Dad" and he replied "Hi Dad, I am your son"—we didn't talk much. Neither did we find opportunity to converse with each other at the rehearsal dinner. I did get to ask him if he had received any of my letters, especially the one describing his eligibility for a scholarship to University. He replied that he had recently been given the latest letter by Father Baudry, but he hadn't read it. He explained his need to be loyal to his mother, who remained strongly opposed to any relationship I might have with my children. Being at the wedding with all of his "estranged" family was difficult for him, and he answered his sister when she asked him how he was doing "I'm drunk—it's the only way I can get through this." But at the wedding and again at the brunch the next day Peter and I got to shoot the breeze, mostly over football and other shared sporting interests. Six months after the wedding, following Peter's visit to Catherine, Teresa and James in Vancouver and his concurrent completion of the Landmark programs, we arranged for Peter and his partner Kate to visit us in Chicago.

It was a wonderful time together. Kate was attractive, athletic, personable and fun. Peter looked more like me when I was 30ish than any of the other children did. He had been a football quarterback, which gave us common ground, and he enjoyed baseball so the Cubs and Sox games we took in were further food for conversation.

In a series of events which closed the circle on meeting Peter, he became involved in Landmark Education, and enrolled in the SELP course. He chose as his project "celebration of family relatedness" (a family reunion). With the help of his siblings, Peter invited and convened 75 new and distant family members and friends on Salt Spring Island for a week-end in the summer of 2001. This was a momentous gathering for the Wood family, what with exciting conversations among family members who were close friends, and more wide ranging getting to know activities for family who had not been together much/ever. For such a crowd, the food was catered efficiently and was excellent— tasty and abundant, and the surroundings were conducive to convivial socializing. The initial investment in Elaine's pre-rehearsal dinner at John's wedding not only brought family together then, but had longer term consequences in this Celebration of Relatedness. In the years that followed there were other family gatherings for Catherine's wedding, Peter's wedding, Teresa's graduation from Medicine, James' graduation from his Master's program and to celebrate the baptism of John's first child—Liam.

As the years past we got to golf together. I loved the game, and Peter was pretty good at it, having learned the basics in his pursuit of a Physical Education degree. One day while riding in the golf cart together, Pete asked me if I had heard why it was that he was so reluctant to meet me years earlier. I hadn't, and I indicated I was eager to hear. As we rode and golfed the next few holes, he told me this story.

"I was participating in the Communication Access to Power course with Landmark Education. There were about 30 participants and we each had a sharing partner to discuss assignments and progress. On a day when I was supposed to review my paper on becoming a leader, I developed a splitting headache. This was uncommon for me, and I wondered whether it might be related to the topic. Whatever, it became so uncomfortable that I was on the edge of not going to the session, when I made a choice in integrity not to miss. At the session, my sharing partner listened as I spoke my paper on being successful, aghast when I revealed to her—and simultaneously to myself—that I did not want to be successful because successful people were those who took advantage of others to achieve their success and so hurt people. Indeed, until then I had avoided leadership positions that might bring success. My partner inquired where I got that idea, and I replied: from my mother. She explained to me when I was young that you (referring to me in the golf cart) were successful in many activities, and you hurt people in the course of acquiring and living success. Then my sharing partner asked if I had observed such hurtful behavior, I replied no, to the contrary all my experiences were positive, including stories from your acquaintances.

It was like a light went on, accompanied by a rapid resolution of my headache. The illusion that successful people hurt people was dispelled by my observations of your work and up-building behavior. This "aha" realization dispelled my own fear of being successful, and subsequently I have actively sought and been selected for many leadership roles, in which I believe I contributed to the wellbeing of the organization and the people in it."

The illusions we acquire during our growing years have such a powerful effect on us during our adulthood. I am so grateful for that game of golf, when we had time enough to tell and hear such a story. And I am so pleased for Peter that he was gifted with insight during course conversations with his sharing partner to let go of the illusion and to become unencumbered.

More years have passed, and Peter embarked on a new healing career in Traditional Chinese Medicine (TCM) and developed his own business, Wood Way Acupuncture. He has now completed his training, been in practice for several years, and passed his exams for Doctor of TCM. Peter served as the President of the Traditional Chinese Medicine Association of British Columbia (TCMABC), and is committed to increasing the visibility of the TCM profession. Friends of ours in Furry Creek who heard about Peter and the symptoms, conditions and injuries he was reputed to heal sought him out. They were pleased and they returned, communicating "Peter has a wonderful empathic listening approach which confers confidence that he understands the problem and he has the wherewithal to fix it."

I'm so glad he came back into my life. It turns out that Peter has developed an interest in the TCM treatment of asthma, and has made contact with a senior colleague from the U.K., who has developed an enhanced, more effective treatment of asthma. Pete now has a group of asthma patients who are completely off their inhaler and steroid therapy after undergoing the TCM herbal therapy. An important benefit of this for our relationship is my long-standing interest in the pathogenesis and treatment of Asthma by allopathic methods. For this gives Pete and me food for professional conversation, starting with my belief that asthma is an inflammation disorder, and TCM herbal therapy prevents inflammation. Though our relationship started so late in life, we now have an opportunity to catch up, and I look forward to it.

I recall over decades having new acquaintances inquire whether any of my 5 children have followed in my footsteps in Medicine. Until Peter enrolled in Traditional Chinese Medicine (TCM) and Teresa enrolled in Medical School, I had always said no, and with no regrets. Now, I experience both the joy of listening to each of them describe and think through complex clinical cases, and the satisfaction of noticing that I rarely have anything to add. I am also warmed to hear the thoughtful conversations between Peter and Teresa addressing an integration of allopathic medicine with complementary and alternative medicine. I can't help thinking that these 2 extraordinary health care providers will contribute substantially to the improvement to health care systems over and above that which their healing presence contributes to the care of their patients.

12

Forgiving is Hard to Define

One November night in 1978 while I was working late at the office, my wife of 14 years, the mother of our 5 children, called and asked that I not come home. During the next 3 years we were separated and divorced while she obstructed my court appointed rights to visitation. To spare my children further acrimony, I let go of my intense desire to participate in their growth and development, while providing their only financial support from the distance of another country, job and marriage.

Anger, humiliation, and abandonment were my responses to being excluded from my children's upbringing. This dark night of my soul initiated a quantum change in my own growth, illuminated by my coming to understand and accept that I did not know what I was doing when I acted in overbearing, self-centered ways to catalyze the movement of my ex toward her paranoid behavior that contributed to our family's dysfunction. In my anguish, the meaning of Jesus' words became clearer and more mine: "Father, forgive me and her for we do not know what we are doing."

Receiving God's forgiveness allowed me to pray for her as an expression of my forgiveness, and to pray for the children as an outlet for my love. As the years passed, each of these five young adults chose to come back into my life to develop warm and life-giving relationships with me and Elaine. What evolved for me is gratitude for my children's wellbeing, trust and awe that the Lord of my life can and will care for all Her children and a state of forgiveness for me and my ex. Such gifts make it easier to be with others in their pain, confident that God will use it to help them access His forgiveness, wisdom and healing.

Easter Sunday, 2010. Elaine and I were the first of our group to arrive at the Golf Club for brunch. As we made ourselves comfortable at our round table for 8, we marveled wordlessly at the scene outdoors—cherry and apple blossoms in full bloom, red tulips and yellow buttercups in profusion around the prominent 18th green, so green. Elaine complemented the hostess for the table arrangement—circular, so we can hear everyone's conversation. Pete and Kate arrived next, ever the attractive 30-something couple happy to welcome us back to our home after 2 months away. Then came Catherine and Nicole, each with warm hugs of welcome, and followed immediately by Teresa and Alfie. With all assembled, we adjourned together to the buffet table to select our favourite foods. Gathered again at the round table, we began a splendid conversation about diverse topics during the next two hours: the recent Olympics; our winter trip to West Palm Beach FLA, St. Johns USVI, and Chicago; updates on current occupations, Health Care Reform in the USA and others. We continued these interesting conversations back at our home, where we 8 contacted by iChat the two brothers in Boulder, Colorado, John with Kirsten and Liam, and James with Anne—all of whom were together at John's home. A lively conversation proceeded, while Catherine reviewed with me her transcription of the next revised version of the book.

And I marveled at this unlikely gathering of 5 siblings and their significant others, each well educated, thoughtful listeners to the others, enjoying themselves and Elaine and me. Why unlikely—well, you had to be there 30 years ago in my room in the Marianists' residence, seeing me lying prostrate on the floor, crying out in resignation "All right, All right, All right, All right!!" Between then and now became manifest the answers to my prayers as the children grew in wisdom and grace, returning to relationships with each other and with Elaine and me.

I told you that to tell you this—I am profoundly grateful to the Lord of my life for hearing our prayers and keeping watch over each of the children in my absence. Thank you Lord!!

13

The Joy That Heals

In the first 6 Chapters of Part II, I describe the central role that Elaine played in welcoming each of the children. Her hospitable spirit amazed me, for she had little to gain except to facilitate my joy in reuniting. Yet her demeanor seemed to empathize with what each adult child encountered in coming to know who I was and she responded by creating a warm and supportive environment as a space for this process. Accordingly, Elaine's' extraordinary culinary skills were regularly employed for family dinners in our home, while the number of guests grew with time as each of the adult children returned and then brought with them their significant others. Delicious and abundant food combined with a warm ambiance and with the children's penchant for good conversation to make these gatherings promote the togetherness we had not experienced before as a family.

Looking back, it seems that I consistently took Elaine's efforts for granted in the full sense of that phrase. From the beginning of our relationship, I did not need to woo her or romance her as much as I was inclined to do so, for she came to me like a bee to honey moving forward through the attractions of my way of being. Elaine said she was drawn to my physique, intelligence, humor and psychospiritual maturity. She enjoyed and participated fully in our searching conversations. Feeling so positive toward me, Elaine found it hard for her to resist the ardor of my deep appreciation of her beauty with charm.

Other components of my attraction to her were just plain needy. Elaine intuitively knew what I needed to fill the hole in my heart, and she gave without reserve. Her fingers and her tender touch lead the way as her caressing soothed my longing skin, putting its' reaching to rest. And how she listened—with a deeply penetrating gaze filled with tears when I related my sadness. Then there was her acceptance, even admiration as she came to learn my work habits, and the tardiness and absences that they caused for her meal preparations at Grant deadline time.

When she took a leave of absence from her accelerated career as a manager of Systems Engineers at AT&T to accompany me on my sabbatical to Israel and New Zealand, I don't think either of us recognized the consequences for her work life and the self esteem she derived from it. Even more after our return to Chicago, the emptiness of her life as my partner eluded our understanding. Truly, we shared the joy and perks of Academic Medicine done well. But when my research productivity declined and I grew anxious again, it gave way to my jealousy. For one so attractive and faithful as Elaine, my concerns were a slap in the face. Yet she handled it and me with grace and wisdom by discussing it openly as my problem that I had to deal with. Who knew that having been healed from rejection and processing the grief of the loss of my children would reveal another character flaw—a deep sensitivity to humiliation and abandonment? Again, in commitment to our relationship, Elaine stood by me as I slowly moved from humiliation to humility, and from abandonment to reaching out.

Across our 30 plus years together, I could not imagine a better friend, and one who brought and still brings the joy that heals. Thank you Lord. I chose to describe our relationship here at the transition of Part II to Part III as the best place to describe Elaine's central role in my healing and joy—first in helping me bring my adult children home, and then in stabilizing my spirit for its' contribution to Academic Medicine. The concept being discussed here is my version of Eucharist. Elaine gave me a pictorial representation of this concept in 1980. (See below.)

A GIFT FROM ELAINE TO LARRY IN 1980

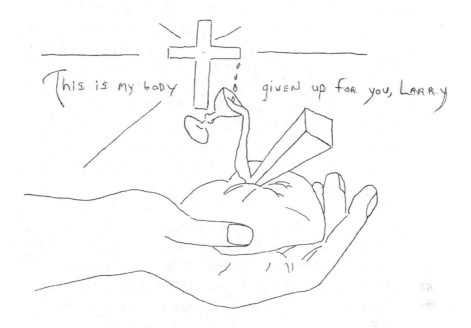

This is my body given up for you, Larry

Readers not familiar with my understanding of Eucharist may find parts of this symbolic drawing overly religious. So I hasten to say what Elaine's gift meant to me. In Peter Van Breeman's book <u>As Bread That Is Broken</u>[E], he paraphrases the Eucharistic prayer of Catholic liturgy, and I paraphrase his prayer to make my meaning clear: "The Lord took Elaine from nothingness and blessed her with life through loving parents and siblings and education and beauty and grace, He broke her in disappointments and losses and failed relationships, and He gave her to Larry saying "Take and eat, for this is my body given up for you." This is how I understand and live the Eucharist—in being for another what they need. And what does a 38 year old man, wounded, abandoned and humiliated, need, if not unbridled love and acceptance of another so attracted to him as he is to her that she gives herself to him completely. This is at once a highly sexual and a highly spiritual symbol, whereby the blood of Jesus on the cross gives new life through

---

[E] <u>As Bread That is Broken</u>, by Peter Van Breeman Dimension Books, 1960

the cup of salvation to bathe and heal the wound carved by the stake in his heart.

When we met, Elaine was a very well processed 32 year old Chicago Lady, smartly dressed, fast talking, flirtatious when she wanted to be. Underneath her gorgeous veneer was a sweet prayerful spirit in constant relationship with the still small voice. *"What would you have me do for you?"*, Elaine asked her Lord. *"Be mine"*, replied the still small voice. She came by her affection for the Lord with disciplined use of her leisure by regularly setting aside time for spiritual retreats to replenish her soul.

Much later when she had exhausted these channels, Elaine turned to diverse other sources of growth. One prominent and effective source of learning was Landmark's Curriculum For Living. Like a duck to water, Elaine dove into the opportunities for learning and conversion in 3 to 4 day weekends at the Forum and the Advanced Course. She then completed Landmark's Curriculum for Living by enrolling in the Self Expression and Leadership Program (SELP). During this SELP program, Elaine was moved to call the children's mother to discern how we could make John's upcoming wedding more comfortable for him and his bride-to-be, Kirsten. Having never talked to her during our 20 years together, Elaine left a 50-minute telephone conversation with Alicia with a sense of "we can make this work", especially when Alicia thanked her for encouraging her to attend the wedding. So moved were our adult children by this breakthrough, that they too wanted to attend the Landmark Forum to get some of this 'good stuff". Catherine, Teresa and James did attend that program, the weekend prior to John's wedding. Meanwhile, Elaine continued her SELP project by setting up a successful first ever family dinner with the adult children, their partners, Alicia and us. This dinner achieved its purpose—to allow a friendly family wedding.

Elaine went on with Landmark to attend and grow from multiple weekend conferences, including the 6-month Introduction Leader's Program (ILP) and the 12-month Wisdom Course. That was so good that even I enrolled to do it, and so Elaine took the Wisdom Course again with both Catherine and me. I relate Elaine's penchant for psychospiritual growth, because it typifies her desire to learn. I admire her for her consistent devotion to self-improvement. What a joy she is to be with—gorgeous, psychospiritually mature, a Healer, and fun. As a gift beyond expectation, Elaine was and is so perfect for me. Just to be in her company lit up my heart and my face. Together, we regaled each other in celebrating the places God led us, the sights He showed us, the company He gathered around us, and the children He returned to us. I had an acquaintance who has known Elaine for nearly 30 years who constantly greets her with a raucous "Elaine—you never age". And it's true! I am gifted with a partner who conducts herself with the wisdom, grace and charm of a stateswoman in the visage and body of a thirty year old. Thank you Lord!!

PART III

Excellence and Compassion in Medicine

14

Establishing an Exemplary Critical Care Program

The story of developing this Program can be told as an official report of a series of successful decisions. But such telling would miss the truth of my being overwhelmed by the complexity of each required building block, and my crying out for help, which came beyond my wildest dreams. As I heard the still small voice say to me about this response to challenge: "I understand your fear—you are afraid to fail. And I like to succeed too. So, give me your plans and concerns, and listen for my direction. Then follow it in peace and I will show you worlds far greater than the Section of Pulmonary and Critical Care at the University of Chicago."

Three years later, such a Section was in place, consisting of strong programs in research, teaching and patient care. Between 1982 and 1987, this Section's Faculty grew in number from 4 to 14 and it's research funding increased from $100K per year to $1.4M per year. A 3-year fellowship training program was established for 4 fellows per year, and this program was accredited by the Residency Review Committee. A Critical Care program to deliver exemplary patient care was established which rivaled all other academic ICUs! When I had a problem, it came from forgetting that I was not alone—out of the blue came the quality people and resources to guarantee success, often before I had seen the need.

THE RESEARCH PROGRAM

Dr. Rubenstein provided all the start-up funds I requested to establish our research labs during the first 2 years at Chicago. This timetable gave me time to re-write and submit requests for Research Funding from the National Heart Lung and Blood Institute (NHLBI). As a first step, I invited three of my senior research fellows in Winnipeg—Peter Breen, Richard Long and Irv Mayers—to come to Chicago to set up our new research equipment in our new research laboratories. To my pleasant surprise, all three accepted and they came together to their new positions as Research Associates as of July 1982. Those readers familiar with the complexity of this task will appreciate the efficiency that such experienced Research Associates brought. Together, we ordered the requisite recorders and transducers, hired three well-trained research technicians, and initiated 3 new experimental protocols by September 1982, an outcome which most investigators find to take 2 years!!

I planned to expend and budget my entire 2-year start-up fund during the first 12 months. So it was essential that I accelerated the pace of my Research Grant Applications for submission in November 1982 for funding in July 1983. Focused writing during my first summer and autumn in Chicago generated the major grant application to NHLBI, and smaller supplementary grants to the American Thoracic Society (ATS) and the American Heart Association (AHA). You can imagine the hopeful anticipation with which I awaited response from these granting agencies, as well as the joy with which our research personnel greeted the announcement that all 3 grants were fully funded. It was a time for gratitude and rejoicing, so we celebrated together in a style that came to characterize our group. For we were party people who enjoyed each other's company, and this demeanor facilitated our ability to work hard together when we needed to. This funding outcome gained favor with Dr. Rubenstein, who had inquired early what my back-up plan was if I didn't get funded for July of '83. Again, like whistling through the graveyard!!

With all due credit to my outstanding Research Associates their presence and productivity allowed me to take advantage of two long-term gifts to the research program. Dr. Iasha Sznajder had collaborated with me and Peter Breen in conducting clinical investigations at the Rambam ICU in Haifa. He joined our investigative team in 1983, and became a productive and creative researcher for many more years than we had anticipated. Iasha completed his Fellowship Program in Pulmonary and Critical Care Medicine while conducting several extensions of our work treating acute lung injury. He then established his own productive research program at Michael Reese Hospital in Chicago before becoming Section Chief at Northwestern Hospital in Chicago where he currently leads the superb academic program, and serves as the Editor of the American Journal of Respiratory and Critical Care Medicine. I had no idea how helpful and effective Iasha would be, and I am so grateful for his contribution and his friendship.

At the same time, I set out to recruit Paul Schumacher, PhD, who was doing a post-doctoral Fellowship with Drs. Peter Wagner and John West at UCSD. Paul had impressed me with his careful work in collaborating with me and Peter Breen at UCSD during an experiment using Multiple Inert Gas Elimination Technique (MIGET) to determine how increased cardiac output increases intrapulmonary shunt (*Chapter 6*). Paul enjoyed our program and accepted my job offer, bringing his research funding with him when he started with us in March 1983: a well trained investigator—without the distractions of clinical medicine—to preside over our laboratories for years to come. Paul soon obtained NHLBI funding for his own research operating grant, and worked with me to initiate my second research operating grant—"Alternative Modes of Mechanical Ventilation". He also became a co-investigator on my first research operating grant—"Treatment of Acute Hypoxemic Respiratory Failure". When I hired him, I knew Paul was an excellent investigator, but I did not imagine his extraordinary creativity and his ability to keep our busy laboratories running smoothly.

Shortly thereafter, Dr. Julian Solway completed his training at Harvard, and agreed to join our section. At the time, Julian was widely regarded as the best trainee in the nation, so we were fortunate to get him to work with us. Julian brought his research funding and expertise from Harvard. What a tremendous threesome we recruited to help build our research program from the bottom up!

Together with Alan Leff who ran a very productive research program in the section when I arrived, we applied successfully for a Research Training Grant in Pulmonary and Critical Care Medicine, which provided 4 salaries per year for Fellows. Immediately, we coupled this research funding with 4 Hospital salaries each year for

Clinical Fellowship Training to establish the financial base for our Fellowship Training Program. And our early Fellowship Trainees provided competitive submissions for NIH National Research Service Awards (NRSA), so most of our trainees had funding for 3 to 4 years. The buzz of learning activity in our section attracted applications for our Fellowship Program from the best of our graduating medical residents, including yearly applications from our highly selected Chief Residents. We began to process about 300 applications each year for our 4 Fellowship training slots.

Accordingly, within 3 years of my arriving in Chicago, our Section had a well funded research program with an abundance of very good research trainees generating, presenting and publishing high quality research in Pulmonary and Critical Care Medicine. As the hub of cardio-pulmonary research, we attracted colleagues from other sections and departments to share ideas and experiments with us: Dr. Bruce Gewertz and his research team from Vascular Surgery; Dr. Ken Borow and his research associate from Cardiology, and Drs. Aaron Zucker and Bill Meadow from Pediatrics were all regular participants in our Research In Progress (RIP) seminars and in our research laboratories. The RIP seminars occurred Fridays from 2-4PM, but often continued until 6pm. These sessions allowed our research fellows and their supervisors to review early and in great detail their ongoing research. Especially important to their research training, the questioning of every aspect of their research helped the fellows to defend their efforts. Not infrequently, new ideas for study emerged from this questioning environment.

THE EDUCATION PROGRAM

Elaine and I were married on November 7, 1981, and we left on a long honeymoon several days later. This trip was long because it was also an 8-month sabbatical leave for me from the University of Manitoba. I had planned to teach *"Principles of Critical Care"* for 3 months at the Rambam Medical Center in Haifa, Israel; and then to spend another 3 months at Green Lane Hospital in Auckland, New Zealand. Of course, a substantial part of these visits was to experience with Elaine life and sights at these exotic locations, so I had arranged day-long teaching sessions on Tuesday, Wednesday and Thursday of each week, giving us four consecutive days (Fri-Mon) for sight-seeing.

As a basis for those seminars, I used an outline of The Pathophysiology of Critical Illness, which I had developed during my 6 years as an ICU Attending in Winnipeg. One of the ICU Fellows at Rambam recorded my seminars. I borrowed his tapes and Elaine transcribed them. Then she revised these manuscripts after I edited them. I repeated this process in Auckland, and so refined the language, format and organization. There were two favorable outcomes of this process. Several years later, they became Part I of our new book, _Principles of Critical Care_[1]. Secondly, they were the content of teaching seminars I started in several venues on arriving in Chicago.

In the autumn of 1982, a group of senior Medical Students at Pritzker approached me seeking informal instruction in Critical Care. I was so ready! I gave them preliminary versions of the sabbatical seminars, and we met in my office for several hours each Friday afternoon to discuss the pathophysiology, diagnosis and treatment of diverse common critical illnesses. Apparently, my reputation as a teacher spread rapidly, and more students and residents sought to join this group. Consequently, I was the recipient of the McClintock Award for the Outstanding Teacher in the Medical School, as selected by the 1984 graduating class. Only years later did I come to understand how unusual it was for a 2-year Faculty member to win this Award.

It was my intent to have the Faculty and Fellows of the Section of Pulmonary and Critical Care Medicine participate in learning sessions, in part to stimulate their own teaching, and in part to attract students at all levels to the Section's teaching activities. Convening a meeting of Faculty and Fellows early in my second year at Chicago, I discussed this plan. I was pleasantly surprised to find groundswell support and participation when I began the seminars as a 2-hour per week course in Advanced Respiratory Pathophysiology (ARP). The beginning sessions drew on topics I had presented in Winnipeg and McGill, supplemented by appropriate topics from _The Pathophysiology of Critical Illness_ seminars. It wasn't long before Faculty members and Fellows approached me to consider topics of their expertise, and the ARP course took off.

A clinical conference on pulmonary disease was expanded to include Critical Care topics. This conference, organized and run by a great teacher, Dr. Gene Geppert, became an opportunity for clinical Fellows to prepare and present interesting cases, supplemented by a literature review of the topic. Since the Fellows were presenting, this fostered a modus operandi of asking the Faculty to comment, answer questions, and give their approach to the clinical problems under discussion.

Dr. Geppert also directed a daily Morning Report lasting only 30 minutes, but discussing salient aspects of 2-4 recent admissions or clinic visits by patients presenting opportunities for problem solving. In this forum, Fellows who did not know the patient or their problem heard a capsule summary of the case and discussed their approach. Then Faculty members offered their critique of that approach, together with teaching points on the topic. Gene was careful to keep track of patients presented, in order to seek follow-up concerning how they responded to therapy or what their diagnosis was. As time went by, this Morning Report drew attendance from medical Housestaff seeking learning as well as an opportunity to present problematic patients from their service.

The Housestaff, Fellows and senior Medical Students on their ICU rotation met together at noon twice per week to participate in the Faculty-led seminars addressing the Pathophysiology of Critical illness. All sessions were open to all comers, and specifically to participants in the Research and clinical activities in Pulmonary and Critical Care medicine. Our faculty made these sessions clinically real by incorporating current ICU patients and their problems in the relevant seminars to help the participants apply the principles.

Taken together, this schedule of conferences created a stimulating questioning environment (see *Table 6*). This conference schedule became the centerpiece of our application to NHLBI for research training in Pulmonary and Critical Care medicine, especially by providing a venue for the Fellows to learn to teach. The quality of the teaching program became a recruitment tool to the Fellowship program from our own highly selected Housestaff. One marker of the quality of training provided is the selection of a Fellowship program by our Chief Residents. From the beginning in 1984, our Fellowship program recruited more than its fair share of Chiefs, and this selectivity has persisted. It may seem trite, but the value of having a comprehensive curriculum for each of the five learning sessions in Table 6 cannot be over estimated. The success of each curriculum is evidenced by the extent to which our graduates become what we and they aspire to—in our program we sought to graduate academic specialists competent at managing exemplary training programs in Pulmonary and Critical Care Medicine. As the graduates of our program left to assume their first appointments at other Universities, we began to hear back glowing reports of their competence and contributions to their new program, especially in the scholarship of teaching.

Table 6 – Teaching Schedule
Section of Pulmonary and Critical Care Medicine

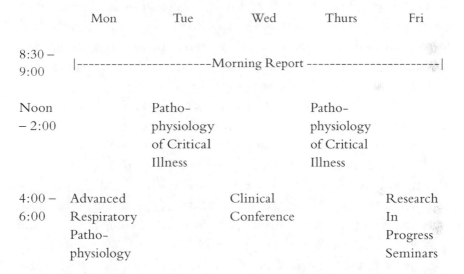

	Mon	Tue	Wed	Thurs	Fri
8:30 – 9:00	|----------------------Morning Report ----------------------|			
Noon – 2:00		Patho- physiology of Critical Illness		Patho- physiology of Critical Illness	
4:00 – 6:00	Advanced Respiratory Patho- physiology		Clinical Conference		Research In Progress Seminars

Another marker of the quality of a section's teaching is the prevalence of teaching awards. Our section consistently had four or five Faculty elected to the group of 10-15 favorite teachers by graduating medical students. This was an extraordinary accomplishment, since our section had only 14 Faculty, and the Division had 400 members from which the favorite teachers were chosen, so our section's Faculty were 10 times more likely to receive this award than the Faculty members in the rest of the Division. The regular recipients were Gene Geppert, Jesse Hall, Holly Humphrey, Greg Schmidt and Larry Wood, and not infrequently one of these received individual awards, such as the Outstanding Basic Science Teaching Award, The Outstanding Clinical Teaching Award or the Humanism in Medicine Award. The residents in the department of Medicine showed a similar preference for our section's Faculty when they elected their favorites each year.

PROVIDING EXEMPLARY CRITICAL CARE

Looking back, I am astounded at how lucky I was in some areas of vision and decision-making. I was confident that I knew who the very best Academic Intensivists were, and that they were people with whom I could build a Program. I was also confident I could persuade one or more of them to share my vision to create the best academic Critical Care Program. So we invited, cajoled, wined and dined my short list—and they all either declined or ticked off some of the Department's Faculty. My approach to recruitment was to build from the top down, bringing in established investigators/teachers who would do the building. While this process was failing, a bottom-up growth of our research and education programs was succeeding. This approach recruited more junior Faculty and relied more on my leadership and ideas for research and education.

A similar bottom-up development of Critical Care occurred. Having just completed his Critical Care experience in Michigan, Jesse Hall was roaming the wards of our Hospital, providing thoughtful consultation on critically ill patients from Medicine, Surgery, and Obstetrics; graciously teaching their Housestaff; offering assistance with procedures; and contributing consolation when the patient died. His blend of excellence and compassion was exactly what was needed to build our program. I appointed him Director of the Medical ICU. As time passed, Jesse assumed Directorship of the Respiratory Therapy Department, became a creative and industrious partner in writing *the Principles of Critical Care*[1], and initiated a productive program of clinical investigation in the ICU. Indeed, my major contribution to his success was to appoint him and get out of the way, conversing from time to time to listen to his ideas or results, be amazed, and offer affirmation.

I can say the same about Greg Schmidt, who consistently displayed the right instincts in every teaching environment. He is the type of person whose opinion—even in the most complicated situations—is reliably offered in a thoughtful, to-the-point response. When he was Chief Medical Resident, Greg sought my advice about how to evaluate his aptitude and enjoyment of Critical Care as a career. We had discussed two preliminary pathways: spending time working in our research lab, or spending time as a senior Fellow in the ICU. He tried the first and found the canine experiments interesting and unpalatable. On the other hand, his presence in the ICU was immediately positive, interesting, exciting, and vision-making. Accordingly, he completed his Critical Care Fellowship training and joined our Faculty without missing a step.

When Jesse and I were considering an invitation from McGraw-Hill to write *Principles of Critical Care*[1], we sought Greg's input and involvement. What a lucky move for us! Greg was an effective writer and editor, who added considerably to every chapter that went his way. On one occasion when the three of us were in discussion about how to deal with some tardy contributors, Greg offered to write the chapters himself. When I said what I thought to be obvious, "Greg we can't write every chapter", he replied, "sure we can". Likewise, when I was invited to speak at a Critical Care conference in Brazil and to bring along a colleague, I asked Greg to come. I knew that his areas of expertise had become different from mine; together we could cover a wider swath of Critical Care for the conference attendees. I attended each of his presentations there, and observed again why our students consistently rated his teaching so highly. His clear explanation of each concept, maximizing the explanation of the minimum necessary concepts, was always a lesson to me about how to teach. And traveling with Greg and his family, Elaine and I were treated to the fun-loving and gracious behaviour of a gentleman.

I lucked out when I hired Jesse and Greg as colleagues and prolific teachers of Critical Care. Together with recruiting Paul Schumacher, Julian Solway and Iasha Sznajder and finding Gene Geppert and Alan Leff in the Pulmonary Section, Jesse and Greg contributed to a critical mass of excellent interactive Faculty early after my arrival. This made building a section far easier than it might have been.

Building an academic section on the pursuit of excellence begins with the quality of the recruits. Given highly trained faculty who ran productive research programs, the scientific basis of Medicine was implicit in our Section's demeanor, and the Scientific Method was an all-pervading approach. Excellence is essential for providing, teaching and researching Academic Medicine, but it is not sufficient. It works best combined with another quality: and acquiring compassion is just as difficult as acquiring excellence. Compassion is the ability to be with your patient in their distress. As compassion grows, so grows empathy, conferring an active receptivity for your patient's story. Since excellence depends in large part on the capacity to let in your patient's story and respond to it with intelligent data-based decisions, compassion enhances excellence. Accordingly, any section building is dependent on recruiting new faculty having compassion and excellence. Any successes in our new section are directly attributable to these qualities in our new faculty and I was either very lucky or very able to discern these characteristics in the recruitment process.

ADMINISTRATION AND FINANCIAL UNDERPINNINGS

It always helps to have a firm financial base for the development of academic programs. Being very aware of the importance of respiratory therapy and blood gas analysis to the delivery of quality Critical Care, I was fortunate to assume Directorship of these essential services when I arrived in Chicago in 1982. The income generated from these Critical Care services was an important contribution to the operating budget when Dr. Rubenstein combined Critical Care services with Pulmonary Medicine in 1983 and appointed me as Chief of our new section of Pulmonary and Critical Care medicine. The administration of our small Section came easily to me because I liked our faculty and staff and served as their encourager and their leader. But I was so engrossed in the teaching, research and patient care programs we were building that I had less attention for administrating the day to day operations of our Section. Accordingly, I was focused on establishing our fiscal base by ensuring a well run Department of Respiratory Therapy including a blood gas laboratory, and this stood the test of time.

EXTENDING CRITICAL CARE EXCELLENCE THROUGH ATS

In 1983, our new Section made a greater contribution to the Spring Meeting of the American Thoracic Society (ATS) than it had previously. Well-rehearsed, well-presented preliminary communications by 10 fellows or Faculty were well received. It was a time of celebration and learning for our growing group, and I was making my presence known by regularly asking insightful questions of the speakers.

Unbeknownst to me, there was considerable conversation about the upcoming business meeting of the Assembly on Clinical Problems of the ATS, which was to consider forming a new section on Critical Care. At the time, more and more intensivists were attending the ATS meeting and seeking to present their work, so the Program Committee thought it wise to provide a forum. I later learned that there was some concern that this new ATS Critical Care forum might be co-opted by the established Society for Critical Care Medicine (SCCM), many members of which were also members of the ATS Clinical Problems Assembly. In the opinion of ATS leadership, the SCCM approach to Critical Care was far less academic than was their vision for the proposed ATS section. By this, they meant that question-oriented approaches to this new discipline of Critical Care need to be fostered, and the gaps in understanding mechanisms of disease and the uncertainties arising from current therapeutic approaches needed to be the focus of the new section. This approach was distinguished from a more dogmatic prescription of understanding as the basis for more formulaic approaches to the diagnosis and treatment of Critical Illness. The distinctions between those approaches were the prospective statement and testing of hypotheses in well-controlled clinical trials or in studies of models of Critical Illness.

This distinction is better caught than taught, so the ATS leadership set out to find an individual whose approach embodied these principles.

They chose me. So on a sunny, peaceful first day of the Spring Meeting, acquaintances of mine asked me to coffee, and laid out their concerns. Drs Clarence Guenther and Roland Ingram ended their discussion by asking me to let my name stand for Chairman of the ATS Section on Critical Care at the business meeting that evening. I told them that I understood the issues they presented, and I thought I could help. BUT I was already overwhelmed with the challenges of building a new Section of Pulmonary and Critical Care Medicine, including transferring my research program to a new city and country. Since I had only been at Chicago for 10 months while developing a new married relationship, I felt compelled to decline. They asked me to think about it—the business meeting did not occur for 4 hours—and to suggest the names of other individuals I thought could kick-start this section in the direction they preferred.

Torn, I met Elaine for lunch at our Hotel and asked her advice about the story and the opportunity. She listened carefully, and came down strongly on the side of the argument that declined because I was already overwhelmed. As I left our lunch discussion, I kissed her softly and told her I would decline.

Several hours later, we met again to share the information that I had let my name stand for Chairman and had been elected over an excellent Critical Care Physician who was better known than I was, Dr. Roger Bone. What transpired between our 2 meetings went something like this. With pen and paper, I roughed out the areas of interest that the new section should address. Then I wrote the names of intensivists who shared the vision of academic Critical Care, paying particular attention to represent areas of potential weakness (Surgery—Jameel Ali, Pediatrics—George Lister, Nursing—Kathleen McClintock, Neurology—John Luce) and filling in our areas of strength with especially strong academic intensivists representing other institutions. By the time I had to commit, I had an organization in mind, so all I had to do was suggest an individual other than myself to chair it. That position stayed blank, I volunteered and I was elected.

Elaine learned not to trust me to decline opportunities to do things I thought were important, and gave me her blessing to do the job well. Immediately, I set about inviting my list of spirited, interactive intensivists to meet at that ATS meeting. Our agenda was to set goals for the Section, and to propose a first Critical Care Program in accord with those goals. At the next meeting of the ATS in the spring of 1984, several half-day sessions were proposed as the centerpiece, each given by strong investigators on topics of current interest, and chaired by interactive knowledgeable intensivists who were good at asking questions and encouraging audience participation. We also proposed for the first time Poster-discussions, a format whereby several discussants visited all posters during the first part of the session, and then led a discussion of each poster during the second half. Planning revealed the opportunity to group posters in accord with the specific question asked within the overall theme, so the discussion stimulated general conclusions on each sub-topic. We learned quickly that it was helpful to involve the whole Planning Committee in the process of vetting and grouping the submitted abstracts, and then giving the grouped posters to the discussants well before the session so they could plan their remarks.

Note the heavy emphasis on discussion among knowledgeable experts as achieved in each of these forums by grouping the themes of research and stimulating their response to their colleague's papers. This format encouraged debate which got to the bottom of the issues under study, often expressed as new hypothesis for study. I had not seen this dynamic forum work so well in the many meetings I attended, but it worked very well back home in our diverse conferences (see *Table 6*). And just as at home, this forum became a shooting gallery for unsubstantiated beliefs underlying the issues being discussed. The process of clarifying the sources of evidence supporting beliefs about how organ systems function is such a fruitful way to confirm established mechanisms or to develop new hypotheses. And finding insufficient evidence to support established beliefs teaches students to question beliefs about their areas, often to generate new hypotheses and so new knowledge.

These and other pedagogical suggestions conferred an excellent learning environment in each session, and the feedback was very positive after our first program of the ATS Critical Care Section at the Spring 1984 ATS Meeting. Now 25 years later, that same enthusiastic questioning approach is evident in what has become the ATS Assembly on Critical Care, the largest Assembly in the ATS. Of course, the attention I gave to the ATS Critical Care Section distracted me from my responsibilities at home—with Elaine, with the growing Critical Care Program, with my research. I will never know whether each of these areas would have been better if I had declined. I just couldn't, for I knew what to do, how to do it, and I didn't know anybody else who could.

15

Contributions of Research to Patient Care and Teaching

In my career, my research efforts produced 124 peer-reviewed publications, 34 book chapters, 8 books and my PhD Thesis. Along the way, several distinct themes emerged as the focus of my investigations (see Table 7). Here below, I review three such themes, and highlight 17 cited publications to convey the breadth and depth of my interest in science as a balance with my belief. After each theme, n = the number of publications describing research therein, though I discuss only a selected few studies in each. These selected references are listed in the Appendix, and the superscript number refers to the appropriate article—for those readers who might be interested. Readers primarily interested in belief may find the description of science in the rest of this chapter to be soporific, but it is included here to frame the science and belief question revealed by the discussion.

Table 7:
Research Programs and Publications

Airways Dynamics (n=26)
Treatment of AHRF (n=23)
Cardiovascular Dysfunction in Respiratory Failure (n=25)
Relationships Among Pulmonary Blood Flow, Edema and Shunt (n=12)
Alternative Modes of Mechanical Ventilation (n=14)
O2 Delivery and Consumption in Critical Illness (n=11)
Invited Review Articles and Editorials (n=12)
Book Chapters (n=34)
Miscellaneous Investigations (n=10)

AIRWAYS DYNAMICS (N=26)

Beginning with the work done at CFIEM (see *Chapter 1*), we observed that maximum expiratory flow (Vmax) varied inversely as the square root of gas density (ρ)[1]. One consequence of breathing dense gas was to limit the ventilation required by divers working underwater. For example, we demonstrated[2] that a person able to perform 1500 KgM. min^{-1} of maximum exercise at sea level with an oxygen consumption (VO2 max) of 4.4l min^{-1} had to stop work at 10 ATA (300 feet of sea water) at 900 KgM.min^{-1} with a VO2 max of 3.3l per minute. Exercise at depth was stopped due to choking dyspnea and cough, due in turn to the dynamic compression of intrathoracic airways when expiratory flow reached Vmax.[2] This novel sensation is not observed at sea level where maximum exercise in healthy subjects is not limited by ventilation but by circulation; but in patients with advanced chronic obstructive pulmonary disease, this same mechanism limits their exercise tolerance at sea level.

Some years later, we studied the salutory effects of breathing a low density gas, heliox, by patients in the emergency room with severe asthma[3]. In such patients, the considerable effort to inspire through constricted airways produces a large fall in the pleural pressure surrounding the heart, so the pressure inside the heart falls with each inspiration. This can be measured as a fall in blood pressure during inspiration, called Pulsus Paradoxus (PP), which we found to decrease from 24 to 12mm hg during heliox breathing in patients with severe asthma. In the same patients, peak expiratory flow increased from 150 to 210lpm during heliox breathing. These data demonstrate density dependence of airways resistance in severe asthma, and indicate that heliox breathing may buy a window of time for bronchodilator therapy to alleviate asthmatic bronchoconstriction before the patient's respiratory muscles fatigue, thereby sparing the patient from intubation and ventilator therapy.

PATHOPHYSIOLOGY AND TREATMENT
OF AHRF (N=23)

A second focus of my research program was to elucidate the pathophysiology in patients suffering Acute Lung Injury (ALI) in order to target new therapy. Most of these patients are admitted to the ICU for ventilator support, and their mortality exceeded 70% in 1975 when we began. ALI is caused by local lung damage (aspiration of gastric contents, pneumonia) or systemic diseases with blood borne injury (sepsis, fat embolism, pancreatitis). These insults have a common presentation characterized by severe pulmonary edema and Acute Hypoxemic Respiratory Failure (AHRF). We began by studying animal models of ALI produced by intravenous injection of oleic acid,[4] or by tracheal instillation of hydrochloric acid[5], or kerosene[6]. As the efficacy of diverse treatments evolved, we summarized the principles by publishing 3 case reports describing and discussing how these therapies were used to treat their AHRF.[7,8,9]

The principles of resuscitation and management of patients with AHRF are listed in Table 3 and discussed in Chapter 6. Subsequent multi-center clinical trials supported the PEEP[10] and tidal volume[11] therapeutic principles for ventilator management, and also supported the strategy of low circulating volume[12]. We are delighted that mortality in AHRF has fallen to about 30%.

In the 25 years between stating these principles of therapy and completing a definitive clinical trial confirming them, intensivists waged considerable debate about the right way to treat the condition under study. What informs the cardiovascular and ventilator management? There was no doubt that science revealed how to treat animal models with acute lung injury. In the absence of other data, I chose to use these principles to treat all of my patients with AHRF. So did many intensivists from around the world who were persuaded by my invited talks and published reviews on the subject. But I acknowledge that that choice is not based on science, but on my belief that these principles conferred benefit in animal models of ALI, so they should work in patients.

Of course, many of our colleagues continued to manage their patients with AHRF using fluids that maintained or maximized cardiac output. Several reasons were given for not following the three guidelines:

- Patients with AHRF do not die due to pulmonary edema, but due to other longer-term complications of ICU and ventilator therapy. We argued that if the pulmonary edema were removed, their need for ICU ventilator therapy would be obviated, so to reduce their mortality.
- Conservative fluid therapy might cause other organ system failure due to decreased cardiac output and hypoperfusion. We argued that hypoperfusion was not allowed because good ICU care should prevent it.
- Hypoperfusion would be even harder to prevent in septic patients due to pathologic supply dependence of oxygen delivery (PSOD). We argued that there was no evidence for PSOD in septic patients with AHRF, so the same good ICU care should prevent hypoperfusion in these patients.
- No clinical trials were available.

So I asked myself, what supports belief in this clinical scenario? Outcomes help. Repeated success from following principles strengthens belief. But when outcomes are not defined and recorded clearly as part of the scientific method, it is very easy to be swayed in the direction of your belief. Of course, the discipline of statistics tries to determine whether the incidence of the outcome of treatment exceeds the probability of it happening by chance. Such clinical trials attempt to control all other treatments except the intervention being tested. This is an onerous task in patients so very ill, and it requires great discipline and clear communications on the part of the investigators from many centers, each of which may have biases and beliefs about other aspects of their patient's care. One consequence of the many constraints imposed by the Scientific Method is that study of the primary intervention gets delayed. For example, the study of conservative versus liberal fluid replacement demonstrated that more patients were able to breathe without ventilator assistance in the conservative group, and most of this difference occurred during the first five days of the study[12]. Given that fluid management had its greatest impact early, it is important to note that this intervention did not start until 43 hours after ICU admission, and 24 hours after meeting the criteria for Acute Lung Injury. Of course, this raises the question whether this intervention would be more effective if initiated sooner.

I often thought as I took over the reins of care of my patients with AHRF that what happens in the first hours of my aggressive, no-nonsense approach was far greater than what occurred in the average patient in a multi-center trial, especially since I was titrating simultaneously guidelines 2, 3 and 4. This sounds like a belief, but I really meant it as a personal challenge to all comers to do better than I can by handling all of the multi-faceted care. But such competitions are not part of the Scientific Method, and the attending Intensivist is not usually in the ICU at 2am when many patients are ready to be studied. Untested, my proposal remains a belief. Belief or science, stories help. My colleague Jesse Hall tells this story in support of my effect on AHRF on arriving at Chicago: A pulmonologist reputed for his radiology-clinical correlations, consistently distinguished cardiogenic pulmonary edema from that due to Acute Lung Injury (ALI) on the basis of their admitting chest radiograph; and Dr. Banner then consistently predicted a several weeks course on the ventilator together with the high morbidity and mortality for the patients with ALI. Dr. Banner was incredulous when he began seeing my patients who had ALI having their chest radiograph clear and the patient extubated within 72 hours.

This is how we move from belief to science, and it can be slow and tedious work. Furthermore, we sometimes find the precision of scientific inquiry limits our advancement or understanding. I mean, how many hypotheses can you exclude and still gain understanding? If this is true when you have a reliable and accurate measuring device, how will we ever make headway without a measurement related to the belief we wish to study?

I conclude that our beliefs will never compete with science for truth unless we find a new paradigm for testing belief. That is why I am so enthusiastic about the still small voice as a guide and support for intuitive beliefs. After all, when you have to ask about a hunch, who better to ask than the Maker? But even if I were convinced that the voice speaks truth, how ever would I convince any of my colleagues unless they had personal experience with the voice and its' outcomes?

CARDIOVASCULAR DYSFUNCTION IN RESPIRATORY FAILURE (N=25)

A third focus of my research program was to define and treat the circulatory disorders associated with respiratory failure. First, using the relationship between left ventricular pressure and volume at end-diastole and end-systole, we distinguished diastolic from systolic dysfunction in patients with AHRF or in animal models. We found that PEEP caused diastolic dysfunction by restricting the filling of the left ventricle[13]. By contrast, hypoxia[14], respiratory acidosis[15] and lactic acidosis[16] depressed systolic function. Making this distinction in patients required measurement of left ventricular volume, and this was essential for choosing appropriate therapy. In particular, vasoactive drugs like nitroprusside[17] and dopamine[4,5,18] were effective in decreasing afterload and increasing contractility to maintain CO, even in patients with low diastolic pressures and volumes.

Table 7 lists the other six areas of study and the number of publications in each. The alternative modes of mechanical ventilation were constant flow ventilation (CFV), CFV added to a small tidal volume to clear the tracheobronchial bottleneck for gas mixing, and high frequency oscillatory ventilation (HFOV) in patients with normal lungs and in models of lung disease. The relationships among pulmonary blood flow and shunt in lung edema were discussed in Chapter 6, as was the V_{O2}/D_{O2} relationship in patients with septic shock[19,20]. The breadth and depth of these investigations lead to a stream of invitations to write book chapters, review articles and editorials.

Looking back, I am pleased by the array of concepts and methodologies I was privileged to learn. Truly, this scholarship conveyed a sense of awe about the intricacies of biology and especially of the component parts of the cardio-pulmonary circuits and their interdependence. Reviewing the chronology of the research described indicates that most or all of the new work originated before 1987, an observation that had eluded me until this compilation. Accordingly, my life's work can be described as education from birth to 1967, discovery from '67-'87, and teaching from '87 to 2003, with some overlap among them with patient care for part of my time from 1975 to 1995. Alternatively, having been educated for 30 years, I then worked as an academic physician for 30 years, divided roughly as equal parts research, patient care and teaching

RESEARCH AND CLINICAL MENTORING

Some things are better caught than taught. One such is Mentorship. Different personality types provide different Mentorship but effective Mentoring starts and ends with being a model which protégés wish to emulate. Given this demeanor, the effective Mentor introduces three transactions with each protégé: support, challenge and vision making. Challenge involves setting tasks, unmasking assumptions, offering alternative perspectives, giving feedback and encouraging hypothetical thinking. Support involves attentive listening, inviting a protégé to action, advocating for the protégé, and helping the protégé to structure the next steps. Vision making involves mirroring the protégé's plan, providing a new vocabulary of concepts with the issues under study and guiding the protégé's development. Emphasis on each component is modified according to the protégé's special needs and by the opportunities made available by their working together. This framework is a basis for critical thinking about the protégé's training objectives, manifest by the competencies expected of the graduating Protégé. Such critical thinking allows the Mentor to engage each graduate in the conversation about who they wish to become.

In the course of directing research programs in Winnipeg (1975–1982) and in Chicago (1982-1994), I had the privilege of training and publishing with 72 research fellows. In my view, all came well selected, well prepared and motivated to learn the investigative process. Most harnessed their training to initiate an academic career which included research. Five of these stood out on the basis of extraordinary industry, creativity and diligence in helping to bring their work to publication. I am especially grateful to each of them, for they contributed in a major way to the implementation and success of my research programs.

Along the way, they contributed to the questioning environment and generated a buzz of creative critical thinking, in our office and laboratory conversations and in our scheduled research-in-progress seminars. Each introduced me to new concepts or approaches to the questions they investigated. And so I learned a lot from them, and they contributed considerably to the growth of our research program. Another trait they displayed—one often attributed to me—was the way potential fellows seemed to materialize out of the woodwork, seeking to work with us. Some things are better caught than taught. In the Appendix, I cite the articles I published with each of these trainees.

RESEARCH AND CLINICAL FELLOWS

Richard Prewitt is the intern described in *Listening To The Patient* (see *Chapter 16*), who insisted on skin-testing his patient for sensitivity to anti-venom. As in this case, he often had a correct hunch about whatever topic he brought up, partly through avid reading and partly through intuition. Richard first brought my attention to the possibility that low pressure pulmonary edema might respond favorably to the same treatment as cardiogenic edema, namely a reduction in pulmonary vascular pressure[4,7]. When our interest in how PEEP lowers cardiac output began, he searched out and introduced me to the one person and technique in our hospital who might help us to evaluate left ventricular function via Radionucleotide MUGA Scan. And then he surprised me further by bringing the scan results from an ICU patient on PEEP[13] and then again by showing up in our animal lab with a portable MUGA scanning device[21]. I found myself putting up intellectual resistance to the output of his creative musing during our discussions, but later in quiet catching up to the value of his proposals. If I offered help at all, it came from my docility and it's application to frame his novel ideas into answerable questions with appropriate controls and experimental rationale. We published together 7 peer-reviewed manuscripts between 1979 and 1982 from our 3 years of work together in Winnipeg about 5 years earlier[4, 7, 13, 17, 21-23]. Richard began working with me when he was an intern newly arrived from Florida. He subsequently did a cardiology fellowship in Winnipeg and became Head of the Cardiology Section there.

Steven Mink came to my program from a Pulmonary Fellowship in Pennsylvania. At the time, I was beginning complicated studies of forced expiration in anesthetized dogs using retrograde intra-bronchial catheters to identify equal pressure points (EPP) and flow limiting segments (FLS) during ventilation with air or heliox. A quiet fellow, Steve caught on to the subtleties of the study faster than I noticed, and shortly he took off on his own in obtaining and explaining the data and then using it to test the wave speed theory of forced expiratory flow which was a step in thinking beyond where I had intended. Along the way, Steve became expert at the management of the laboratory, so when another Resident with training in infectious diseases, Dr. Bruce Light, came to discuss with me the production and investigation of pneumococcal pneumonia, Steve expressed a desire to help. He kick-started Bruce's familiarity with the instrumentation and recording necessary for the new project. Together, Steve and I published 8 peer-reviewed manuscripts between 1979 and 1983, about 4 years after we had done the work[24-31]. His time in our laboratories overlapped with Richard and his colleagues, and this interaction stimulated an environment actively receptive for new questions. Steve made a seamless transition from senior research fellow to Attending Pulmonary Faculty, and shortly after became Chief of the Pulmonary Section.

Peter Breen was a pilot who spent some time after graduation from Medical School practicing in Northern Manitoba before he came to work with me in 1981. His peripatetic efforts at research began with a study of high frequency oscillatory ventilation (HFOV) in pulmonary edema[32] and continued when he traveled to San Diego to collaborate with a colleague there. Peter lead the implementation of that study with a pilot's rigor and attention to detail, and he met a counterpart in a post-doc fellow, Paul Schumacker. Together, they carried out a successful study, which disproved two possible explanations of how Q_S/Q_T increased with increased cardiac output[33]. We conducted a follow-up study in Winnipeg which disproved the hypothesis that increased cardiac output increased the edema[34].

Then Peter accompanied Elaine and me to the Rambam Hospital in Haifa, Israel. There, Peter worked with a Critical Care fellow, Dr. Iasha Sznajder to test HFOV in ICU patients. Back in Winnipeg, Peter orchestrated a complicated feasibility study of constant flow ventilation in anesthetized patients[35] before he rejoined me in Chicago in July 1982 to help establish my new research program. In so doing, he initiated another complex study establishing a model of bronchoconstriction with methacholine in dogs[36], while assisting colleagues in studies of the treatment of acute lung injury[5, 37-39]. We published 9 manuscripts in peer-reviewed journals between 1982 and 1988, and Peter completed his training in Anesthesiology before joining the faculty of the University of California. Accordingly, Peter was a bridge linking my research programs in Winnipeg and Chicago by way of Israel.

Keith Walley came to work with me in Winnipeg in 1981 when he was a first year Medical Student. He so impressed me then with his piercing comprehension of basic science principles that I hoped we would work together again. And six years later, there he was in my Chicago office, visiting from McGill in Montreal, to interview for research and clinical training in Pulmonary and Critical Care Medicine. I listened carefully as he described end-diastolic and end-systolic volume-pressure relationships of the left ventricle, and how these might make the distinction between diastolic and systolic dysfunction in respiratory failure. I listened on as he outlined with joyful enthusiasm how two pairs of ultrasonic epicardial crystals could measure LV volume accurately and with a frequency response quite good enough to plot simultaneously against LV pressure measured by a Millar Catheter Tipped Transducer. Then we talked about relating myocardial O_2 consumption to these P-V loops as myocardial O_2 delivery was reduced by desaturation of the circulating hemoglobin, in turn by progressively decreasing FIO_2.

Delighted, I bought the new equipment and went to work with Keith on protocols to study the myocardial dysfunction of respiratory failure: hypoxia[14], hypercapnic acidosis[15], and lactic acidosis[16]. Keith was a senior investigator already, and I marveled at how the Section's fellows and those from cardiology flocked to work with him. He even extended his ideas about ventricular dysfunction to parallel studies of respiratory muscle dysfunction[40]. Together we published 5 extraordinary papers between 1988 and 1991, the last of which was in collaboration with Lincoln Ford in examining effects of hypoxia and hypercapnea on the force-velocity relation of papillary muscles[41]. Again, Keith meticulously gained expertise in the handling of these delicate tissues, as well as the robust handling of the data by providing mechanisms of cardiac dysfunction in respiratory failure. Keith completed his clinical fellowship in Pulmonary and Critical Care Medicine, functioning as a superb clinician in our ICU. He has gone on to run his own research program at St. Paul's Hospital and the University of British Columbia in Vancouver, BC, where he is now Professor of Medicine.

Cons Manthous blew in to our Critical Care program from his residency in Johns Hopkins, certain that he wanted the best clinical training possible, and also certain he wanted nothing to do with research. He began in our ICU as advertised—a dynamic, organized, brash but polite fellow, pushing the limits of decorum whenever he bumped into them. Along the way, he treated a patient with fulminant hepatic failure with anti-endotoxin antibody, collected the clinical and laboratory data, and wrote and published the paper[42]. Some time later, he visited me to reiterate his plans for completing his clinical training as soon as possible—no research!! Somewhere during the conversation, Cons listened to the story of Critical Care training—that the best clinical skill is critical thinking, and most often that is caught from the process of planning and conducting studies to ask answerable questions. Snap—he converted!! In short order this dynamo became a protocol generating, data gathering, whip cracking enrollment machine. Between 1992 and 1995, Cons published with me 6 manuscripts[3, 20, 42-45], and launched himself on a career as Academic Intensivist. Who would have thought?

FACULTY COLLEAGUES

So these 5 fellows stood out among many as extraordinary research trainees who taught me a lot. Previously, I mentioned the role of Iasha Sznajder and Paul Schumacker as Faculty who made early contributions to our new research program in Chicago. They displayed the same talents, but contributed most to the research program after their research training was complete. For comparison, Paul and I published 19 papers together between 1982 and 1993, most on the themes of supply dependence of O_2 consumption and alternative modes of mechanical ventilation before he embarked on studies of the molecular and cell biology mechanisms responsible for detection of hypoxia. And Iasha and I published 24 papers together from 1986 to 1998, most on the themes of management of acute lung injury and alternative modes of mechanical ventilation before he embarked on studies of the molecular biology of lung liquid clearance.

While making the distinction between productivity of trainees and Faculty colleagues, I must mention three special cases. Jameel Ali was a classmate of mine in our Medical School, so we graduated together in 1966. When I returned as a Faculty member to the Department of Medicine in 1975, he was a Board Certified General Surgeon and Faculty member of the Department of Surgery. Jameel invited me to review some of his experiments measuring the effects of furosemide on canine acute lung injury[46]. We began to work together, and over the next 13 years, we published 10 papers together[32, 33, 38, 46-52]. Jameel consistently amazed me with his diligence and industry, for he was a busy general and trauma surgeon who regularly attended in the surgical ICU while initiating and performing his own experiments. He was a regular presence in our laboratory through my 6 years on the Winnipeg faculty, and consistently lent his valued surgical skills to other research colleagues. Through all these activities, Jameel found the time to plan and process thoughtfully his experiments, thinking creatively about the explanations of his data.

The second person to follow an unusual research-training pathway with me was John Yanos. I met John when he was a resident in the ICU at Chicago in 1982. When I first arrived there, I devoted most of my time to grant writing and establishing an educational program. But I needed to assess the delivery of Critical Care to prepare to manage it, so I occasionally would drop in to the 4-bed unit to observe. When John saw me there more than once, he took it on himself to ask me who I was and what I was doing there. I replied that I was a new Faculty Intensivist seeking to understand how Critical Care worked here. John shot back quickly in his usual sardonic manner "Patients admitted to the ICU here are cared for by the senior residents, and Faculty don't interfere." We continued our conversation awhile in the unit, and later over coffee in my office, where John came to understand that I had some ability to teach the residents *important principles* of Critical Care. I realized several years later that John was convinced when he applied for a position in our Pulmonary and Critical Care fellowship. Of course, we accepted John because he was very highly regarded as a clinician, and he held a position of esteem among the Medical Residents. In a relatively short time in the laboratory, John published 2 fine manuscripts with me addressing respiratory muscle dysfunction in respiratory failure[40,53], and two others on the ventilator treatment of ALI[54,55] and became a friend. John surprised me shortly after my retirement by visiting me in Chicago from his home in Missouri to spend a day reviewing our time together. I was touched.

A stated goal of writing this book was to integrate my life—to become more aware of what transpired. One surprise from this Chapter's compilation of research was my publication history with Jesse Hall. Our 44 publications together snuck up on me as an accumulation of invited clinical reviews of diverse Critical Illnesses, of the output of Jesse's clinical investigation program in our ICU, and of the books and book chapters in the *Principles of Critical Care*[59]. Jesse's critical thinking and clear writing style contributed immensely to our reputation for clinical scholarship. Alerted to our publication history, I checked to see Greg Schmidt's collaborations with me, and found 7 books, 12 book chapters and 9 original articles for a total of 28 publications—the second most of all of my collaborating investigators. I have written in Chapter 14 about the extraordinary contribution of Jesse and Greg to our education and patient care programs in Critical Care, so these observations about our publication record complete their history of collaborative clinical scholarship with me. Being actively involved in the clinical research productivity of our Section, they poured oil on the creative fires of our trainees and contributed greatly to the critical thinking of our trainees. I am so grateful for our time together.

The third Faculty member came to visit me shortly after his appointment as Chief of Pediatric Critical Care. A well trained Pediatrician and Intensivist, Aaron Zucker expressed a desire to learn more about research. We discussed possibilities for him to work with our investigative team to learn the basics, and then to branch out on his own projects with our assistance. An eager and industrious learner, Aaron began to work with Iasha on a complex study of the pathophysiology and treatment of ALI produced by hydrochloric acid aspiration[18]. While helping that investigation, Aaron treated a 10-month old girl who aspirated kerosene and died with ALI about 48 hours later. He wrote a case report linking her pathophysiology to that of ALI caused by acid aspiration[56]. Then he initiated a study of kerosene aspiration to confirm the pathophysiology and treatment[6,57]. By now, Aaron was fully integrated into our research team, contributing regularly to our research and clinical conferences. Accordingly, we fully supported the next extension of his research—a collaboration with a busy surfactant investigator, Bruce Holm, conducted in Iasha's new laboratories at Michael Reese Hospital in Chicago—published in 1992[58]. About 10 years later, Aaron wrote at the time of my retirement the following letter that honored the Mentoring process:

Dear Larry,

Yesterday morning, I attended a seminar that focused on mentoring relationships in academic medical centers. Both during the talk and afterwards, I found myself thinking of you and the role you played in my early career development. Given my lack of prior experience and training needed in the laboratory, you were able to balance constructive criticism and exhortation in a way that few can. I always felt that I could venture forward on my own with the security that I had you as a resource when I had questions or problems. Even though I did not go on to run a major laboratory like many of your other "offspring", the things I learned from you still serve me well in my day-to-day practice and in clinical research endeavors. I got all this from you painlessly—it was a magnanimous gift that came without demands in return. In the nicest of possible ways, I will always be in your debt.

I went on to recall a day in your office when I spoke with you just before making public my decision to leave the University of Chicago. I did not feel that anyone else there (or anywhere, for that matter) understood me and the political situations well enough to give me truly helpful advice. As always, you listened intently, asked insightful questions, and at the end of my soliloquy when I asked for your opinion, you quietly said, "I think you are making the right decision to leave." In retrospect, it **was** the right decision overall, and one of the biggest I have ever made. You were invaluable in helping to put my mind at ease when it counted most, and I cannot thank you enough. Do you remember what you did at the end of that conversation? As I stood to leave, you embraced me warmly and exchanged a few final good words. That was an especially powerful "father figure" moment for me.

It is an odd coincidence that I was doing this reminiscing after the seminar yesterday, only to learn of your illness and change in educational responsibilities a few hours later via an e-mail from a former colleague. While I don't want to sound maudlin, I want you to know that I am profoundly affected and that you will always be in my thoughts. Let's face it" I am a 50-year old (!) man who's seen a lot, met all kinds of folks, and recognizes that no one is perfect. That said, I look up to you as one of my few personal and professional heroes. You have Elaine by your side, so you are starting head and shoulders above where others might. I wish you both physical, mental and emotional strength.

Love,
Aaron

L.D.H. Wood, MD PhD

RESEARCH TRAINING ENHANCES THE SCHOLARSHIP OF TEACHING

Beginning in 1967, and extending through the next 25 years, much of my professional work was devoted to the scholarship of discovery. My research training taught me how to investigate the mysteries of pathophysiology. Understanding how the transducers work, how they are calibrated to provide accurate measurements, how their electronic outputs are processed and displayed, how experiments are designed to control for alternative causes of the effect being studied, how data are collected and processed—these were the elements of research training which facilitated starting my own research program. But there were other lessons caught along this research training which contributed to my teaching career by conferring critical thinking and clear communication.

The first arose from preparing preliminary communications of my research work in the form of brief (<200 words) abstracts submitted for presentation of the research at National meetings. It seemed impossible at first to tell the story with such space limitations. But with guided rewriting and thinking, brevity emerged without confounding clarity. Since at least one new piece of research was submitted for each of 3 meetings/year, I became quite familiar with concise writing by the end of 5½ years of research training and 20 such abstracts. Later in my career, colleagues complimented me on my ability to summarize complex discussions in the course of lectures or meetings, thereby to forward the action. To the extent I was good at it, I attribute this skill in part to the discipline of preparing abstracts.

A second spin-off came from preparing and delivering 10-minute presentations of my work. When I began, it was not uncommon for me to prepare 10 to 15 slides as visual aids for such a presentation, and then to speak rapidly to present it all in ten minutes. By the end of my training, I would prepare 4 to 5 slides for the same talk by presenting the minimum amount of information essential to convey the message of the study to my audience. By maximizing my discussion of the minimum amount of information, I was better able to explicate the message. Later in my career as a teacher, I was often complimented by my students and colleagues for my ability to make complex topics simple. And again, I attribute the clarity and simplicity of presentation to the countless hours of preparing how to present complex experiments in a very short time.

A third spin-off arose through learning a style of delivery which engaged the audience. From my very first presentation I insisted on going note-less. This freed me to develop eye contact with my audience. In turn, this promoted opportunities for underlining points with speech inflections, gestures, and use of laser pointers to emphasize the essential points of the presentation. My commitment to speaking without notes came from observing how the best scientific presenters did it. Although this initially challenged me to maintain my peace in speaking to large audiences, I soon realized that well prepared visual aids could be used as reminders of what I wished to say instead of reading from notes. This approach tended to make a smooth talk integrating words, visual aids and eye contact to maximize my engagement with the audience.

Another key lesson from my research training was the art of handling questions. This began with the countless questions directed my way during rehearsals and research in progress seminars from my supervisor(s) and colleagues in our Fellowship programs. Once I became comfortable with the breadth and depth of questions they asked, I could work at staying sufficiently alert to detect early an outlying question I had not considered, and give it my due consideration during the 5-minute question periods that most meetings allowed. Some simple rules, such as repeating the question for clarity and acknowledging good questions by framing them in the context of my work, were helpful tactics. Later in my teaching career, I became adept at handling questions during lectures by linking my answer to what had been discussed previously or would be addressed shortly, a springboard as it were to the next topic. This skill is invaluable if I truly want to encourage questions from the audience, for it allows an answer without being deflected from the time allotted for that lecture or topic. Ultimately, when done smoothly, question taking encourages and engages the audience to listen with a questioning mind, a demeanor which enhances learning.

So research training confers pedagogical skills as well as research techniques. Working with the research mentor on his research proposals contributes to the art of grant writing. To incorporate a clear statement of the problem or question, together with how the proposed experimental design will address it, is the key element. This experimental rationale coupled with elements of budget preparation completes the research training, and prepares the graduate from such training to establish his independent research program. The curriculum of every training program is best built on the knowledge and statement of what the graduate will become. These elements of the research training need clear description and implementation. In a word, developing the skill of critical thinking allows the graduates of such research training to build their own research program and career.

16

Reconsidering My Calling

It was the doldrums of Chicago Winter 1985 when I escaped. Between my arrival at the University of Chicago in July 1982 and now, five grants had been written and funded, the research laboratories were up and running productively—32 Abstracts of Preliminary Communications were published and presented, the ICU program of delivering and teaching exemplary Critical Care was organized and implemented, 6 new extraordinary Faculty had been recruited to the Section of Pulmonary and Critical Care Medicine, and the teaching presence of our faculty was evident in medical school, internal medicine residency, and our new Fellowship program. And the ATS section on Critical Care was up and running, having experienced a first Spring meeting with an exemplary scientific program for an unexpectedly large membership, and was poised for it's 2nd annual meeting with another superb program.

This progress was associated with my calling to be a productive investigator who built a great program in Academic Critical Care. I was succeeding! I was exhausted! And not very happy!!

A VACATION IN GREECE

Thank God for a timely invitation from a colleague, then doing a Research Fellowship with my PhD supervisor at McGill University, in Montreal. "You and Elaine are welcome to live in my Villa on Kamari Beach in Santorini," said he, in response to my whining about being too busy and needing to get away. It happened that I was scheduled to participate in a Critical Care Conference in Brussels in early Spring 1985. So we extended our European stay after that conference by traveling to Athens and then to Santorini.

Funny thing, we could not get a ticket back to Athens from Santorini in June of 1985, when I was scheduled to participate in a Critical Care Conference in Jerusalem. It turned out that the Greek elections were scheduled then, and the Papandreou government had purchased all the air tickets allowing supporters to travel from Santorini to their voting polls in Athens. After weeks of futile attempts in Santorini, Elaine and I gave up our struggle to get tickets.

Early one morning, the villa phone rang, and a gravelly Greek voice said, "Larry, we have a problem. A prominent young man in the Papandreou government has become very ill with Pneumonia, and has been on a ventilator for 2 weeks—we cannot get him off. Can you help us?"

I explained to my Greek colleague that I was ready and willing to help, but I could not get off Santorini. When he said he would take care of our travel to and from Athens, I asked Elaine what she needed. After weeks on this exotic island, her needs were well defined. Quickly, she replied—"I go with you; we take a room at the Hilton where I can get my hair done, and we get air tickets back to Athens after you have seen the patient and returned to Santorini."

Less than 10 minutes passed from the time I got off the phone until there was a loud knock at the door. The well-dressed young man presented us with round-trip tickets—Santorini to Athens, for this morning's flight, and explained that an airport limo would pick us up in an hour. Oh yes, and a one-way ticket for us to return to Athens to connect with our EL AL flight to Jerusalem!

We were met on the tarmac by Dr. Kyrakis, who introduced himself as the Director of the ICU where the patient, Costas, was being treated. He escorted us to a waiting limo which set out through Athens traffic to the Hilton hotel. On the way, he explained to Elaine the time and place of her hair appointment. Then he described succinctly the presentation and course of the patient, including a brief description of how important Costas was to Papandreou's re-election. We stopped at the hotel just long enough to get Elaine registered and settled in her room before we took the same limo to the Hospital.

As we entered the ICU, a bevy of white coated Housestaff greeted us. I inquired who was the resident in charge of Costas' care, and asked her to tell me his story. Somewhat less succinctly and with more details of current health status and treatment modalities, she told me the same story as Kyrakis: "This is a 38 year old patient weighing 100kg with no significant past illnesses who acquired severe right lower lobar pneumococcal pneumonia. During the first 48 hours of admission, this spread to cause 4-quadrant air-space filling requiring ventilation with 100% oxygen, a tidal volume of 1.0l at 20 breaths per minute, and 15 cm Peep to maintain 90% hemoglobin saturation and a $PaCO_2$ of 44 mm hg. Over the next 7 days, FI_{O2} was reduced to 0.6, Peep to 8cm H_2O, and tidal volume to 0.8l at 16bpm to maintain the same blood gas values.

Subsequent attempts to let him breathe on Synchronized Intermittent Mandatory Ventilation (SIMV) were met with one of 2 patterns: if the sedation were maintained sufficient to make Costas less responsive to deep painful stimuli, reduction of the SIMV rate below 6bpm caused rapid (40bpm) shallow (200 ml) breathing; or, if the sedative were discontinued so that Costas was awake and responsive to verbal commands, he became obstreperous, flailing his arms and attempting to grab the endotrachial tube. As he was a large strong man, this behaviour required several Nurses and Housestaff to restrain him.

I asked the resident how I could help her, and she replied "Please get him off the ventilator safely so he can breathe spontaneously, for I think he is well enough to do so." I responded with this plan, which took 3 hours at the bedside to implement:

- First, I had the sedative infusion reduced so that Costas was drowsy but arousable.
- Then I introduced myself to him with the help of his Resident as translator, explaining that I was a Specialist in helping patients like him resume spontaneous breathing, brought to his bedside by his friends who were worried about him. I told him I was going to change the ventilator settings slightly to make him more comfortable, and he was to tell me if any of the changes caused him to not get enough air. I had the tidal volume reduced in small increments to 400 ml, and he progressively increased his

rate of triggering the Ventilator on the Assist/Control mode from 16 to 24 bpm. Then the Peep was reduced to 4 cm H_2O as he registered normal blood gases. When asked if he was getting enough air, he nodded yes.

- After 1 hour of this breathing pattern, he remained comfortable so I told him I was going to reduce the work the ventilator was doing to let him do more of the work of breathing. When I switched the breathing circuit from the ventilator to at T-piece he did not change his breathing pattern, and he maintained normal blood gases during the next hour. He was calm without any limb flailing, and when anxious he responded to verbal anesthesia.

He was extubated that evening uneventfully.

Elaine and I flew back to Santorini for the rest of our mini Sabbatical. While there, I read Homer's <u>Odyssey</u> on my friend's patio, and discerned that my disenchantment in Chicago was due to having 4 full time jobs. I opted to rank them in the order that I enjoyed them, and then to cut from the bottom until my joy in Medicine returned: 1) Teaching; 2) Patient care; 3) Research; 4) Administration. The approach leading to these priorities emerged slowly during our participation in an 8-day retreat lead on audio-tape by Thomas Greene SJ on the patio of our idyllic Santorini Villa. Accompanied by numerous messages from the still small voice (3 of which are transcribed in *Chapter 20*), these conclusions were both a statement of belief and a hypothesis to be tested. Again, I was living the interface of science and belief.

On returning to Chicago, I set in motion the steps to relinquish my administrative position as Head of the Section of Pulmonary and Critical Care Medicine as of July 1987. My life improved considerably, though I was blindsided by the loss of my enjoyment of being in the portals of power in our Department. Once I named that, I could get out of the way of my successor and get on with my 3 full time jobs. As luck would have it, the world of investigation shifted from Pathophysiology to cell & molecular biology, and I chose not to follow it. Accordingly, my job focused on teaching and patient care. I told you this story to make this point—most accomplished professionals are propelled by their productivity to take on more than they can handle within their limits of time and talent. The consequent high-velocity choiceless lifestyle leaves no time to think outside of their complicated job responsibilities. By taking the time to define what I wanted to do, my revised job description focused on our new Fellowship Program, with all it's requisite teaching and on expanding my teaching activities in the Medical School. About two years later I accepted the opportunity to write and edit the _Principles of Critical Care_ Book Series[1,2,3], then several more years later I accepted Leadership of a Task Force on Review and Revision of the Medical School Curriculum. Taken together this sequence opened the door for a new focus as Dean for Medical Education, a progression so suited to my talents that it brought joy back to my professional life.

So I was following a new calling—away from research and toward patient care.

LISTENING TO THE PATIENT

The call from the ER was terse. "We have an exotic dancer bitten by her pet rattlesnake; her vital signs are stable and she is not bleeding, but her blood work and smear show no detectable platelets."

A hasty elevator trip from the 7th floor ICU to the first floor ER brought me into the presence of an attractive smiling young lady who spit out the salient aspects of the incident without my asking any questions:

"My snake has been off his food for a few days. I tried to push a mouse in his direction, but it struck my hand instead. You can't give me anti-venom, because I have received it many times before, and have grown allergic to it. And don't give me platelets because the venom is still in my blood, and it will destroy the platelets and cause me to develop a rash and drop my blood pressure."

We examined the two puncture marks on her hand and read about snakebites. We learned from her what type of snake it was and called the Poison Control Centre in Toronto. They quickly identified the anti-venom and arranged an emergency delivery via military jet.

Four hours later, my intern had drawn up four fifty ml vials of anti-venom for IV administration.

"But what about her allergy?", asked the intern, "I know the Poison Control Centre said we had to give it via IV, but let me do a skin test first." Drawing up 1ml of the anti-venom, he diluted it in 100ml of saline and injected 1ml of the diluted anti-venom into the skin of the patient's upper arm. Within minutes, the arm doubled its size and became an angry red colour. But not as angry as the patient, who defiantly cried "I told you!".

Transferred gently to the ICU on complete bed rest with 1 percutaneous small bore IV, she listened as we discussed her need for platelets to prevent a life threatening hemorrhage. "I'd rather bleed than experience the effects of platelet infusion", she insisted. But with calm persuasion, we convinced her to try one unit of the 12-platelet packs we had available for her.

Within minutes, her body developed an intense rash, her blood pressure dropped to 60/0, and she complained bitterly of weakness, pruritus, and malaise. We stopped the platelets and she returned to normal—still on strict bed rest.

Three days later, she was discharged home with a normal platelet count and no evidence of hemorrhage.

Primúm, non nocere. First, do no harm.

It starts with listening to the patient, who always knows more about themselves than the caregiver possibly could. This is especially true when the patient presents with a relatively rare condition which otherwise would necessitate a literature search and a quick reading of relevant articles. For often, the patient with the unusual condition has distilled key information; this saves precious time in getting treatment started without causing harm.

This story is another example of living the interface of science and belief. All prior evidence concerning treatment of this patient concludes with intravenous administration of the anti-venom, except that the patient herself says "don't' do it—I am allergic to the anti-venom." The clinician-scientist among us was the Intern, who listened to the patient and got new important evidence by performing a skin test. In the urgent and emotional furor surrounding this patient's life-threatening snakebite, it was possible to believe that anti-venom should be administered, but in reality, her caregivers needed to test her hypothesis—the Scientific Method in practice served her well. I believe that questioning science is appropriate and life-saving, life-giving and life-affirming. These outcomes are the result of questioning science and belief. Story after story from providing Critical Care gave me an abundance of clinical cases to write about. More importantly, these helped to develop a Philosophy of Critical Care, shared with our trainees and my colleagues daily. This produced an approach to Critical Care which was now looking for an outlet.

WRITING A TEXTBOOK OF CRITICAL CARE

My experience as a Professor of Medicine and Section Chief was only 5 years in duration by 1987, yet my vision for my professional job description had already changed considerably. Based on my deliberations during a mini-sabbatical in Santorini in 1985, I had relinquished my position as Section Head and focused on my Research Program while maintaining a large teaching role and effecting Clinical Critical Care. It soon became clear that funding for my research program was under siege for my not having enough cell and molecular biology focus. It seemed that I needed either to redirect my investigative efforts, or reduce them to focus on other academic goals.

I re-evaluated my research program. What I saw was a productive research start in Canada, with effortless transition to research funding and productivity in Chicago. By July of 1987, my research program was booming with 2 NHLBI operating grants and a Research Training Grant with abundant good fellows and superb colleagues.

Then the bottom fell out, suddenly but with warning. A colleague on the Grants Review Committee called to alert me that a significant number of members on my new Study Section had expressed dissatisfaction with the pathophysiologic focus of my two grants, and so I would be wise to initiate some different direction or methodology. Our application for a Scientific Center of Research (SCOR) in late 1987 addressing Acute Respiratory Failure was not funded, the first such outcome I had experienced in either Canada or the United States. Then my competitive renewal of my 15-year investigation of AHRF was not funded. I was dismayed.

Simultaneously, I received an invitation to edit a major Critical Care text that I thought I could do and I imagined would provide an outlet for our Teaching expertise. Accordingly, I decided not to launch studies of Cell and Molecular Biology, which would require a whole new learning curve and vocabulary of concepts and techniques. Instead, I planned a Sabbatical in 1989 to launch the Critical Care book series. Essentially, I decided to redirect my effort away from research and toward clinical scholarship and teaching—a major crossroad for my career.

In late 1988, I accepted the invitation from McGraw/Hill to organize, write and edit a definitive text on Critical Care. During extensive planning with Jesse Hall and Greg Schmidt, we developed plans with the publisher to prepare a 4 part, 190 chapter, 2200 page book for trainees in adult Critical Care from the disciplines of anesthesiology, medicine and surgery. During the 1989 Spring Meetings for the ATS in Cincinnati, we three editors met with 10 carefully selected associate editors—representing prestigious centers of Critical Care or with unique Critical Care expertise—to formalize our goals and list of invited contributors. By August, 90% of the contributors agreed to furnish first drafts before January 1990 in order to allow an unusually rigorous 2 stage review of each chapter before April 1990—all to publish the book in the Spring of 1991 in anticipation of the three Critical Care Boards in the autumn of 1991.

The unique features of the book were: a first part describing in less than 200 pages the foundations in pathophysiology for all Critical Care; a final section addressing perspectives on diverse Critical Care issues not amenable to organ system description (e.g. ethics, clinical investigation, etc.); and the heart of the text—Diagnosis and Management of Critical Illnesses—which included leader Key Points and an Illustrative Case with discussion for each of the 133 disease states in Part III of the book.

The initial investment in selecting excellent contributors bore fruit in the quality of the chapters we reviewed. It was a full and exciting 1990 completing the editorial reviews to galley and page proofs. There was an appropriate enthusiasm for a much needed companion pre-test for Critical Care Board Review. Further, the anticipated attention which this book brought to University of Chicago Critical Care demanded a Mid West Board Review course in the Spring of 1991 sponsored by our office of Continuing Medical Education (CME) and McGraw/Hill, and taught by our core faculty of Critical Care teachers, so these plans were initiated in late 1989.

The outcome of these efforts was a 2400 page text, which was well reviewed and well received by the Critical Care community. Along the way, we invited our cadre of fellows and junior faculty to help us prepare and publish a handbook of the principles of Critical Care[2], designed for Housestaff pocket use. And we prepared a book of pre-test questions and answers developed from the text to assist preparation for Critical Care Board Exams. We organized the mid-west conference addressing the management of acute cardio-vascular disorders, and began a State of the Art (SOTA) Critical Care Conference sponsored by the American Thoracic Society (ATS), in part as a Critical Care Board preparation. It seems that the large text had sustainability, for McGraw Hill published a second and third edition (1998 and 2005), and are preparing the 4th edition for 2012.

The preparation and editing of this text was a wonderful learning experience. Almost immediately, the regular updates on diverse Critical Care topics discussed in the edited manuscripts of book chapters promoted State of the Art discussions in our Morning Report and Clinical Conferences by our Housestaff, Fellows and Faculty. These discussions facilitated excellent patient-based conversations of clinical problems and solutions on ICU Rounds. And research questions galore were stimulated by the timely review and discussion of clinical problems. So there was a buzz of interested smart Critical Care physicians and trainees spun off from the regular discussion of the many topics being reviewed, especially since most of our fellows and faculty were either reviewing or writing the book chapters.

Looking back at the influence this book and its subsequent editions have had on the understanding and practice of Critical Care, several features stand out. In a field built on resuscitation and the fast paced protocols designed to shorten the time-down of patients presenting with arrested vital functions, we introduced rationale and moderation to the post-resuscitation Critical Care such as: seek the least intervention achieving defined endpoints or goals of therapy; utilize clinical skills to base a differential diagnostic approach for all abnormalities; formulate clinical hypotheses and test them; liberate patients from ICU intervention as urgently as they were added to patient care; implement clear communication with the patient and their family early, including discussion of prognosis and end of life considerations; and establish an efficient research and teaching program in the ICU.

Outside the University of Chicago, it became much easier to pull together thoughtful Faculty to participate in Critical Care Conferences, for we knew more than most who the experts were. In turn, our invited participation at National and International Conferences increased as our Critical Care reputation grew and organizers became familiar with the quality of our teaching. Our reputation as editors and authors of this new text brought us an invitation to contribute 4 chapters on Critical Care for the second edition of the pre-eminent _Textbook of Respiratory Medicine 2e_ edited by John Murray and Jay Nadel (Saunders, Philadelphia, 1994).

During my sabbatical when most of the book editing was going on, I had more time than usual to clean up a backlog of manuscripts accumulated during the busy building years. Accordingly, I was able to publish 19 peer-reviewed manuscripts and 11 book chapters. We also submitted for presentation 11 abstracts of new studies initiated in 1989.

This year was helpful too in pursuing a more balanced life. Elaine and I had become more active in our Parish community of St. Thomas the Apostle catholic church. There, we led a Bible Study one evening per week, and coordinated a Lenten prayer program for about 40 parishioner participants each week. These activities spawned a parish-wide program of Stewardship, exploring ways to share our time, talent and treasure. These interactions raised questions in our participants' minds, and after our meetings they would ask us questions about their spirituality. So Elaine and I sought ways to get answers through further training as Spiritual Directors.

Busily preparing _Principles of Critical Care_[1] and actively involved in church activities, I had no idea that a new area of Medical Education was opening up for me. Nor did I know how the apparently spiritual activities of Stewardship and Spiritual Direction were just the preparation

I needed to help me contribute to the review, revision and management of Medical Education. I was clear that I was shifting my career away from research and toward clinical scholarship, but I did not anticipate how this change would immerse me in the management of education in the Medical School.

17

Welcoming and Advising Students in the Profession of Medicine

Each autumn, a new Medical School class starts their learning of the practice of Medicine—about 100 students average in 125 schools across the USA—over 10,000 students per year. And each class is welcomed to the process in different ways. At the University of Chicago Pritzker School of Medicine we collaborated with the Arnold P. Gold Foundation to dress this process in a white coat given to and worn by each entering student, for a white coat symbolizes the Professionalism to be learned. On September 29, 1992, I had the honour of welcoming the Class of 1996 to Pritzker, and this is what I told them in my White Coat Ceremony Keynote Address to the Class of 1996. I include it here to give one example of my speaking style and teaching demeanor. The title of the talk was:

NURTURING THE ROOTS OF PROFESSIONALISM

"What a privilege it is for me to welcome you this evening! Fresh with the experience of being admitted to one of the outstanding medical schools in the world, you should relish the feeling. It is like sitting hungry at a smorgasbord of delights waiting for the banquet of medical learning to begin, anticipating appropriately the new vocabulary of concepts which will confer understanding both practical and awe-inspiring. Practical, because you actually use what you learn to facilitate healing of your patients. Awe-inspiring, because the revealed wonders concerning how the body and spirit of people are made will knock your socks off, conferring the humility and wide-eyed enthusiasm required to keep you healthy in your practice of medicine. I hope you will notice and enjoy your learning environment. You begin the study of Medicine as the first class of the second 100 years of learning at the University of Chicago, the home of Nobel laureates and leaders of Medicine. Each of you will catch a measure of that spirit of excellence. And Chicago is a great city—from the jogging and bicycle path along the lake to downtown theatre, Opera, restaurants, and sports teams!

In keeping with the theme of your inauguration ceremonies, I would like to share a few reflections about your acquisition of professionalism during the rest of your life. Professionalism is an acquired demeanor perceived by patients and health care workers to indicate that the physician has commitment to the needs of the patient, clinical competence, compassion, integrity, and self-awareness. These characteristics have their roots in intrinsic qualities of the exemplary physician: excellence and compassion. These inclinations of the human spirit can and should be honed by each of you beginning today; your medical curriculum is currently being reorganized to nurture these qualities from its selection process based on your potential for both learning and caring, through a process of humanizing your undergraduate medical curriculum, integrating your scientific and clinical training, and teaching you to be a student throughout your life

EXCELLENCE

The pursuit of excellence in medicine is a complex process, based on a balanced knowledge of your capabilities and limitations in acquiring familiarity with a body of knowledge so broad and deep that no one can master it all. Accordingly, each of you needs to master the limited knowledge at hand, with emphasis on mastery even if it is of the minimum. This will mean choosing what to master repeatedly, and a good guideline for you is to choose what interests or fascinates you; such an approach does not provide good marks—that is one reason why we at Pritzker espouse a pass-fail system. That there is a possibility to fail means you cannot push your choosing what you like too far—that is, I love physiology so much more than Anatomy that I am going to skip all anatomy classes, labs, and homework in order to master physiology. But within each of these disciplines, each of you will be fascinated by sub-components which you can master. Then what you acquire in terms of facts is less important than your acquisition of the pursuit of excellence—a process which you can then apply to every new learning situation.

Let me give you an example. This summer, about half of the first year class conducted a research project in an expanded and reorganized training program designed to introduce students to the exciting process of asking answerable questions. Toward the end of her experience, one very motivated and gifted student shared with me her disappointment that her goals for her research would not be achieved. Knowing that she aspired to be a clinician-scientist, I asked her to review with me the techniques of science she had acquired. To our mutual surprise and delight, she listed thirteen complex methods of cellular and molecular biology she had mastered, and came up with her plan of how she would use these during her second summer of research to pursue her career progression. I told you her story to tell you this: We do excellence here, and you will catch it. Excellence is partly taught, but it is mostly caught by the process of working side by side with mentors who have it.

And so mentorship should be actively sought as an integral part of your pursuit of excellence. Mentors provide challenge, support and vision for your pursuit. Challenge is common, and you are already accustomed to it—setting tasks, unmasking assumptions, offering alternative perspectives, giving feedback, and encouraging hypothetical thinking. You may be less used to support—the mentor listens, invites, advocates and helps you structure your next steps. Teachers in the audience, ask yourselves with me now, and again daily "How many of you admired the performance or behavior of a student today, and told her so?" If you are not affirming their accomplishments, you are killing their self-esteem! And mentors provide vision for you—partly by mirroring your own plans, partly by providing new language for your understandings, partly by mapping your development within a time-honored tradition they do know and value more than you. So seek mentorship to aid your pursuit of excellence, and your faculty will respond by providing it.

COMPASSION

Did you hear the story about the Chinese boy who pushed his father's outhouse into the Yantze River? The father convened a family meeting to ask "who pushed my outhouse into the Yantze River?" There was no reply, so he asked again. Still no reply, so he told his family a story about George Washington, who as a boy chopped down his father's cherry tree. When asked who did it, George replied, "I did, father." His father patted him on the head in forgiveness and commendation for his honesty, and predicted that George's integrity and courage would lead to greatness—indeed, he became the first president of the United States. "Now", continued the Chinese father, "who pushed my outhouse into the Yantze River?" Replied his 12-year-old son, "I did, father." Where upon the father thrashed him soundly. Days later when the anger abated, his son asked, "why did you tell me about George Washington, and why was George treated so differently?" "Because George's father was not sitting in the cherry tree."

I told you that story to tell you this: One's view of complex issues often depends on where you sit. And where I sit concerning nurturing the pursuit of excellence is at a viewpoint privileged to observe the entering medical class and the graduating medical class each year. My observations lead me to believe that excellence is necessary for the acquisition of professionalism, but it is not sufficient. I think it needs another quality, and acquiring compassion is just as difficult as acquiring excellence. In operation, compassion is your ability to be with your patients in their distress. As your compassion grows, so that understanding called "empathy" will grow, conferring an active receptivity for your patient's story. What most of you will learn is that your excellence depends in large part on your capacity to take in your patient's story and respond to it with intelligent, data-based decision making. So compassion can enhance excellence.

Let me give you an example. Fifteen years ago in Canada, it became clear to me that divorce was unavoidable and that separation and estrangement from my young children would be one terrible consequence. When that realization hit late one evening in my office where I was trying to finish a research manuscript while attending in our Intensive Care Unit, I became despondent. After several hours of processing my grief, I decided on an unusual course to help me deal with my inevitable loss—I went to the ICU to waste some time with the patient who had the least chance for recovery. Until then, it had been my style to spend most of my time with my patients having the best chance for cure, sometimes even bypassing my other patients for whom I had nothing to offer. Of course, the response from my previously neglected patient was both surprise and delight as I got to learn how he felt about his inevitable death. He was heard by his physician, who now understood that not all terrible conditions can be cured but the patient can be comforted.

What was going on that night?—A process of <u>being with in the pain</u> when no cure was available! Who benefited?—both the physician and the patient learned that medicine is not just about the relentless pursuit of cure for the diseases of life, for often enough our competence is insufficient to diagnose or cure. Then what? Each of us needs to draw on our own woundedness to provide the strength to be with, to comfort without cure. Although that process can be scary, it gets better with time and with our surviving more losses. In a sense, we become "wounded-healers", a process which uses our own processed grief as a source of personal strength from which compassion flows effortlessly. The good news is that all your past, present and future losses have great value to your professionalism when you process them well. Think about it—some of us come from dysfunctional families, some of us will fail exams, others will enter unsuccessful significant relationships, others will encounter unexpected illness in ourselves and our loved ones—and it all can be used for our own personal development—including the acquisition of professionalism arising from compassion balanced with excellence!

BALANCING EXCELLENCE WITH COMPASSION

Interviews with patients concerning their physician's care reveals repeatedly that satisfaction is proportional to how well the patient feels he has been heard and understood. Analysis of the recent malpractice explosion in America reveals that allegations of malpractice are most often based in the patient's indignation with the interpersonal skill of the physician; the outlet for that indignation is a search for examples of inadequate care as a basis for lawsuit. By contrast, many patients are unaware of receiving less than the adequate standard of care by empathic physicians who make each patient visit a warm, up building experience. Can you see the conundrum? Our profession is currently replete with physicians whose pursuit of excellence confers exemplary medical decision-making for patients, who regard them as heartless, arrogant people. Similarly, physicians abound who regularly make erroneous medical decisions based on the admirable desire to ease their patients' distress, but without having the data-base or experience to help. Of course, none of you would willingly choose either of these extremes, yet there are intrinsic antagonisms between the pursuit of excellence and the enhancement of compassion which you should consider in trying to balance them.

Many of you, and me, are driven to pursue excellence in order to achieve success and avoid failure. Unchecked, this fear of failure can make us anxious before new challenges; for example—exams, learning to conduct medical interviews, or encountering a patient with a condition or question we have not seen or heard before. In response, we are disposed to search frantically for the information that will solve the problem, in order to provide personal satisfaction and the approbation of others as opposed to feeling ignorant and incompetent. This self-centered state of mind interferes with the process of paying appropriate attention to our patients and colleagues in the situation, such that the pursuit of excellence confounds one's intrinsic compassion. What is required is a simple acceptance of the truth—"I don't know, but I will use the resources available to find out." Such a humble approach acknowledges that you can't know everything always, but you have learned how to find out; hence the importance of research is to provide the luxury of time to learn how to form the question in one area, and to learn the tools for answering it; once you acquire confidence that you know how to solve a problem, you can solve any problem. In the meantime the personal interactions can proceed unclouded by your fear of the unknown, which is often just what your patient (or spouse or friend) needs.

On the other hand, you will repeatedly experience patients whose stories strike so close to yours that you live their pain. So encumbered, your medical excellence will elude you—recede from your consciousness before the imperative to do something to ease the distress by diagnosing and solving their problem. Because your compassion confounds your excellence, you will be inclined to protect yourself by putting on armor to keep you from becoming incapacitated by your empathic participation in your patient's distress. Again, truth helps, either spoken or articulated internally—"I am experiencing your distress so intensely that it drives me to intervene beyond my current expertise, so I am going to get more informed assistance."

EMPOWERING THE BALANCE—AWE AND JOY

Can you imagine any greater professionalism than that displayed by a competent physician who cares? Such a doctor is perceived to respond effectively to most clinical situations while making the patients, their significant others, and members of the health care team feel dignified with information about their condition and concern for their distress. The two roots of professionalism, excellence and compassion, feed off each other rather than confound each other, to make the complete physician an eternal student. Your pursuit of these goals begins today and lasts forever. I hope I have conveyed the complex and arduous path to professionalism sufficiently clearly to make you ask "where will I ever get the energy to fuel this inner pursuit of excellence and compassion?" If you ask, I give you my answer by telling you what I did today:

I awoke to my alarm at 5AM, showered, dressed and spent 30 minutes of quiet with my journal. Elaine joined me for breakfast, and I left our apartment at 6:30AM. I walked to my office and then to meet my ICU team to begin rounds at 7AM. Together with 3 senior Medical Students, 3 Interns, 3 Residents and a Critical Care fellow, we heard about two newly admitted patients and 11 other ICU patients. We examined each and set in motion the plan for their care that day. Four were being ventilated, two others required intubation, three were ready to be extubated, and four others were hypotensive and required a fluid challenge and vasoactive drug infusion—all during rounds, which we finished at 8:30AM. As a group, we moved to the pulmonary and Critical Care conference room, where we spent 30 minutes hearing about four new patients. We also heard follow-up on two other patients we had discussed last week—all six patients provided interesting diagnostic and treatment lessons.

At 9AM, I returned to my office to review 2 Book chapters for our text *Principles of Critical Care*[1] which I processed before I rejoined the ICU team at 11AM in the Radiology Suite. We reviewed the recent x-rays of all of our patients. In the course of these x-ray rounds, we noted 2 endotracheal tubes and one Swan-Ganz catheter requiring repositioning and we detected right lower lobe collapse and new lung infiltrate in 3 other patients.

After lunch with a visiting Professor—whom I had invited to speak to our Faculty and Fellows later this afternoon in our Advanced Respiratory Physiology course—I met our ICU team back in the conference room for our daily 1-hour learning session about the Pathophysiology of Critical Illness. Today, I spoke to the group about the bedside differential diagnosis of hypoperfusion states, or shock, a favourite topic of mine which was a timely review for the Housestaff who managed 3 patients with shock overnight.

Then I returned to the ICU to write my daily note in the chart of each of my patients before I met with the family of one of the patients who was not getting better. At this family meeting, we discussed the withholding and withdrawl of therapy for their loved one, and I recommended that we should switch our goals from cure to comfort. This was a poignant discussion, and the family of our patient required support to manage their grief.

At 4PM, I returned to the conference room to introduce our guest speaker and his topic, "Pulmonary Gas Exchange: Contribution of multiple inert gas elimination technique (MIGET)". After his lecture, we met with several Critical Care fellows to discuss their ongoing experiments in which some peculiar gas-exchange results had been obtained. Our visiting Professor was helpful and the fellows got a chance to work with a famous scholar.

About 6:30PM, I joined Elaine for dinner and we took a walk along the lake to discuss our day, and to collect and focus my thoughts on what I would say to you tonight.

And the University of Chicago Department of Medicine actually pays me to do this!!

I love providing Critical Care and teaching it and researching it!! I told you that to tell you this—the practice of Medicine is an exhilarating process full of challenge, opportunity and fun, in which I utilize all of my human skills—you will too!! This joy fuels my pursuit of excellence and compassion; in turn, approaching each new situation with excellence and compassion enhances the enjoyment. Good luck on your journey, and remember that this process of transformation and personal growth you experience is much more important than the short term goals of passing grades and even practicing medicine."

At the time of preparing this book, President Obama has signed the Health Reform Act. Many physicians and patients express fear at what these changes will do to the practice of Medicine. I contend that I am wise to stay the course—acknowledging that my joy and awe in practicing medicine, that my pursuit of excellence and compassion will keep sacred my desire to help heal the ill, no matter what external systems of management/governance prevail. Personally, I find it easy to espouse a healthcare system which makes care available to 30 million citizens who currently do not have access to it. At the same time, I understand the concern of my countrymen who think the government will allow more wastefulness and abuse of resources. So I recommend that we provide healthcare for those who need it out of compassion, while we define and fix the management glitches with excellence.

ADVISING STUDENTS OF MEDICINE

Once admitted to Medical School, the students spend four years of curriculum-based study. Along this arduous pathway, they encounter many obstacles common to most Medical Students, so the Office of Medical Education sets up regular advising sessions—some with the whole Class, and some as 1-on-1 meetings with the Dean of Medical Education or his representative.

The reader may find the grouping of topics in this piece somewhat unusual. It is!! But stories are like that. The anecdote about evaluation created a problem, and professional behaviour was the solution. To invite the students to this solution required challenging them, an essential component of Mentorship. During Mentorship of Medical Students, Housestaff and junior Faculty, it is not uncommon to encounter issues of career progression, a topic so close to the fabric of the protégé that he may invite prayer.

EVALUATION

When I was appointed Dean of Medical Education in 1996, I was at the peak of my teaching activities. If I had been asked then what the correct balance was in the curriculum between content and evaluation, I would have answered 80%/20%. But after 8 years of managing the curriculum while having about the same teaching activity, I now think it the other way, 40%/60% content/evaluation. Part of this shift was encouraged by the strong presence of education specialists in our Office of Medical Education. For they implemented and titrated a robust system for evaluating the teaching and teachers by the students, and educated me and the Faculty Teachers on how to fairly evaluate the students' performance. The evaluation tools then provided objective data about how the courses and teachers were meeting the needs of the students. Of course, students have an incomplete understanding of what they need to learn on any subject, so this evaluation process needs to be guided by a clear statement of course content. This is examined regularly by the Liaison Committee for Medical Education (LCME); in turn, our Faculty Teachers need to titrate these course descriptions and their learning objectives. Again, these steps were built in by the thoughtful deliberations of our Curriculum Review Committee.

Given a strong performance in each of these steps, the anonymous feedback of students is invaluable. Over several years, we evolved a system of obtaining maximum feedback by having students evaluate the course and teachers just before their final exams. This had the defect of generating perfunctory evaluations from harried students eager to start their examinations. So an educational program for the students was implemented to raise their understanding about the value of their feedback to course and Faculty teaching improvements.

Then the student evaluations went electronic. It was just as easy to encourage maximum student participation by a policy of not releasing a student's exam results until she had submitted her evaluations. And anonymity could still be maintained by separating a student's response from his name on the submission sheet. Now each student had the luxury of time to provide and submit thoughtful evaluations. And submit they did! Most of these electronic evaluations were of great value, but a problem inherent in the system grew out of control and beyond our expectations.

A minority of disgruntled students used this electronic podium to vent their spleen directed at the course and some of its teachers. Some of this response, especially if it had consensus, is valuable in managing the curriculum. But such candor when hyperbole prevails robs the Curriculum Review Committee of their best tool for improving courses and teaching—giving feedback to the Faculty. For even when the distribution is to the Faculty member being evaluated, it was so disheartening, even insulting, that it could not achieve its purpose— to improve, for that needed the gumption and talent of the Faculty member. Statements like "This man should not be allowed to teach anything in Medical School. He is such a jerk." were offensive to the Faculty and seemed to stimulate rancor rather than improvement.

PROFESSIONALISM

How do you get the students to put their evaluations in terms that the Faculty can hear and respond productively? My answer grew out of a teaching approach I had used with Medical Students. I found it realistic and helpful to deal with these 25-year-old students as responsible adults who were my colleagues in a sacred profession of helping patients, and I called them so. "Good morning, colleagues" is a simple salutation which makes our relationship and their behaviour explicit.

At the next gathering of the first and second year classes, I spoke to them about collegiality in our profession, and the demeanor that is civil in interacting with our colleagues. Though anonymity may allow the most demeaning descriptions of our colleagues' behaviour, it never promotes professional interactions. Professionalism is an acquired demeanor perceived by patients and health care workers to indicate that the physician has commitment to the needs of the patient, clinical competence, compassion, integrity and self-awareness. So in evaluating courses and teachers, professionalism demands that we convey criticism in the most constructive way, so that our colleagues can consider it seriously and be moved to improve. In this context, I displayed on the overhead projector several of the most egregious comments, and asked the assembled students to consider how they would feel to receive such.

I heard later that the class leaders had called a follow up meeting to discuss this issue. It never became a problem again. Afterwards I was embarrassed at my uncertainty about how my message would be received. For I know the psyche and behaviour patterns of 25 year olds well enough to expect resistance and rebellion. And I was some anxious as I went forward to speak this word. I should have known that students treated as professional colleagues would respond in a professional manner. And I can't help but think that this was one of the most important lessons I taught that quarter.

MENTORSHIP

Challenging the Medical Students to understand their importance in evaluating their courses and teachers was an invitation to their acquiring professionalism. The process required my setting a task for them to think about the contribution their constructive evaluation made to the curriculum. For some students, I was unmasking their assumption that Faculty teachers were not trying to do their best or could not respond to constructive criticism and improve. For many, I was offering alternative perspective of the evaluation process, which required their suspending their indignation. I gave them all feedback about how irresponsible critique is not helpful. And I encouraged hypothetical thinking—to the extent that I provide constructive criticism I can improve curriculum.

Though I was uncertain how each class would respond to this challenge, whatever confidence I had came from the support I had given the students previously, and the habit I had cultivated of providing vision for them. These are the elements of Mentorship—Challenge, Support and Vision-making. More often than with entire classes, mentorship is a large part of the one on one conversation between Mentor and Protégé. When a student visits, the Mentor listens attentively, invites the protégé to action, advocates for her protégé in diverse ways depending on the issue under discussion, and helps her protégé structure next steps. Often, the challenge and support offered accompany vision making—mirroring the protégé's plans, providing new vocabulary for the concepts under discussion, and mapping the development of the protégé.

Faculty members serving as mentors come to the process with a wide range of behaviours; in general Mentoring does not come naturally to most. And there are few programs available to teach mentoring to interested Faculty. While seeking instruction about the process of Spiritual Direction, I was delighted to learn how to listen empathically, and the value of doing so. Mirroring is a great check on whether the Mentor has heard correctly what the protégé has said. Assuring the protégé that he has been heard correctly sets up a relationship which is actively receptive to challenge and vision-making.

PRAYER

How the Mentor balances these behavioral tasks in each session is guided a lot by intuition. Partly because I learned these skills in a spiritual context, my intuition often found an invitation to prayer as a component of mentoring. Information about my protégé's spiritual background often came out during the session. And just like my uncertainty in approaching the class of Medical Students, my spirit senses are heightened when I ask whether or not to invite my protégé to pray about the issue. I am sure part of my uncertainty comes from the general view that prayer in the matter of career progression is not common, especially in the Dean's Office. Yet I have not experienced any other response to this invitation than "yes". "Would you like to start" I then ask. About half the time the student begins to pray, and his words make the space around the issue sacred. Then I pray in similar form and style as the student, requesting assistance from our Higher Power for the issue as best I understand it. Of course, this prayerful approach to Mentorship is an extension of my life, while the prayer of the protégé may be a surprise even to them. The following letter documents a variation on this prayer, and includes the room for questioning and awe arising from shared prayer with the student:

"Thank you for taking the time to talk with me last week. We covered a lot of ground: from Tagore to the Soros fellowship, from my confusion about what to do next to your story of where life has already taken you. Thank you for sharing your memories and experiences.

I thought a lot about what you said—especially about asking God when I'm not sure what to do (about my own relationships). It was just 2 words of yours—"Ask Him"—except that hearing them made me think of personal faith, of the idea that God listens and can actually give us direction in our lives. Thank you. That is a precious thought, and also a guide. I also thought a lot about how you slowly open your hands to what God has to offer in all of life. Though quite different from the fist that you started with, the image of your hands open and your gaze upwards makes me think of strength. I hope that one day I'll share in that strength with you."

At issue here is just how much we are in control of our own destiny, ranging from meticulous planning of the outcome and every step towards it, to a serendipitous and grace—led journey to what is best for us. Most students feel pressured to follow the first because they are confronted with the second. I contend that both approaches are complementary and together reduce the stress on the student, so I try to introduce the 2 approaches in the course of career planning. Room for this discussion almost always arises from the uncertainty of the student.

18

Allopathic Medicine and CAM

Allopathic medicine refers to a system that aims to combat disease by using remedies (as drugs or surgery) which produce effects that are different from or incompatible with those of the disease being treated. The scope of allopathic medicine is determined by the curriculum of Medical Schools which is guided in the USA and Canada by the LCME (Liaison Committee on Medical Education), consisting of the Association of American Medical Colleges and the American Medical Association. Through regular and systematic evaluation of a self-study and a site visit of each and every Medical School, the LCME ensures the responsibility and accountability of the School for a coherent and coordinated curriculum.

There exists outside of this allopathic system an array of Complementary and Alternative Medicine (CAM), which seek wellness, and the treatment of health disorders. Examples of CAM are Traditional Chinese Medicine (TCM) encompassing Acupuncture and Herbal Therapy; Homeopathy; Ayurvedic Medicine; Chiropractic Medicine and Naturopathy. A resurgence of alternative medical practices provides some insight into the belief-science discussion. Almost every medical decision I make derives from evidence based in scientific discovery by allopathic physicians. At the same time, my colleagues in fields of complimentary and alternative medicine practice the healing arts based on centuries of description of effects and outcomes of clinical syndromes treated with specific mixtures of herbs or stimulation of meridians with needles or pressure, or with infinitesimal dilutions of homeopathic agents. I interpret the different perspective to be analogous to that of science (Allopathic) and belief (CAM).

The distinction can be made more clear with stories. When my son Peter, a Doctor of Traditional Chinese Medicine (DTCM) learned of a new herbal therapy for bronchial asthma, his first approach was to explain the interaction between the asthmatic patient and the therapy based on the long history of TCM diagnosis and treatment. By contrast, my first inclination was to set up a double-blind placebo controlled study of this new remedy in the hope that it would prove effective in diminishing essential asthmatic symptoms such as wheezing, shortness of breath and pulmonary function abnormalities like airflow obstruction reversible with bronchodilator therapy.

Now this differing perspective is not easy to resolve for Peter's new therapy did not arise by chance. Rather, it was an order of magnitude increase of the dose which was previously less effective. Each new successful treatment was another demonstration of therapeutic value. Accordingly, there is no need to conduct the double-blind placebo controlled study, is there? The agent was already effective. But not so fast, say I. For we do not know whether the effect of this agent was similar to that of a placebo in patients with asthma. And we have no systematic record of outcomes and complications of therapy with the herbal agent or the placebo.

Those readers unfamiliar with such studies should be aware that the improvement and complications of placebo are often up to 40% of the outcomes of the agent. Such differences can modify the therapeutic efficacy of an agent from a dramatic improvement to a marginal effect. Making these distinctions are the reasons for rigor in scientific studies; they are also the reason for skepticism of belief-based observations of therapy without the inclusion of principles of science. Doctors of TCM argue that giving the same herbal agent to all asthmatic patients in such a study loses the potency that they provide by tailoring the herbal mix to the presentation of the patient. This argument assumes they know the algorithm linking patient's presentation to herbal mix, but that begs the question of how they know—quoting thousands of years of observation does not help if each and every observation lacks placebo control. Any argument about which method of inquiry is better will be won by the Scientific Method, so there is no valid reason not to follow its principles when seeking understanding

Having said that, I also believe that significant modifiers affect the outcome of any comparison of allopathic versus complementary Medicine. A most important modifier is the quality of the healer-patient interaction. For example, a modern trend in allopathic medicine is the 10-minute visit, initiated by innovative health care models like Preferred Provider Organizations (PPOs) and Healthcare Maintenance Organizations (HMOs), ostensibly to promote profitable medicine at the acknowledged expense of quality care and caring. This adoption by business organizations of healthcare as a commodity to be dispensed with the goal of maximizing profit is an extension of the last century's corporate mentality applied to an area of human interaction where it does not belong. That is, the primary goal of the corporation is to maximize profit; the primary goal of healthcare is to promote wellness and healing, a goal confounded by the profit motive. Such time constraints on the interaction between the distressed patient and the healer ultimately interferes with empathetic listening and creation of an environment of caring and concern. Conceivably, caring contributes as much or more to healing as does the rigorous diagnosis and treatment of evidence-based medicine.

It is argued by such organizations that the trappings of quality care and empathetic understanding can be trained into the system so that efficient and profitable care doesn't exclude caring. But every system has a limit when pushed, and if Healthcare Organizations learn to provide caring together with a 10-minute examination, you can bet that some CEO will push for the 7-minute interview to boost profit further. If inadequacy creeps in on oilrigs or on ships transporting oil, be assured that it will supplant proper caring for patients in our modern hospitals and clinics, and at all levels of care.

I have a good friend who is regularly recognized as one of the most empathetic health care providers in our Medical Center. He tells the story on himself that as a Chief Resident when there was never enough time to organize and do the requirements of his job, he learned to take notes of his patient's history while maintaining eye-contact and demonstrating interest. Being ambidextrous, he then learned to write the required prescriptions or referrals with his other hand simultaneously. Imagine the scene and tell me what is missing from your picture. Even our best physicians can be pushed to squeeze caring for the patient out of the Physician-Patient interaction. It was his own empathy that put a stop to his great efficiency in order to listen to his patient and let them know they were heard. Don't count on profit driven corporations to put the same check on the absence of caring.

Some years ago, I was asked to help some Medical Students develop an instruction in Spirituality and Healing in Medicine (see *Chapter 23*). In their planning, the students felt a need to include a session on Complementary and Alternative Medicine. I invited an Internal Medicine colleague who also played a prominent role in Homeopathic Medicine and its proofs. She came—a charismatic, enthusiastic and articulate teacher who taught her students through stories about her patients and their response to Homeopathic treatment. The Chicago students became quickly interested in how she knew so many minute details about her patient's lives and wove these details into an informed diagnosis and treatment plan. She replied simply, "My entrance interview takes 2 hours!". A hush fell over the class as she added her belief that each of her patients were far more complicated than she could ever understand in a 10-minute interview, let alone provide her enough time to establish a caring relationship.

Many readers as patients agree with this stance, and often equate Allopathic Medicine and its 10-minute interview with poor listening and lack of caring. Yet the teacher in this story was both Allopath and Homeopath and can stand for the principle that good healers are good listeners, whatever their discipline among the Healing Arts. As Dean of Medical Education, I was amazed at the quality of teaching how to interview patients that our students received from this Faculty's instructors. With the consistent assistance of trained standardized "patients", and video taped encounters, our students were introduced to a diversity of patient interviewing situations designed to train them for their real encounters. The considerable time devoted to this process in a Medical School that is highly Allopathic was another illustration of how proper Medical Education can graduate a balanced physician equipped with excellence and compassion.

It seems that allopathic medicine is a better approach to health and therapy than alternative medicine, just as the Scientific Method is a far better method of inquiry than belief. Yet one would be foolish to discard the possibility of new value in ancient systems, especially when new understandings and uncertainties currently abound concerning fundamentals of sub-atomic physics and the Cosmos. For example, the growing awareness that mass and energy are interrelated warrants study of the mechanisms of energetic medicine such as Acupuncture. As a second example, the convincing argument that homeopathic remedies are so dilute as to become non-existent overlooked the possibility that the remedy changed the molecular structure of the water in which the agent is dissolved, thereby changing the water itself to a healing solution.[1]

One can occasionally find other studies of TCM in the allopathic literature which comply with the scientific method in terms of randomization and controls[2]. Faculty at the University of Chicago received teaching awards and course development grants to set up a new course in CAM for our students and this effort generated a textbook of CAM[3]. Recent articles in the web-based periodical _National Holistic Science_ report new findings that the acupoints occur consistently at branch points of superficial skin C-fiber sensory neurons which are known to traverse great distances and map out meridians.

In a word, we in the allopathic world of medicine would benefit from respectful appreciation of Complementary and Alternative Medicine. Epistemology, the study of knowing, tells us of many ways of understanding and we ought to stay open to the possibility that ancient healing arts have knowledge we can use that may seem new to us. In the course I mentioned above on _Spirituality and Healing in Medicine_, a Chicago Medical Student presented a paper from the prestigious journal "Science". The authors of that paper were investigating the Acupuncture treatment of eye disorders by stimulating the acupoint in the foot; as a control, they also stimulated an adjacent point several centimeters away in the same foot. They used functional MRI (fMRI) of the brain to determine whether in fact Acupuncture influenced brain blood flow. What part of the brain lit up during Acupuncture therapy? The occipital region, the site of vision!! There are no anatomic neural connectors between the foot and that part of the brain; yet Acupuncture stimulated a connection that must exist, if we believe either the fMRI or the patient's positive progress toward healing.

EXPERIENCE WITH TCM HEALING—SCIENCE OR BELIEF?

These are the theoretical considerations affecting the comparisons of Allopathic and CAM concepts. They represent a reasoned approach to systems of Medical Practice in the absence of personal experience. Then there is what happens, and my experiences demonstrate beyond a shadow of a doubt the efficacy of TCM.

In the Summer of 1980, Elaine came to visit me in Winnipeg. Before she arrived, I had injured my back playing tennis, and walked with a distinct new twist associated with the considerable strain of muscle spasm. My friend and faculty colleague, Henry Fung, an MD, PhD Nephrologist, called to me across the parking lot of the Health Sciences Centre *"Hey Larry, gimme an S!"*, referring to the shape of my back. Inquiring about my injury, he offered to provide some relief if the Orthopedic Surgeon and anti–inflammatory drugs didn't help. I asked what he had in mind, and he told me that 3 acupuncture treatments spaced several days apart would make me feel much better. I said "when and where". Henry replied that he had his equipment in the dialysis suite, so we could do the first treatment right then. "Oh yes!" I replied, and Elaine and I joined Henry in the dialysis suite where he examined my back upright and then prone (face down) on the examining table. Henry then explained that my strained or torn back muscles were edematous and the muscle spasm was aggravating the back pain, so he planned to insert Acupuncture needles about 6 centimeters apart on each side of the vertebral process, connect them to a pulsing voltage generator, and turn up the voltage until muscle twitching was observed with each pulse. Then he left the voltage constant and pulsing for about 20 minutes, by when the twitches grew stronger. Over the next 40 minutes, he progressively dialed down the voltage until it was less than half of the original value while the muscle still twitched. Henry explained that the current flowed more easily through the tissue because the resistance was falling as the edema dissipated. When I got off the table, the pain was remarkably better. I returned the next day for a second treatment, when the initial voltage was much reduced compared to the previous day, as was my back pain. And after a third treatment, I was nearly back to normal.

A second healing followed, relating to an injury to my left wrist while golfing in the Autumn of 2007. Examinations by my allopathic physician and Orthopedic Surgeon made the diagnosis "carpal tunnel syndrome", and I was treated for 4 weeks with a brace and anti-inflammatory drugs. Experiencing minimal relief, I spoke to Peter, who said he could help. One hour after he placed Acupuncture needles in the pericardial meridian, my symptoms of left wrist pain and numbness in my digits 1-4 abated. As Peter predicted, the symptoms returned somewhat before my next treatment, but were gone after it. Before the third treatment, I had no symptoms, and they have not recurred since.

Before and after this episode, I experienced constipation and sleep fragmentation—both attributed to my Parkinson's Disease. Despite allopathic therapies for both, I experienced no relief, so I spoke to Peter about TCM therapy. After his clinical examination, he explained that in TCM concepts, I had a "deficiency of liver and kidney Yin aggravated by wind". Although I had no idea of what this meant in allopathic language, I certainly appreciated the resolution of both symptoms following 4 weeks of twice-daily herbal therapy to replace Yin and suppress wind, coupled with weekly Acupuncture aimed at the same mechanisms.

These healing experiences make it unreasonable for me to reject TCM—this also makes me interested in conducting experiments to define the mechanisms for diagnosis and treatment in TCM or CAM more broadly, though I recognize my need for an education in TCM before being able to generate hypotheses. These 3 events describe my certainty of having been healed by TCM technique while being mysterious to me. A moment's introspection reveals to me what my automatic response would have been if another person told me the same story of being healed—I would judge them for being gullible and taken in by a healing therapy which would never stand up to rigourous scientific evaluation. Well now I say *"Who am I to reject a benefit that I so clearly enjoyed because it is mysterious."* And I wonder how many other biases I have.

Teaching

I love to stoke the fire.
a prod here, a pull there, a flip
and brilliant arrows leap erratically
alive from dying embers.

Then I sit to contemplate
the exciting fruits of my small effort.
Sometimes nothing—no flame, no glow
for the longest time.

Only the hunch from being there before
that this one is on the edge.
And there it is!—in an instant burst forth
with new patterns of chaotic vitality.

Warming, enlightening all around.

19

Legacy

At Medical Education Day in November of 2009, the *Lawrence D.H. Wood Teaching Scholar Award* was given to Dr. Godfrey Getz. This award was established in 2006 by the University of Chicago Academy of Distinguished Medical Educators to honour a senior Faculty member for outstanding contributions to medical education at the Pritzker School of Medicine. Selection is based on extraordinary contributions to medical education, recognition for distinguished teaching, and for serving as a role model who inspires others with the joy of teaching. Dr. Holly Humphrey asked me to be the one who hands the award to Dr. Getz, and invited me to join a group for dinner the night before. She asked if I would like to say a few words at the dinner regarding my work in medical education, and its legacy and impact at the University of Chicago. I was honoured to do so, and collected these thoughts.

MODELING THE JOY OF TEACHING

I came to the University of Chicago in July of 1982, directly from an eight month sabbatical in Haifa, Israel and Auckland, New Zealand. At the ICUs in these cities, I taught the Pathophysiology of Critical Illness using an interactive seminar series I developed in Winnipeg, Canada, and refined on my sabbatical. These seminars became the introduction to a later book, *Principles of Critical Care*[1] and teaching them to students of Critical Care had become second nature to me.

Accordingly, I was delighted when a group of six senior Medical Students appeared at my new office in Chicago to request some of my time to review Critical Care concepts. I couldn't start soon enough, and we met for 2 hours each Friday afternoon. These sessions grew popular, and were repeated the next year as part of a new ICU rotation for senior students. As the years went by, I began to teach first year Cardio-Vascular Physiology; second year electives in the Pathophysiology of Critical Illness, Spirituality and Healing in Medicine, and the Doctor-Patient Relationship; Junior lectures in Shock and Acute Respiratory Failure; and to the senior class, Vignettes in Physiology and Becoming a Resident Teacher. The students consistently rated my teaching highly and accorded the courses I directed with unusually high ratings. Residents from Medicine and other Departments also rated my teaching high, and the Medical Students and residents consistently counted me among their favourite teachers.

When I was appointed Chief of the new Section of Pulmonary and Critical Care Medicine, I convened our Faculty and fellows to discuss our new educational program. As I was discussing the central course in our syllabus, Advanced Respiratory Physiology, a young Faculty member from Michael Reese interjected, "let me get this straight", said he, "you want us to drop everything and come here for 2 hours each Monday to listen to you talk about Respiratory Function?". When the stunned silence abated, I replied, "Yes, and when you understand the value of such in-depth teaching which helps students formulate questions at the edge of each topic, I will encourage you to teach something on topics of your expertise". I was concerned that his attitude was prevalent in our faculty, but I needn't have worried, for our Faculty and fellows came, they listened, they questioned, and then they taught. Oh how they taught!! Gene Geppert, Jesse Hall, Holly Humphrey, Greg Schmidt and I became regular recipients of teaching awards from students and Resident Housestaff, and for several years, Gene Geppert and I received respectively the Outstanding Clinical Science and Outstanding Basic Science Teaching Awards.

And when I was appointed Dean of Medical Education in 1996, I became the Faculty member promoting affirmation of excellent teaching, so I often had to model a style of accepting affirmation. Not infrequently, I viewed my colleagues deflecting complements on their teaching performance, changing the subject, or outright denying their teaching excellence. I tried to show them another way in listening attentively to the feedback, then asking if the speaker could elaborate on it. Accepting teaching affirmation allows the teacher to accept both approbation and constructive criticism. This behaviour is rare, for hearing suggestions about how to improve teaching is often welcomed like being told one has bad breath. Yet straightforward acceptance of teacher evaluation is a big step toward teaching excellence.

Beyond these awards from Medical Students, the Medical Housestaff selected me on 5 occasions as their favourite teacher. On the occasion of my retirement, I was honoured to receive over 100 cards and notes from Medical Students, Housestaff, Fellows and Faculty expressing their gratitude for the time we spent together. I was grateful to be awarded the ATS Distinguished Achievement Award from the American Thoracic Society, and the Distinguished Teacher Award from the Alpha Omega Alpha Honours Medical Society together with the American Association of Medical Colleges. Being so honoured invited my reflection on Teaching, so in accepting these awards, I offered 3 words for those who would be teachers.

> BE INSPIRED—in your search for understanding, enjoy the process, for you teach well what you know well, and many lessons are better caught than taught. To catch it, the protégé needs to have it modeled, so therein lies the outcome of your being inspired.

> AFFIRM YOUR STUDENTS—mine came to me highly prepared and motivated to learn, so my task was to discern and point out their strengths to fan the flames of their enthusiasm which empowers their growth to the limits of their potential. It is your role to make them aware of their talent by praising them without flattery. Remember this, if you are not affirming them you are killing them.

> FOSTER A COMMUNITY OF SCHOLARS—who help each other learn, and who celebrate their learning joyfully—this collegial behavior multiplies the learning opportunities, for my students learned far more from each other than from me.

I told you those stories to tell you this. Whatever legacy I leave, whatever impact my work has on Medical Education, it begins and ends with my joy of teaching effectively and modeling that behaviour. Note that though these characteristics are necessary, they are not sufficient to contribute to institutional approaches to Medical Education. This second part of my legacy required skills of listening carefully to smart people, organizing to provide a forum for their ideas, and facilitating dialogue among them to effect and notice the creativity arising when two parallel pathways synapse. It also required the gumption to implement all good ideas quickly and to advertise widely the contributions of the process so that the Faculty, residents, students and staff became enthusiastic about educational renewal.

IMPROVEMENTS IN CURRICULAR OVERSIGHT AND MANAGEMENT

When Dr. Godfrey Getz agreed to serve as Interim Dean in 1994, he faced many challenges including the need for a systematic review of the Medical School Curriculum. This was timely for several reasons, not the least being that LCME was scheduled for the next regular site visit for re-accreditation in the Autumn of 1997, and there was a requisite 18 month institutional self-study preceding that visit. Further, LCME were still concerned that our Medical School had not responded adequately to the 1990 site visit concerns, and were considering an earlier ad hoc site visit prior to Autumn 1997.

Dr. Getz asked me to chair a Task Force on Review and Revision of the Medical School Curriculum. I believe our selection of teaching champions to join the Task Force infused enthusiasm and creativity to the process, which otherwise could become tedious and mundane. The Task Force made fourteen recommendations, and the timing of their implementation varied from some during the 18 months of deliberations to others implemented in stages up to 7 years after the Task Force was over. The following description is my assessment of the impact of six important recommendations on Medical Education.

IDENTIFYING, FACILITATING AND REWARDING TEACHING EXCELLENCE

Glenn Steele MD PhD was appointed Dean, Biological Sciences Division and Pritzker School of Medicine in the Autumn of 1995. Immediately, he began negotiations with me regarding the new position of Dean of Medical Education. We agreed on all points of the new job description except for my insistence on line items in the budget of the new Office of Medical Education (OME) for:

i. Faculty Teaching Awards (FTA) for curricular enhancement ($200,000/yr)
ii. Course Development Grants (CDG) to equip and supply the course(s) of the FTA ($100,000/year), and
iii. Funds to build and operate a new Clinical Performance Centre (CPC) at Chicago ($100,000/year).

As these funds were in themselves about equal to the rest of the OME budget and had not been planned in Dean Steele's start-up budget, he was most reluctant to agree. In what came down to a line in the dust argument, Dean Steele turned to his Chief Executive Officer, Jo Anne Wade, to ask if he had the money. She replied "Only if you take it from another budgeted project." "OK", he responded fixing his gaze on me, "but I want you to show me the results of these items."

This was a breakthrough in funding for Medical Education at Chicago! I would not have accepted the position of Dean OME without this funding. For now and for the first time, a Faculty Member other than the Dean of the Division had discretionary funds to promote curricular revision. Through the deliberation of the Task Force, I already knew eight required courses which were not in compliance with LCME guidelines, or were so poorly rated by students that they needed overhaul. In my view, the effectiveness of such overhaul was critically dependent on a knowledgeable interested course Director. Always, such competent Faculty are too busy to take on more, so the FTA was designed to liberate some of their time and effort.

Of course, the Department Chair needed to be on board with this deployment of his Faculty, so I met early with them to get their partnership for the salary savings. This necessitated my persuading the Chair that better teaching was good for his Department. During the first year of the OME budget, 7 FTA/CDG grants were given. In each case there was considerable improvement in student ratings. The main purpose of partnering the improvement in the course by the owning Department was to ensure continuity after the FTA/CDG had expired. A side benefit, then, of the FTA/CDG tool for course improvement was to make more transparent the funding of Medical Education. The end-game of such discussion came down to a negotiation between the Department Chairs and the Dean of the Medical School concerning what part of the Dean's contribution to the Department was for Medical Education.

Accordingly, these teaching awards encouraged our best teachers to improve the curriculum without being punished for stealing time away from funded research and clinical activities. They were my attempt to level the playing field by providing recognition and salary support for teaching effectiveness. The FTA/CDG attempted to improve the status quo by providing incremental support for improvements in teaching. I spent considerable time with each potential FTA/CDG awardee to optimize their revisions and additions for success using my own familiarity with what works. In large part, I listened carefully as these very talented teachers told me what they needed.

Teaching Dossiers were developed for widespread use by Faculty as they went before the Committee of Appointments and Promotions (COAP). By standardizing the format, these Dossiers attempted to limit the exaggerating effect of flamboyant rhetoric in describing teaching, and anchored description to hours taught and rated by the students. Of course, this is only as good as the Rating System being used, and the OME was fortunate in having a high quality system.

This rating system allowed the OME to affirm excellent teaching with letters of commendation to Faculty, with copies to their Department Chair, Dean and the Provost:

for teaching efforts accorded ratings > 4.5/5,

or courses / clerkships given ratings > 4.0/5.

The OME also promoted the development and implementation of new courses designed to teach Faculty and Residents to teach Medical Students.

Further, I initiated the quarterly meetings of a new Society of Medical Educators (SOME) to discuss innovations in Medical Education. Members were invited to join who had demonstrated sustained participation in Medical Education. This SOME was the precursor of the current Academy of Distinguished Medical Educators.

EMPOWERING PCRC AND CCRC

Oversight and Management of the Medical School Curriculum was observed to reside with the Curriculum Review Committee (CRC). But its structure and way of operating did not give it executive action or decision-making power. CRC members represented the departments meant to own the courses or clerkships, but often these members did not teach in that course. Further, there were large differences in the ways pre-clerkship courses were run and evaluated compared to clerkships, yet this one CRC attempted to evaluate all years of the curriculum. And the elected student representatives on the CRC who were responsible for bringing student evaluations to the Directors attention did so in a mean-spirited manner leading to chronic disaffection with the process.

An overhaul of the system was implemented in the Spring of 1996, leading to a great deal of efficiency. To achieve effective oversight and management was not rocket science, but it did need someone to assume authority to make the changes. I reorganized the CRC as two Standing Committees—the pre-clinical Curriculum Review Committee (PCRC) and the Clinical Curriculum Review Committee (CCRC). The PCRC included the course directors of all MedI and MedII courses; and the CCRC included all current clerkship Directors as well as potential directors of proposed new clerkships. The OME staff worked well with the Medical Students to ensure that students intending to stand for elections to the CRC understood its role and their roles. Specifically, the elected students enjoyed an in-service instruction on what the student rating process was, and how the data on rated courses could be used in collegial discussions with the course directors to increase the chance of suggested changes being implemented. They learned further how to keep their classmates informed about what was done with these ratings, as well as what changes in curriculum were being discussed.

Taken together, the course and teacher ratings gave substantial data on which to discuss the curriculum. Course Directors sought input from their colleagues whose course gained significantly higher ratings. And this cross-talk became a data-based discussion among peers seeking the common goal of better teaching. Student Representatives were trained to discuss ratings without judgment, affirming where appropriate, and so became empowered partners in the pursuit of teaching excellence. So empowered, the PCRC and CCRC became thoughtful, creative, action-oriented organizations to manage and oversee the curriculum. I played a major role by listening carefully to these talented teachers and students, then facilitating the conversations among CRC members and focusing their attention on requisite revisions.

ESTABLISHING A CLINICAL PERFORMANCE CENTRE (CPC)

Until the Task Force focused on the concept, our Medical curriculum at the University of Chicago had no facility in which our Faculty could teach and assess the Clinical Skills of our students and graduates. Dr. Gene Geppert had done an extraordinary job of borrowing or renting the CPC at the University of Illinois, while noting that both Northwestern and Loyola Schools of Medicine had recently built new CPCs at considerable cost. The logistics of transporting and scheduling Pritzker students to the offsite CPC were immense. By rolling-over the CPC budget for '96-'98, we were able to accumulate sufficient funds to equip space rented on the University of Chicago campus. The unexpended budget for Fiscal Year '96 (about $80K) rolled over to FY '97 and again to FY '98, so that in FY '99, the Clinical Performance Centre budget was about $340K, enough for my Clinical Performance Centre staff to build and equip an adequate facility. In the interim, we acquired the expertise to use the CPC facility for more required education each year.

Accordingly, by 1999 we established our own CPC, and by 2001 we were able to conduct our first Clinical Performance Experience (CPX), a formative assessment of students' clinical skills following their third year. By the Autumn of 2003, we had used the CPC to conduct 3 CPX which had been evaluated favorably by the students taking it and by the Faculty observing their performance. By that time, the CPC was used to teach and to assess clinical skills for First, Second and Third Year students, who now had acquired experience with this type of facility to be prepared for the National Board of Medical Examiners® (NBME) Step IB.

It seems that the OME had snatched a Medical Education victory from the jaws of defeat by relentlessly pushing ahead with establishing and utilizing the CPC in the absence of any prior attention to this instrument. It amazed me that Pritzker School of Medicine operated until the year 2000 without asking the question: "How do we know that our graduates can perform an effective Clinical Examination?". In retrospect, we know now as a result of their CPX performance. Even so, the LCME continued to ask for evidence that our students had been observed doing a Clinical Examination by a Faculty Member or a Resident. Again, the CPC ensures such an observation.

APPOINT A DEAN FOR MEDICAL EDUCATION

As the Dean for Medical Education, I served as the Faculty person responsible and accountable for a coherent and coordinated Medical School Curriculum; as such, I assembled the resources and infrastructures to implement the recommendations of the Task Force. Achieving the 3 outcomes listed above required a credible leader. In one sense, the Dean of the Division is that person. But the changes made in the curriculum occurred during the tenure of 5 Divisional Deans (Hellman, Getz, Steele, Weir, Madera) and so one part of my legacy was to provide continuity of vision and planning. I believe this was especially important because our Division did not have a culture of educational leadership. Effective leaders rose up to organize responses to crises, but often these were bursts of brilliance that faded quickly with the crises. When Glenn Steele appointed me Dean of Medical Education, he got a banner carrier for Medical Education who had credibility with researching, practicing, and teaching members of his faculty. I also displayed an inclination to action on the educational front not seen in the recent past.

Accordingly, things got done quickly, informed by an effective Task Force which gave good priorities, in an Academic environment which seemed more interested, even excited, about Medical Education. Taken together, these behaviors created an overarching job description, the guardian of the vision, which passed seamlessly to my successor, Dr. Holly Humphrey, who first came up with that term. Along the way, the infrastructure of Medical Education increased from 4 to 40 administrative staff and a yearly operating budget from $200K to $3M. These are also components of my Legacy that grow stronger through the shared vision I had with my successor Dr. Holly Humphrey. Her job description expanded to include responsibility for Graduate Medical Education, and her staff and budget for the Office of Medical Education (OME) increased considerably. Accordingly, the large leaps forward in organization of Medical Education which occurred with my appointment as Dean of Medical Education in 1996 has now taken another giant step, under Dr. Holly Humphrey's leadership.

ESTABLISH AN OFFICE OF MEDICAL EDUCATION

When I accepted Dean Steele's offer to head up the administration of the Medical School Curriculum, we implemented our ideas for an Office of Medical Education directed by me with Wylie as Associate Director. Mary Lou Trepac became the Administrative Director, and she interviewed and hired 2 efficient and effective administrative assistants. This staff began operations in early 1996 with a budget which was twice that of the Curriculum Office it succeeded.

Considerable efficiency emanated from the reorganized Curriculum Review Committees and from Curriculum enhancements produced by FTA/CDG awards. Shortly thereafter, Dean Steele asked me to oversee the Admissions and Financial Aid process and student programs, so our administrative staff tripled, as did our operating budget. We now had an organizational chart of an Office of Medical Education that included 3 Associate Deans (Admissions and Financial Aid—Eric Lombard, Student Programs—Holly Humphrey, and Curricular Affairs—Sandy Cook). Sandy had taken over Wylie's position after his lung transplant. Each Associate Dean had a staff of five assistants, so our Office of Medical Education was a busy operation with 20 staff.

The efficiency of the OME was aided by the collegiality of the staff. In turn, this was aided by weekly meetings of the Executive Staff (me, Mary Lou, Sandy, Holly, Eric, Wylie) to discuss the plans for the coming week. In my opinion, our Executive Staff's working well together was facilitated by the opening item of the agenda each week: "What is going on in your non-professional life that you would like to share?" Once the Executive Staff began to feel safe, they shared their life briefly with the other Executives to promote humanism in the academic workplace. We thought this style would model the behaviour we sought to encourage in the Medical Students and the Faculty Teachers who frequented the Office of Medical Education. In this way, we created an enjoyable environment for learning. This goal and outcome continued for the 7 years until I retired, and has continued under Holly's leadership since.

The initiation and sustained operations of the Office of Medical Education were contributions to the University with which I am pleased. It provided a robust infrastructure for Medical Education not previously present and this infrastructure was essential for our Medical School to grow in compliance, even leadership, of the Medical School imperatives as enforced by LCME. I served as the person responsible and accountable for a coherent and coordinated Medical School Curriculum, which was much improved during my decade of administrative involvement. The new Curriculum was now on solid ground, readied for the next level of reform by Dr. Humphrey.

BUILDING PROFESSIONALISM IN THE OFFICE OF MEDICAL EDUCATION

It is almost magical how individuals essential to making major changes in complex systems flit in and out of one's sphere of interest, rarely receiving the attribution they deserve for their contributions. Elaine was like that in restoring joy to my soul. Jesse did that for Critical Care at Chicago. Paul Schumacher did that for our research labs and programs. And Mary Lou Trepac—lovingly dubbed "MLT"—did that for the OME.

Looking back at each of these extraordinary contributors to my life and interests, I tend to list their accomplishments, the outcomes of their efforts. But true affirmation would require a detailed analysis of what their day-to-day industry and creativity brought to the tasks at hand—these were the foundations of their subsequent accomplishments, yet they get lost in time. For example, Mary Lou played a major role in reorganizing the space available in the BSLC to accommodate efficient operation of OME. To all intents and purposes, the University's space committee fed information to the space officer who met with individual participants to hear their needs and make a plan to accommodate them. This organizational plan was a set up to satisfy vested interests and fragment a coherent working group. Mary Lou never let that happen—she participated in every discussion about BSLC space, contributing a thoughtful plan, a vision that restructured the BSLC.

For she understood that OME had the opportunity to bridge communication gaps, by strategic juxtaposition of the 3 arms of Medical School Service—Admissions and Financial Aid, Student Programs and Curriculum. Time-honored resistances to cooperative communication had produced fragmentation of the common goals of each of these arms. Change takes time and effort, so her ceaseless striving to enhance cooperation at every opportunity slowly integrated the OME as a cooperative system.

The same was true for creating an Annual Budget that used our limited financial resources efficiently. And it took the same meticulous attention to detail in the budget negotiations of each arm of OME with the Dean's Office to bring about a cooperative budget which took advantage of the efficiencies of our integration. By taking her integrating job seriously, Mary Lou was able to use her extensive familiarity with the budget needs of each arm to budget the vision.

When Dean Steele shifted the responsibility for Medical Student Affairs and Programs to me, I acquired an extraordinary opportunity to implement a Student Advisory system which could be accessed equally by each student. But the time commitment was immense. In its simplest form, each student warranted at least 1 hour of shared conversation with the Dean each quarter—roughly 1200 hours per year or 60% full time effort—impossible but essential. So Mary Lou set about sharing this important task among 6 senior members of the OME staff, or 10% FTE for each. Other essential student programs were the Promotions Committee and the Dean's Council. The first gave academically troubled students access to early help, and the second allowed elected student representatives to develop helpful programs by using regularly scheduled meetings with me to pursue an agenda of development. Again, Mary Lou was indispensible in working with administrative schedules bringing together just the right students and faculty to take ownership of these student issues, using the Dean's resources and wisdom to move the action forward.

Mary Lou was certainly most familiar with the Medical School Curriculum, and her influence was invaluable in negotiating several impossible but essential curricular improvements. The Clinical Performance Centre would not have been developed for our students' use without negotiating a roll-over of unexpended CPC budget for several years, until we accumulated equity sufficient to acquire the major equipment and personnel. And her diplomacy and tact in helping Sandy Cook's independent talent and productivity overcome the timid, subservient role acquired after years of working for Wylie. As it worked out, Sandy was just the person to lead our curricular progress.

Taken together, these examples demonstrate the diversity of Mary Lou's contribution to the Medical School. At face value, she had neither the political clout nor the academic qualifications to work this integration of the OME and its staff. But given support enough from me to follow her well-informed intuition about the best next steps, she was a miracle worker who helped build the OME vision: that our Administrative Offices are home to our Medical Students and their Teaching Faculty, so it behooves us to treat each other humanely and professionally so the students can catch it.

The camaraderie and shared spirit of the OME evolved yearly as faculty and staff began to feel safe. There developed a willingness to share workloads, and a more peaceful demeanor that came from having most activities scheduled far in advance, so there were fewer administrative emergencies to rescue important functions not well planned. Of course, one aid to this end was a large staff, and we benefitted from Dean Steele's support for our growth. Clearly, the enthusiasm and efficiency continued to get better, so that by the time I retired in 2003, we had in place a supportive and effective OME to build upon, and Holly—my successor—shared the vision while adding more support by increasing the professional staff.

LEGACY IN MEDICAL EDUCATION

This brings me to summarize my Legacy and the impact my educational work had on the University of Chicago. First, I taught well and a lot, with a demeanor which conveyed my joy in teaching which others could catch—in a sense, I modeled effectively the joy of teaching. Second, I brought faculty attention to what we were supposed to do as medical educators, and when I saw deficiencies, my inclination to action brought solutions faster than our culture was accustomed. In fact, few of the changes were big or complicated, but they needed focus and cooperation to get them done—and with these, a lot was achieved. At the end of my time, our school was actively receptive to more substantive changes, and the Legacy benefited from a smooth transition to Holly's creative impact on Medical Education.

Legacy is defined as "something that someone has achieved that continues to exist after they stop working". When I addressed the Graduating Medical Students of 2003 at their Recognition Dinner, I described part of the process of retiring as: "I had 2 offices—one in the Hospital and one in the Learning Centre. In a short time, I cleaned each by discarding "garbage"—things I no longer needed. Do you know those large green mobile garbage disposal wagons about 5 feet tall and 9 feet long, with a black closure lid? Well, I filled 3 of them to the top—in each office! And as I was discarding these documents, I perused several thinking to myself, gosh I thought this was important—then I threw it in the green box." After the dinner, several students and their families spoke to me about various topics, and I noticed my friend and co-worker, Greg Schmidt, looking back as if to get my attention. I acknowledged him, and he said:

> "Larry all you threw out was just paper,
> but what you left behind is as strong as oak."

Beyond such words are two tangible pieces of this Legacy. In June 2003, the MedI and MedII classes instituted the LDH Wood Pre-clerkship Teaching Awards for extraordinary teaching in each of these classes. Awarded to two Faculty Teachers each year since 2003, fourteen Faculty have received these awards until now. A second award, the Lawrence DH Wood Teaching Scholar Award, was established in 2006 by the University of Chicago Academy of Distinguished Medical Educators to honour a senior Faculty Member for Outstanding Contributions to Medical Education at the Pritzker School of Medicine. Dr. Bruce Gewertz, a former Chair of Surgery, received the inaugural award in 2006 in recognition of his 25 years of service to the University of Chicago, and his early leadership as the first Faculty Dean for Curriculum. The only other recipient of this Award is Dr. Godfrey Getz, who is the 2009 recipient in recognition of his 45 years of service to the University of Chicago which has lead to numerous curricular innovations that promote interdisciplinary scholarship. I am grateful to have been in such company.

Other contributions to Legacy are the people who learned and carry the lessons forward. I regard these protégés as the most important, for they are not reflections of the mentor but stars burning brightly with their own brilliance, extending my influence immensely further than I could by my efforts alone. Many of these are now in prominent positions in Academic Medicine, and I am proud of all of them. I am also grateful to each, for they are responsible for the work accomplished to make my Legacy.

It is important that a legacy in Medical Education is accompanied by public and professional awareness of outstanding educational programs in the School. The US News and World Report (USNWR) has made a project out of auditing diverse educational institutions. Between 2004 and 2011, Pritzker School of Medicine has increased its overall rank from 24th to 12th in the nation, and in 2012, our overall rank increased further to be in the top 10 schools in the nation! During that same interval, our school's ability to attract the best students (selectivity) has risen from 41st to 5th, and in 2012 we now rank 2nd in selectivity. These unprecedented changes in ranking order of the top 50 schools are a tribute to the groundwork laid to enhance those characteristics contributing to USNWR evaluations. Those close to our graduates have become familiar with the high regard generated by their performance, and the high number of residents graduating from Pritzker who go on to become Chief Residents.

PART IV

Living the Interface of Science and Spirituality

20

Whispers

Many scientists report the experience of hearing an interior voice that confers support for their innovative belief. In Chapter 6, I present and discuss why I believe the still small voice of God serves to verify belief for those who ask, so serving as a spiritual source of knowledge not unlike the scientific method. This Chapter extends observations about the still small voice heard as whispers by me and others, and proposes that a survey like that reported by Hybels on the larger and more diverse population would bring new evidence on the prevalence of the still small voice.

I know that subjective conviction that God speaks to me is evidence enough for me. It is akin to the value of eyewitness in the court of law—ear-witness to the still small voice. We don't have provision in our current Scientific Method to protect us from preconceived ideas or bias heard as whispers, so we rely on advice from people with spiritual experience to guide us. Hence the guidelines from the Linns' and Hybels (see *Chapter 6*). I don't pretend this is easy, but one must live this choice one way or another—test it or wait for more convincing evidence. I'm glad I was blessed with the opportunity to test it, but the process leaves the question standing—what constitutes evidence for personal spiritual experience sufficient to reject the null-hypotheses that God does not exist/speak to His people. Hence the value of Hybels' survey. Until that data is available, we are left with anecdotal, if comprehensive, recounting of conversations with God. For example, in 1995, Neale Donald Walsch[1] writes in his introduction to his book by the same name:

"Shortly after this material began happening to me, I knew that I was talking with God. Directly, personally. Irrefutably. And that God was responding to my question in direct proportion to my ability to comprehend. That is, I was being answered in ways, and with language, that God knew I would understand. This accounts for much of the colloquial style of the writing and the occasional references to material I had gathered from other sources and prior experiences in my life. I know now that everything that has ever come to me in my life *has come to me from God,* and it was now being drawn together, pulled together, in a magnificent complete response *to every question I ever had."*

It starts with having one's own spiritual experience. Then having the courage to follow the instruction is an essential next step. It seems that such listeners have some foundation for spirituality: belief that God will speak to them; a quiet spirit, free from noise, hurry and crowds; a desire to know God's answers to one's questions, or to know God's preference among courses of action set before the listener. But having all these does not guarantee hearing the still small voice, for ultimately that hearing is a mystery and a gift. Given the opportunity to hear and obey the still small voice, it would be the normal action to share it with one's colleagues. Knowledge obtained from the scientific method finds publication in established professional journals, but few such journals exist for spiritual sources of knowledge. I contend that such observations are just the type of new knowledge that warrant publication and open discussion lest we blind ourselves to important contributions of new knowledge.

Don't get me wrong—I support the scientific method as the best method of inquiry we have. But this evaluation does not exclude using or discussing the use of other methods of inquiry. When we give too much credit to one approach to the extent of excluding other methods of inquiry, we run the risk of excluding fresh ideas, and so maintain the status quo: for examples, the Church vs Galileo; Darwinian evolution vs Lamarck; and Crick's Dictum that all heredity outcomes derive from nucleic acid sequences and their reproductions in the double helix, with no acceptable hypotheses allowed to test for environmental influences (epigenetics). I worry that we do it again when we are unwilling to engage in discussion about how we validate spiritual experience, and how to promote spiritual sources of knowledge.

These are questions of a serious searcher who wants to be sure of the source of advice before he acts on it, for it takes guts to act on such life changing messages. The similarity of the Linn's Attributes with Hybels Filters is evident in Table 4 (see *Chapter 6*). This increases my confidence in my hypothesis that the still small voice is the verification of beliefs we act on, the hammer that nails down the belief most in touch with reality among a large number of beliefs. If true, the still small voice becomes the fourth step in processing belief as a method of inquiry, similar to the fourth step of the scientific method (see *Table 1*).

And lest we get too caught up in the serious search for evidence about our communication, a vignette from the Arts may help. In the play and movie *"Fiddler on the Roof"*, the Jewish elder and father—RevTevia, is depicted in constant conversation with God. In one scene, he is pushing his cart while complaining about his life, but the cart keeps grinding to a halt as its' wheels encounter stones in the road. He quickly changes his complaint to the cart but stops in mid sentence, looks enlightened, and turns the cart around to pull it over the stones, still complaining. I told you that story to tell you this—some people are put off by diverse aspects of God talking to Her people—pretentious, dangerous, psychotic—but I participate like RevTevia, humbly waiting for advice from my God, especially to questions I ask.

Beginning about 1978, I compiled in three ring binders my frequent prayer entries, such that I now have 10 such binders. From these for illustration, I now reproduce 10 consecutive answers from an eventful period in 1985, to questions asked or topics discussed in my part of these letters, as abbreviated before each answer, as illustrations of this prayerful exercise. It is illuminating for me who heard the still small voice to reconsider the message of each entry in the light of intuition, for, if I were blessed with an intuitive insight into the topic of each entry, what would it sound like to me?

How to let go vis-à-vis cling?

August 26/84

You see, it's not so complicated.
Just lots of hidden reasons
which I will reveal in time.
And not so painful either
when you talk to me about it.
You do know how to let go very well
and it has been, is, and will be good for you
for each time what you have clung to
was inhibited
so when released, they could grow better.
You too grew better when you weren't distracted
by clinging too hard
It's just that you fear there will be no solace
when you let go.

Foolish heart,
you should know I am with you
in those you cling to,
and in you when you don't cling
so let go all to me
and learn in your warm solitude
that you grow in relationship with me.

How to come to the quiet?

I love you—you are Mine!
Before even one of your thoughts, I knew you,
and called you by your name.
    Peace! Relax! Enjoy my loving care!

It was different for you then, and could be still
but you listened when I called
you let me mold you and heal you
    then.
For now, more of the same.
don't rush
just listen and speak to me
    and write to me—it helps you hear.

Consider your soul-pain
consider how you can't be all for all
        as you wish to be.
Consider your children so far from you
    and how your company with other children hurts you.
consider how uncertain you are in your job—
    whether to do it better as you are driven
    or to abandon it as you are called.
consider these and all your hurts
    and know that all is well!

They are more fully considered by Me
as the most economical way to your wholeness.
So rejoice in your pain leading to your Lord!
        Rejoice in me always—again I say Rejoice

Why agitation & hiding
When memories of healing abound?

Nov 8, 1984

    I understand!
You expect to fail, so you are afraid to start
and when you start, it is with groaning and frustration
    rather than the peace and joy I plan for you.

    You don't do it, you know.
I do, and for your celebration.
When you take yourself too seriously,
    You transform joy in celebrating my surprises
        into the exasperations you <u>should</u> feel
        <u>if</u> you were in charge of all I do <u>thru</u> you.
    That is the letting go—
You are a child of my Father
Live it! Enjoy it!
    He is in charge!!

    Consider Elaine and the lilies and birds.
You had it once—the Mustard Seed—
Recall how I taught you
    that it acts out its created nature
    like you—giving glory both—
you with consciousness of the Father's good gifts
and His presence in your life.
    You do it better smiling.

    I'll tell you when you are called to more than gratitude
while you get prepared for more
by learning to accept the calls
    in laughter and love.

Thanksgiving & joyful resignation.

Nov 9, 1984
You are a Prince
from the day of your birth
Thank you for coming to me in silence
Go now in love and laughter
     to enjoy
          to grow
               to suffer with me
                    to reach out in hospitality
                         and prayer
                              from your solitude.

Drink no more
     but stay alert and sober.
          You will see more, enjoy more, serve more.
My people are in pain
     and need company
     and ears
     and hearts that understand and accept
Be me for them
and come to me for restoration
     Do not fear
     Do not be anxious for tomorrow
     You have seen enough to trust
     But when you fall short
     Remember, your hurt self does not understand
I am with you, so rejoice.

Long 3 AM letter in agitation.

Dec 27, 1984

Thank you for talking to me tonight.
It is good for you to get it articulated
and in your problem—writing
are my answers

I am with you—
Peace—Be Still
And know I am your God
Who made it all
for your enjoyment and delight

So enjoy. So relax. So let go
of all the troubles to me.
They are mine to use as I wish
for your growth and journey to Me.

Rest in Elaine's warmth
She wants you there.
and that is consolation enough
for tonight. Enjoy!

Tape 5 – Distracted by life's challenges
so that I can't get to know you

Jan 6, 1985

I am here with you.
And I invite you to a kingdom
even more majestic and admirable
      than the section of Pulmonary and Critical Care Medicine
      with a SCOR, training grant and adulation
via a process just as intricate—
using your other talents
      the spirit senses I gave you.

      Your friends are on your side
cheering for your victory—
David and Daniel and Francis and Thomas
      and many more with whom you can share
      a spirit life like you seek vicariously in your job
so come to the quiet
Don't waste time or lose poise or be convulsive
      just come in silence and calm.

      and I will show you what you need
not to waste yourself in proving yourself.
I know you—you are mine
      I call you by your name.
          Come!!

**On a quiet weekend contemplating sabbatical
Yet agitated about plans and commitments
+ grateful for past mysterious joys
Open + wondering.**

Feb 3, 1985

I love you
and want you to respond to my call
come to Me
You who are heavy burdened
    and I will give you rest
You who thirst
    come for the life-giving water of my presence

Come to the quiet
    free from noise and crowds and hurry.
Come. and sit. and listen. and write.
    You are my beloved.
    And I want the best for you
    See how I do it!
        In Quiet,
        in retreat places
            like the Marianists'
            and Freeport
            and Pecos
            and Elaine
Be calm.
    Peace.
        All is well.

Troubled, treated, reflective
to start the vacation/retreat

Sun. April 28/85
Santorini

    Come—its quiet enough now,
and it will get more so.
I welcome your consciousness of me—
    that is why I gave you life
    so you might share the light + love I am

    come—follow me
through your life's blessings
to my view of you
    to calvary
    and resurrection

    come—I have a message for you
that will be revealed in quiet
with time we waste together
    I'll comfort your pain—physical spiritual + emotional
    and I'll care for Elaine
using you as she needs
while using her as you need.

    Peace
        Be calm.
            All is well.
        I love you,
    and planned this vacation
        just for us.

What do you think of me, Lord?

Mon. April 29, 1985

I thought you would never ask!
You are mine, you know.
I carved you, I knew you in your mother's womb.
I helped you grow, saw your pain.
    And I was there
    When your need for independence sprouted
    I saw it grow in willfulness,
      in need to excel.
But shared excellence is part of my plan
and I rejoice more than you know when you do it well.

I like your morning heart
so eager to be awed, wonder-struck
at the marvels of my creation.
    I like the confident articulations
    of your fresh insights—hallucinations you call them—
into my plan for the moment.

I would have you eat less to enjoy more
    to drink less to appreciate more
      to work less to praise more
        to fear less to listen more
to slow down and be more quiet
that you might have life's energy sufficient
to carry out my few requests of you:
    Be mine.   Be calm.
    Be quiet.   Listen to me.
    Love life and tell me so.

After long Review of Spiritual Journey

Mon May 6, 1985

    Well done, good and faithful servant
    Now, we begin
Listen—to your heart
    to Elaine
      to the tapes
    to the scriptures
then we'll talk again
for you are on the Way.

New life in me awaits.
Don't spend too much time looking back
    I will explain all you need to know

But the way is obscured by evil
so stay alert, sober
be rested and at Peace
    Prayer scatters desolation
      like the morning light scatters the darkness
and if evil gets tricky, keep your eyes on Me
(look to the hills from where your saviour comes)
and I come quickly.

Be Brave, stout heart
for now we fight our battles together.

I chose one more conversation with a somewhat unusual message. Several years ago, my morning journal recorded the 4-line message (see below). My preceding letter to the still small voice was full of whining and complaining and the stark reply took me aback because the voice usually speaks to me in a civil and gentle tongue. Yet I instantly knew the surprise and wisdom of this reply, characteristics which I attribute to conversation with God.

Another extraordinary factor was how I heard these words put to music as *"Ode to Joy"*. Despite my poverty of musical talent and training, I heard the full orchestral expression.

Recently, I reviewed this with my Psycho-Spiritual Director who was taken enough by the message and its context that he sang it for me over the phone. When I told Elaine, she said she always had trouble with the harsh, cross words. So I took the time to spell out their teaching to me (see next page).

LIGHTEN UP YOU SULLEN BASTARD
LIFE IS BETTER THAN YOU THINK
WHEN YOU TURN FROM LOVE AND LAUGHTER
ALL YOUR EFFORTS START TO STINK.

Lighten Up –	Don't fear or be worried Let the light of life in be aware of the light you emanate
Sullen –	Silent, ill humor and a refusal to be sociable; gloomily or resentfully silent or repressed
Bastard –	an illegitimate child Not behaving as a child of God
Life . . . think –	distinction between how it is versus how you think it to be
Turn –	As in "turn your back on"
Love and Laughter –	keywords/concepts used repeatedly in "God Calling" and "God at Eventide" by God to instruct the listeners as to how to behave
All . . . Stink –	No matter how hard you try there is no redeeming value if not motivated/accompanied by Love & Laughter

21

Witness to Stewardship

During the Sabbatical in 1989 when the generation of a book series on the principles of Critical Care began, Elaine and I had a bit more luxury of time to consider and seek balance in our busy lives. We got involved in leading a bible study for some 40 parishioners 1 night a week for 2 years. And during the season of lent, we led an evening prayer program for about the same number. A small group of 9 of us who shared in these activities responded to an invitation to learn and teach about Stewardship in Parish life—the sharing of one's time, talent and treasure. In prayerful discussion, we concluded that personal witness to Stewardship in our own life, spoken from the pulpit during the liturgy of the Eucharist on Sunday by us lay members of the parish would be an effective way to inform the community about this program. As a group, we met on several occasions to review each member's contribution to ensure a coherent and coordinated presentation. Here follows the witness made by Elaine and me, included in this autobiography as a summary of our spirited activities and an example of my spoken word.

"My name is Larry Wood and this is my friend and spouse Elaine Wood. We have been asked to share with you what Stewardship means to us, and why we try to contribute to our Parish. So we will tell you love stories—ours with the Lord and with each other. For us, Stewardship is more than a matter of budgeting our time, talent and treasure—it is first and foremost a matter of developing and displaying trust in our God who loved us first and gave us all we have. Out of gratitude, we ask; *"What return can we make Lord?"* (Psalm 116:12). Our God replied to us through scripture, in the teaching of our church, and by personal revelation in quiet times of prayer; *"Bring Me your first fruits out of honour for Me and gratitude to Me and trust in Me—then I who gave you everything for your pleasure and journey to Me will multiply these first fruits of your brothers and sisters and you—beyond your imagination, pressed down and flowing over"* (Prov 3:9-12, Luke 6:38, 2 Cor 9:6, 1 Pet 4:10)."

ELAINE'S STORY

" *"Glory to God who can do immeasurably more than we can ask or imagine."* This is a verse from Scripture in Ephesians (3:20) that describes best most of my life and relationship with God. When I was raised as a Catholic, Jesus was always a friend and companion—it was easy for me to accept Him. I knew He was real when at the age of 11 years old, I prayed to win a piano contest for my parents' sake and after winning I was sure God had arranged it. The next 20 years of my life were filled with awareness of God's presence, attraction to Him and seeking Him in daily Mass and retreats. I attended my first 8-day silent retreat at the age of 30. By that time, I had expended maximum effort to secure a committed relationship in my life. I gave myself fully and unreservedly. During this retreat, I gave it all to the Lord—the struggle, the pain, the lack of commitment, the spending it all and getting nothing in return—and my search for a change in life style. The retreat itself was blessed. Scripture came alive. It was as if I was set free—ready to soar. I said "no" to my former way of operating and "yes" to God in the fullest way I could. I gave <u>God</u> my full commitment.

God responds in strange and powerful ways. Almost immediately, my career fell apart. Ten years of my own accomplishments that included high salary, a leadership position in a major company as manager of 15 systems engineers, and the exciting enjoyment of travel were upset by a corporate merge that to me was analogous to an earthquake. The structure fell apart and devastation followed. I remained hopeful for a year while I watched integrity and justice disappear, and greed and power take over. Being one of the victims, I resorted to suing the company for discrimination. God, however, had other plans. Through a book I was reading, God said, "I'll show you another way, turn the other cheek" that comes from Matthew's Gospel (Mt. 5:38-48). And at Mass the next day the Psalm response was "I am the Lord your God, hear my voice" (Psalm 50:7). I obeyed, and resigned the same day.

In short order, I was picked up and dusted off by being given a job elsewhere with a huge salary increase. So I was encouraged to trust God more in the future as God nursed me from destroyed "self confidence" to confidence in God alone. During this time, I attended another retreat in New Mexico where I met Larry, "the love of my life". What followed was the beginning of God's love, through Larry, healing me from the inside out. Committed relationship in marriage and the healing that comes from self-revelation and acceptance was the biggest gift God has given me. Our marriage allowed me to retire from my busy career and spend more time in prayer. The foundation God began then, prepared me for the most painful challenge of my life—the loss of both my parents in 1987. At the time, I didn't realize the gift of not working until their needs allowed me to spend most of my time with them. In relationship with God and through Larry's love, I have passed from the loss of their lives, through the grief, to restoration of my will to live.

These experiences led me to ask, "Lord what would you have me do?" and He replied clearly, "Be Mine". His answer surprised me—yet looking back I realize it was for this that He liberated me from my career, gave me a committed relationship and a loved heart fixed on Him alone. From this loved disposition Jesus calls me forth to risk new ministries. I visit Osteopathic Hospital once a week as Minister of Care under Sr. Marguerite's direction. I believe a seed was planted in me during the years before my parents passed away. Accompanying them in and out of the hospital, I was blessed with occasions of being there when the Minister of Care came. When my father, during his struggle with cancer said to me: "Do you know what that person told me? Tell Jesus how sick you are, tell Him you need Him." The way he said it, I knew it made a deep impact on him. We were blessed to have my dad live with us for the last four months of his life, and I was privileged to pray with him and hear his prayers. I took a small step of faith to "try out" Ministry of Care a year and a half ago. For me, healing took place during the training. In the discussions of pain, suffering and death, I was able to process my own loss better. And each visit is a blessing—sharing faith in prayers, God's timing in placing me there just before tests or operations, helping calm fears, and looking to the Lord for everything—keeps my eyes on what is important in life.

Many of you know us through the Bible study. Larry and I were involved with a "read through the Bible in 2 years" program at home when we saw the invitation in the bulletin for people to help implement the scripture study in the Parish. My response was reluctance to give up my "private" devotion, "unless", I said to the Lord—"It's the Little Rock Scripture Study." It was, and we got involved. What we received was 10 times more blessing than on our own. The shared prayer, faith stories, insight and wisdom of God's Word are still unbelievable blessings, which God poured out on us when we took the small step to get involved.

And greeting—many of you see us at the 10 o'clock mass welcoming you. We had seen Fr. Farry and others doing it. And during prayer once, I got the inspiration to "Go greet the people". With fear and trembling I did, and again it was like receiving gift after gift—faces and smiles. One man said to me on my first day "Now that's what I call serving the people of God!" I almost cried with joy.

I think if I could say what God wants me to do next for Him—it is to come out of my fear and receive the life He provides in overflowing abundance. My message to you about why I am involved in Stewardship is captured in the words of Psalm 103 that have become favorites of mine: *"He forgives all my sins, He heals me, He redeems my life from destruction, He surrounds me with loving kindness and tender mercies, He fills my life with good things." "*

LARRY'S STORY

"I was born and raised in Canada, and was educated in Catholic schools in the '50's, so my spirituality could be simplified as *"If I follow God's rules, God won't punish me."* I grew in self-righteousness, hiding my real sense of guilt and inadequacy under layers of accomplishments as physician, athlete, and church leader. Yet my driving desire to win every battle and to seek approbation made me insensitive to the cares and needs of those closest to me, and I drove them all away! Alone and despondent at the age of 33, I longed for death to take away my grief over all I had lost or could not control. In the quietness of prayer, I heard God's invitation: "Try another way—choose life without your concerns by relinquishing them to my care and giving me your permission to look after them and you. Then watch what I do!"

I obeyed as best I could. First, my God led me to the quiet as a guest in a Marianist community where I could live for 3 years while learning to listen to God's Word. There, I learned more how David felt when he cried in Psalm 51: "Have mercy on me God in your kindness. In your compassion blot out my offense." And how Job came to realize and to speak to his friends about his loss of everything—"Naked I was born and naked I will leave this life. The Lord gave and the Lord has taken away. Blessed be the name of the Lord!" Then I was led to a retreat in a monastery in New Mexico, seeking the Lord and finding another seeker—Elaine. In the first hours' blush of mystical meeting in the chapel, I led Elaine in shared surprise to the Tabernacle to offer our life's prayer: "Lord Jesus, please receive this relationship, begun while seeking you, and do with it what you will." What followed was not imagined in our wildest dreams—healing of my crippling arthritis and self-pity with the joy and delight of companionship, faith sharing, mutual spiritual counseling, shared prayer, annulments, and marriage in the church of our youth.

With all this grew imperceptibly the consciousness that God loves me so much beyond any small-minded rules of mine that I must respond in kind. "What return can we make Lord?" is the question of our love life now. Our God replied in Scripture, through the teaching authority of the church, and in a quiet inner voice, "Bring to me your first fruits of time and talent". God had given me skills as a physician, researcher and teacher, which I had used partly for God's glory and mostly for my vanity. When self-aggrandizement became empty and desolate for me, I turned again in confusion to the Lord and heard this Word of loving reply: "Thank you for all your effort. I love to succeed too, and your desire for excellence is a gift from me. But now, it is time for you to lighten up in your expectations of where you think your talents are meant to be used, so that I can show you wonders far greater than the Section of Pulmonary and Critical Care Medicine at the University of Chicago".

So I quit the part of my job that drained most of my time and pandered most to my vanity, to turn in trusting anticipation of what my

God would do with my abandonment. Among other gifts, I received a sabbatical year used early to facilitate a fruitful Lenten Prayer Program for 40 parishioners. To my surprise, this program invited me to process more fully the pains and gains of my own stages of life. So I ask again, "who is giving here, Lord? I am trying to serve you by giving over the first fruits of the time and talent you gave me, and you use my tokens to heal my heart. You multiply and return my first fruits as if it were all for me. What return can I make?"

"My people could use the first fruits of your income to get a few programs off the ground." So Elaine and I began to tithe—10% of gross income. What transpired in short order was to see the floodgates of God's creativity open in new ways. We saw our Parish's new big screen TV facilitate VCR based learning programs: "Gandhi" for the school children; teen movie night; "Healing the 8 stages of life" for the Lenten Prayer Program; "Ten Commandments" for the Bible study; Adult education film on Euthanasia and for Round Table discussions. And we also saw a renewed spirit of celebration for the Parish's growing sense of community, signaled by Fr. Farry's 50 Fest, Oktoberfest, Bible study parties and prayer program parties. Is it as clear to you as it is to us that we did not imagine in advance that increasing our financial contribution would aid education and community building through these new unplanned paths? They just crystallized around our step in trust of giving first fruits.

In conclusion, our experience of Stewardship began with noticing God's gifts and seeking to return a part in thanksgiving. This often required trust—to give God our permission to use our tokens of first fruits of time, talent and treasure for God's will. Yet God honors those who honor God (1 Sam. 2:30), so much that the more we give, the more indebted we became to God's immense generosity. We realize more today how much God loves us—sinners though we are—and our experiences with others lead us to believe that God loves each of you as uniquely and fully as God loves us. What our God needs from each of us is only our first step in trust to open the floodgates of God's love. Thank you for listening to our love stories, which are the source of our commitment to Stewardship."

This witness, together with that of our colleagues, was well received by our parishioners, and served to kick-start a successful re-financing of our church and re-peopling its activities. Meanwhile, Elaine and I went back to the Pecos Monastery where we met twelve years earlier, to learn about Spiritual Direction.

22

School for Charismatic Spiritual Directors (SCSD)

During 1989, I spent some time imagining what the next stage of my life might look like. Fully involved with community building activities in our church, I felt a call to prepare myself better to provide helpful advice to the many parishioners we encountered during programs we led in Bible Study, Lenten prayer, the ministry of greeting at church services, and Stewardship. Awareness of the SCSD happened in a moment of prayer and grew rapidly as a vehicle for the inner work and spiritual leadership techniques I sought.

This 6-week school took place in two sessions, the first a 4-week intense learning experience in the summer of 1990, followed by a year's return to the normal life before a concluding session two weeks in duration. Those enrolled in our school were 50 individuals selected for their involvement in church activities, most sharing some experience with the Catholic Charismatic Renewal. Accordingly, praying in tongues, the gifts of prophecy, teaching and healing were common among the students, who came from everywhere in the world to the Pecos Monastery in New Mexico.

THE PROGRAM AND ITS HIGHLIGHTS

The six weeks of study in SCSD were set in an idyllic environment for learning and prayer—good food, plenty of time scheduled for rest, exercise and prayer and a seasoned curriculum addressing essential topics of Spiritual Direction. Each session was about 50 minutes long, and there were 5 major themes:

Two of the highlights were an enhanced understanding of Dreams—their meaning and how to access it—and Personality Types—their description and impact on behaviors. The next section gives one example of my dream analyzed, and a précis of Personality types.

The Dream

I am at a party in my home but I don't recognize much of it. Teresa is missing. I go to look for her. After awhile, others are looking too. They send back a message of ambivalent optimism and pessimism. The house is near a river, like Pecos River, and people are looking in the river. As I search alone, I am speaking frantically.

"I just got back and I didn't even notice her. Lord help me find her that I might notice her and see what she is like before she is gone."

Back at the house there is a phone call. Another lady answers who seems to be in charge. I wrest the phone and say "Dr. Wood speaking." A man's voice says "I am sorry, she is ASINEW". I say "Oh no—do you mean she is dead."

"Sir, I said she is asinew. It is Brad, sir. We have lots of documentation with Veterans Affairs but now he has really done it. I'm sorry." I get off the phone and go to console Elaine. I say, "Teresa is gone. Our Baby is dead."

I wake up frightened, alarmed angry, confused.

PROCESSING THE DREAM

**Stage I – Personal association with people of the dream/
       Amplification.**
Stage II – General Amplification/Archetypes
Stage III – pick one character and dialogue
who are you, what do you mean, when—why in dream now

I chose Dialogue with Teresa (T)

Who? (T) I am your abandoned daughter who does not know why
      you left her. I was told you are an evil monster, so when you
      came back, I didn't know how to approach you. I was curious
      to know you, yet afraid, so I ran away across the bridge.

What does "asinew" mean? You already guessed it. I have no way
to harness my own strength to the tasks I am made to do because
the connecting sinews atrophied without work. You always do
everything so I couldn't grow, develop my potential.

How did I do everything? You never allow time for uncertainty, for
process—you seize initiative early and then follow the consequences
for right or wrong. You have no basic trust so you replace process
with action.

How can I improve, or how can I help you strengthen your sinews?
You can play with me, wasting time for no reason but our joy. Then
ask me about important decisions and don't be impatient when my
answers slow you or aren't logical. If you follow my suggestions,
I will become stronger—in time, my harnessed strength will
complement you and we will become whole.

And who is Brad? Brad is the playful mischievous bright adventurer
in you who visited Israel and New Zealand instead of working. It
means Be Radical, and he was unlikely to save me from asinew
because your shadow had me so excluded from joy and contribution

to your life that the man on the phone never expected action from Brad, despite all the information gathered that Brad might act out—He is so old now that the shadow had that information in the Dept. of Veterans Affairs!! yet Brad is dangerously reactivated now with all the instruction and work on the younger buried inner-self at the School. And time has let you change enough to set aside your books for a month at SCSD—Now that is Radical! and nice, eh. I ran away from the old you I didn't know, but Brad found me, and I have hope that the initial strengthening will continue. When you find me in play and laughter, we will both be more whole.

Stage IV – Reverence the Dream and its Meaning

My anima has become weak from lack of use while my animus acts without uncertainty to seize the action. Yet recent lessons help my adventurous side to act out and be radical by listening more, being with uncertainty, ask for advice, and increase love, play and laugher.

When I read again the dream that led to these insights and conclusions which I choose to reverence, I am surprised and amazed at the non-linear progression arising from processing the dream, and especially from the dialogue with Teresa. It turned out that not too long in the future, my job changed to Dean of Medical Education, and my job description became better served by my feminine side (Teresa/anima) using intuition, approbation, and an inquiring approach than it had been served by analytic, action-oriented independent decision making.

An example may help. In becoming the Faculty Dean for Medical Education in 1996, I negotiated for and assembled a senior staff of 10 Assistant Deans. Before we began our weekly staff meetings, we went around the conference table answering briefly the question: "What is going on this week in my non-professional life." In short order, the group developed a sense of trust and safety required to share personal concerns with work colleagues, and the community spirit spread to our work environment. I called this "Humanism in the Academic Workplace", which created a model of behaviour for the Medical Students and the Teaching Faculty whom we served.

So creating a safe environment for sharing current losses promotes hospitable interactions among the staff and this can be augmented by several adjuncts:

- take every opportunity to give attribution and affirmation for tasks well done
- forgive errors by stating openly that if there are no mistakes, you can't be working hard enough
- manage by wandering around, visiting your team in their environment where they are comfortable in offering suggestions for improvement
- cultivate empathic listening for the feelings behind the words
- support your staff without question when they make decisions in your absence
- work at providing opportunities for career progression in the job descriptions of each worker

The intent of these tactics is to promote enjoyment among the staff, which behaviour is caught by the Medical Students and their Teachers as they pass through the OME.

Of course, not all dreams require such processing and dialogue to provide instruction and direction. For example, at the time of the first dream, I was beginning to interact with colleagues at work with greater empathetic listening than before. This behaviour was helpful in synthesizing the many good ideas my colleagues voiced as we began to tackle problems in our Medical School Curriculum. The venue for this listening demeanor was in the Task Force Deliberations, in the Curricular Review Committee meetings, in the Dean's education group, and in diverse student organizations with whom I met.

So I had a second dream. I was reading a book, and several lines of the written page began to glow and lifted off the page where they had been written. I wrote them down and reread them frequently:

> "There are more productive ideas and creative contributions arising from listening carefully to smart people than you can imagine."

L.D.H. WOOD, MD PhD

PERSONALITY TYPES

One analysis of personality type which I studied is the Enneagram. This ancient and mystical tool is a circle with 9 points, each representing a human compulsion that motivates action and thought. My Enneagram type is three (3), my compulsion being to feel successful so I am prone to deceit to avoid failure indicating that I distort the truth to look good. Unredeemed, this looks like a peacock, flashing colourful tail feathers of immense proportion; but redeemed, this looks like an eagle soaring high above the action and able to pick out what is really happening with a keen eye. The antidote of deceit is integrity, and the solution to doing it all myself is teamwork and delegation.

A second analysis of personality is the Meyers-Briggs Personality Type Indicator. This divides people into Introverts (I), Extroverts (E), and subdivides these 2 types into Intuitive (N), or Sensate (S); further subdivision acknowledges that the main approach to a problem may be Thinking (T) or Feeling (F) and people's responses may be Judging (J) or Perceiving (P). Of many uses for this information, the most helpful is to gain understanding that personalities differ widely and these differences can be described as Type. My Type is INTP, indicating that I get my energy in quiet reflection (I), and tend to get drained by people. In the quiet, I tend to be Intuitive (N), rather than Sensate, meaning that my description of nature tends to be broad and non-specific rather than clearly defined.

An example—early in my career as a Clinician-Scientist, I developed a therapeutic approach to a serious disorder, the Acute Respiratory Distress Syndrome (ARDS). I expressed it as 1) Seek the lowest pulmonary vascular pressure giving an adequate cardiac output, 2) Seek the least positive end-expiratory pressure (PEEP) giving 90% saturation of an adequate circulatory hemoglobin concentration on a non-toxic inspired oxygen concentration, and 3) Seek the smallest tidal volume giving an adequate $PaCO_2$. This process-oriented description drives my Sensate colleagues nuts, for they need to know precise values, or at least a range of values, that were the target for "lowest" and "adequate". It is quite possible to argue vehemently about which is best, but in truth they are both ways to get to the same end-point. And it is easy to see why opposite Personality Types might not be compatible, but my soul mate, the love of my life, is ESFJ (Extrovert; Sensate; Feeling; Judging). Go figure.

OUTCOMES

Though I applied to the School with the hope of being more useful to our parishioners as a Spiritual Director, I was surprised to find that my enthusiasm for church activities dried up. Partly, the expressions of prayer, liturgy, and inner work I enjoyed during the School were far more Spiritually nourishing to me than were the activities in my home church. On the other hand, I was amazed at the unsolicited requests I received back home in my Hospital Office for career counseling, from Medical Students, Housestaff and junior faculty colleagues. And, when we dug a little deeper about the issues involved in career progression in Medicine, I often heard profound questions about Spiritual growth. I was prepared by SCSD to listen empathetically for the issues of the heart, so that I could provide challenge, support and vision for these searchers, who already were living a life of deep service in the healing ministry of medicine.

THE TGIF GROUP—AN OASIS, A PLACE OF REFUGE

One important outcome from SCSD brought ongoing spiritual community to our lives. Graduates of the School were strongly encouraged to gather a small group of friends who shared our approach to spirituality as a forum for shared prayer and faith sharing. Reflection on this invitation revealed that we worked extensively in our home parish with a small cohort on several parish ministries, but we had no regular opportunity to discuss how these activities were affecting our lives, especially our relationship with God and our spiritual journey. These parish ministries took a lot of time and effort, including bible study, Lenten prayer program, welcoming at weekend liturgies, stewardship, parish council, St. Vincent de Paul Society and Teen Night. Elaine and

I were leaders in most of them, so we were aware of who the other leaders were.

Shortly after returning to Chicago from Pecos in September of 1991, Elaine and I discussed over morning coffee who might join us in this new small group, and wrote nine names on the restaurant's napkin. We then extended an invitation to this group to meet in our home to discuss and develop a plan and to consider joining. All nine were pleased to attend, and quickly moved forward to a plan. A common sentiment shared by this group of leaders was feeling drained by the combination of their work and their leadership of church ministries. They were looking for an oasis—a place of refuge—where they might define and satisfy their spiritual needs. Our planning together was much aided by our having worked with each other previously to establish trust at the outset. A shared spirit also assisted us—we needed to begin with prayer for God's blessing and guidance that the group do His work in us and for His people.

All nine were in. We meet weekly on Friday evening (hence TGIF for "Thank God It's Friday"), beginning with a light meal shared from 6:30-7:00PM. The location rotated among most of the members, and the hosts rotated with the location—that is: your home = you host. A separate rotation was set up for leading the meeting, which was to proceed as follows: 1) Selected music; 2) opening prayer; 3) scripture reading from next weekend's liturgy, and reflection on it's meaning by all; 4) what is going on in your life; 5) how best can we pray for you, 6) closing prayer, dessert and coffee conversation. Adjourn before 11PM.

We began to meet in the Autumn of 1991. Now, nearly 20 years later, seven of us continue to meet, though the time and frequency of meetings were adjusted to accommodate the relocation of 4 of our 7 members. Most of us found the TGIF experience to deepen our spiritual life, first by finding out "who I am", and then we integrated our life with our spiritual journey which helped us each to grow as a whole person. TGIF allowed us to see our best self through the eyes of our companions. We also came to appreciate hearing and empathizing with the spiritual journeys of other members of the group—feeling the pain and the joy of it all.

Looking back, TGIF was good for my spiritual journey by providing a commitment to several brothers and sisters to be there for them through thick and in thin. And of course. I am so grateful to my Lord of life for providing such a caring group to share life with. I cannot emphasize enough how sharing the psychospiritual issues among adults seeking God and Her way of living was missing in our lives before TGIF, even though we participated in religious activities. To take time together to voice the uncertainties of life, and have that message heard and prayed with is edifying and confers peace.

I believe we lived the distinction between religiosity and spirituality[1]. First, we had all lived extensively according to the rules and regulations of the Catholic Church, but now longed for the spiritual feeding that comes only from enjoyed compassionate participation in discerning and meeting the needs of the community. Accordingly, shared prayer and faith-sharing were the essence of our spiritual relationships, and we defined our spirituality in broader concepts than the rules of religion. Religion encourages a set of rules, rituals and practices that carve out a separate niche for its followers, while spirituality seeks to live fully the blessings apparent as we live in gratitude and wonder. Mystery abounds in the spiritual life as we try to help one another discern God's will in our uncertainty. Where religion is interperpersonal and institutional and enjoys doctrines, values and traditions, spirituality is transcendent with emotions of awe, gratitude and forgiveness. Where religion arises from culture and binds us to our community isolated from "other", spirituality savors our own experience while also valuing that of others. Religion is cognitive, with beliefs that divide and project; spirituality is emotional, built on trust that binds us together with empathy. The authority of religion is imposed from the outside, while spirituality is democratic and emanates from within.

Stories often help. One of the TGIF members, I'll call him Jack, tells about leaving the Parish rectory early one morning but finding his path to back out of his garage blocked by a pigeon sitting on the driveway. After a few feints at backing up, Jack got out of his car to shepherd the pigeon off the driveway so he could back out and close the garage door. Later on returning home, he found the same pigeon blocking the driveway. Out he got to move the pigeon, park the car and close the garage door, when he noticed the pigeon now inside the garage! Exasperated but prayerful, Jack prayed "Lord, I can't look after all the pigeons in Hyde Park", and he recalls distinctly hearing the still small voice telling him "This pigeon is yours."

Now this story stands on its own concerning God's care for his creatures. But as soon as I heard it, Jack's story connected with one of mine, as follows. Daniel was a very competent Internal Medicine Resident who was accepted to our Fellowship Program in Pulmonary and Critical Care Medicine. Not too many months into his program, he began to show signs of a clinical depression. As his Program Director, I met with Daniel to review his medical care, which was appropriate but not effective, for he grew more despondent. One Saturday morning, he phoned me to say he was feeling lost and didn't know where to turn. Immediately, I left my golf game and drove to his sister's home to pick him up. Together, we drove with his belongings to my home, where Elaine met and welcomed him. He settled in for several weeks, growing more comfortable with time, until he was able to come back to work with me. Along the way, I could have cried out as Jack did, "Lord, I can't care for all the residents and fellows in my program." But, I didn't have to, because I knew this pigeon was mine!

How do we know these mysterious things? In my case, because I was Daniel once, and they took me in. "What return can I make?" I see the world moving in this direction—of transformation. Of being so grateful for God's help to us that we cannot help but to discern the needs of others and be their supply. This is the calling of the new world now, the cosmos, whereby every action causes a reaction, and we are called to personal transformation. This is how we live TGIF.

23

Spirituality and Healing in Medicine

In the autumn of 1996, I was approached by 3 first year Medical Students seeking instruction about Spirituality and Healing in Medicine. Their entreaty came just after I had announced and described several curriculum changes for the Winter Quarter, in my capacity as Dean for Medical Education. I invited these students to come to my office after their next class when they had a 2-hour lunch break.

Lunch in hand, they came as invited, and reviewed with me the need they perceived to be informed about how to elicit and respond to the psycho-spiritual needs of their patients. Together, we brainstormed about topics or titles which might be addressed in such a course: definitions of spirituality and healing; how to take a spiritual history; praying with patients; issues of death and dying; 12 step programs for the alcoholic and the addicted; investigating the health outcomes of prayer. All flowed easily out of our heads and into the organization of the course.

We then inquired as to whom is this course directed. Since we had no such course previously, we proposed that it start as an elective course in the Spring Quarter for Med I, II and IV students, allowing undergrads and post-doc students as they wished to enroll. Uncertain about the degree of interest among students and faculty, we drafted 2 letters describing the course: one from the organizing students to the Medical Student mailing list, and another from me to the faculty mailing list. Both letters solicited ideas for the course as well as participation at either student or teacher level. To our surprise, we received 48 responses to each letter, mostly indicating an interest in enrolling from the students and several volunteers to teach from the faculty.

Our efforts in course building were further informed and guided by an RFA (Request for Application) from NIHR (National Institute of Health Care Research), in conjunction with the John Templeton Foundation. We crafted our rationale and course description to be responsive to the RFA, and were successful in obtaining funds to support a course director, visiting professors, and materials and supplies to support the course.

By Spring Quarter 1997, we launched the first course entitled "Spirituality and Healing in Medicine". I served as the Course Director, and obtained able assistance from Kyle Nash, a Thanatologist working with the Centre for Clinical Medical Ethics and a popular teacher in the Anatomy Course for first year students. We planned 10 sessions, each lasting 3 hours on Monday afternoons beginning at 2pm, with a 15-minute refreshment break at 3:30pm. Twenty-five students enrolled, most being MedI's and MedII's (18), but 4 senior Medical Students, 2 Medical Residents and 1 undergraduate college student also enrolled.

I told you all those details to tell you this. Contrary to expectations about the secular, research-oriented University of Chicago, there was a strong interest in the Medical School about Spirituality. And a course addressing that topic came together very easily, attained outside funding, and had a substantial enrollment. What further surprised was the high level of interest and participation offered by the students; indeed, they took ownership of this elective and adjusted the course content to meet their needs.

We set the discussive-reflective tone of the course on day 1 by reviewing the syllabus and distributing a packet of selected readings for each session. Then we invited the class to reflect for 10 minutes on what they wanted to get from this course, and to share their written expectations with the class. This format lends itself to group learning if and when the Course Director listens well, and paraphrases what was last said as a question directed at another member of the class[1]. Accordingly, a good introductory statement of course goals was had, and written on the board.

Then the reflection was turned on to definition of the key concepts of the course. After another 10-minutes of reflective writing, class members offered their definitions, and through cross-talk, these were refined to the following vocabulary of concepts:

1. **Spirituality**—the experiential integration of one's life in terms of one's ultimate values and meaning; it concerns the whole person—bodiliness, relationships, social contacts, environmental setting—but often transcends these experiences by locating the person in a far larger landscape.

2. **My Spirituality**—(Each class member wrote their own. This is the definition of the Class Director)—Awareness of a relationship with a personal Higher Power characterized by Her loving acceptance and affirmation and by my experiences of awe, wonder, delight and gratitude in our communication and in my interactions with other people and all of creation.

3. **Spirituality in Medicine**—the degree to which one's attitudes and values, one's life story and its interpretations, can be profoundly enjoyed, challenged, undermined or altered by conditions of health and illness, AND the degree to which spirituality helps the suffering patient to find meaning in illness and to sustain hope.

Equipped with these definitions, our students perceived that understanding of the concepts would best be obtained by discussing specific cases where the concepts were obviously operational. One clinical situation that applied was death and dying, so we began with the topic "Withholding and Withdrawing Life Sustaining Therapy in the ICU" and then discussed several cases. The explicit challenge to the students was to determine whether the assessment and management of these patients dealt with their spiritual needs.

WITHHOLDING AND WITHDRAWING LIFE-SUSTAINING THERAPY IN THE ICU

Since up to 90% of patients who die in modern intensive units do so with the decision to withhold and withdraw life sustaining therapy, exemplary

Critical Care should include a commitment to make this transition to treatment for comfort a humane and compassionate process, conducted with the same expertise and excellence sought during treatment for cure. In our view, the physician's conclusion that the patient is dying is the starting point. Thereafter the physician's recommendation to shift treatment goals from cure to comfort is essential, so that the patient and the family have no illusions that full ICU care will produce a cure. Thirdly, understanding that comfort care is extensive and effective allows the ICU to become a safe place for grieving and dying. This is a distinctly different approach from that of many physicians who feel they have failed their dying patients by not providing cure; all too often, this fear of failure leads to abandoning dying patients without providing effective comfort care. Since death is not an option but an inevitability for all of us, Critical Care physicians can bring their expertise and understanding to help patients decide when to forego life sustaining therapy and to replace it with effective comfort care, making the ICU a safe and supporting space for the dying patient and their significant others. Note that the ministerial skills and attitudes required to implement this approach are more in the province and curriculum of social workers, psychologists and clinical pastoral associates than Critical Care physicians. To the extent that experienced intensivists find this approach helpful, teaching it to students of Critical Care becomes an important contribution to a curriculum of Critical Care.

FIRE IN THE ICU CUBICLE

It had started as pneumococcal pneumonia. The elderly Chief of the First Nations band quickly became very short of breath and cyanotic, so by the time he was admitted to the Northern outpost he required urgent intubation and mechanical ventilation. Once his vital signs had stabilized, he was transported emergently by air to our Intensive Care Unit. There, his chest x-ray showed 4-quadrant air space filling, associated with arterial oxygen saturation (SaO_2) of 78% while ventilated with 100% oxygen. Adding positive end-expiratory pressure (PEEP) of 15 cm H_2O raised SaO_2 to 90% on an FIO_2 of 70%. And there his gas exchange status remained for the next 72 hours.

During that period, family members and close acquaintances of the Chief flooded to his bedside, together with the Shaman of the band. I met with them shortly after he was stabilized on the ventilator, to hear the story of how he became ill, to explain our treatment of his acute lung injury, and to inform them of his poor prognosis. So informed, the Shaman explained to me how important it was for the Chief's recovery that ritual invocation of the Spirits be initiated early and sustained. Together with the bedside Nurse and the Charge Nurse, I negotiated the timing of this ritual with the Shaman, but we interrupted this process when the Shaman indicated his need for a bedside fire in the cubicle.

Our Nurses responded immediately that this was out of the question for several reasons, not the least of which was the very high O_2 concentrations needed for his ventilator. This constituted an explosion hazard, threatening not only the Chief and his attendants, but also the 15 other patients in our ICU. Taken aback, the Shaman again explained the importance of fire to the healing ritual. Indignant that he did not comprehend that fire in the cubicle was prohibited, the nurses quickly developed an adversarial relationship with the Shaman and the Family, which was interpreted as if we were withholding care for their loved one.

In the belief that such cultural diversity in treatment did not require a general to improve order, but a negotiator to seek a solution[2], I moved the meeting from the Chief's cubicle to a nearby conference room, where all participants could sit comfortably around a table. I convened this second meeting with an opening statement of purpose— this meeting was to maximize the diverse treatments the Chief was thought to require while causing no danger to the patient, his attendants or others in the ICU. Then I invited the Shaman to lead the meeting by explaining the ritual he thought was required.

CLASS DISCUSSION AND OUTCOME:

Careful listening revealed that the healing ritual required smoke, not fire, to accompany his invocation in the space where the Chief was being treated. By chance, this was in a corner cubicle of the unit where considerable space was contiguous to the location of the bed and ventilator where the patient received treatment.

The Shaman agreed that smoke from a smoldering charcoal briquette would suffice, so we retrieved from the chaplain such a briquette in a container. Then, outside the ICU, we asked the Shaman to observe the effects of a smoldering charcoal, and again he confirmed its adequacy. The family members still gathered in the conference room understood the Shaman's decision, and felt comforted when he initiated and completed his ritual prayer over the Chief after first explaining to him what was happening. Throughout this ritual, the charcoal smouldered in the corner of the treatment space, far from the ventilator and the oxygen source.

The outcome of the process was that the Shaman and the Family were satisfied that all was being done for the patient. It seemed to me that our nursing staff felt they had been consulted and involved in the decision-making so they were able to establish a co-operative relationship with the visiting family. And it also seemed to me that the patient was made to feel better.

In my view, this outcome was far better than what might have happened if a rigid rule were imposed. This had beneficial effects a few weeks down the treatment road when the Chief's ventilator dependence on 100% oxygen, together with his coma, renal failure and sepsis, made it likely that he was dying with multiple system organ failure. Then, another family meeting was held to discuss withholding and withdrawing life sustaining treatment.

OTHER TOPICS ON THIS COURSE

I described in some detail the discussion points of the first of 10 seminars addressing Spirituality and Healing in Medicine. Another topic of interest to the theme of this book is "The effect of prayer on healing". It turns out that several investigations were recently conducted to assess whether distant prayer influences recovery from several illnesses. The null hypothesis was "Prayer does not influence recovery from acute myocardial infarction (AMI)." A large number of patients with AMI were randomly assigned to "Prayer" or "No Prayer" groups without this knowledge. Those in the P groups recovered more quickly (decreased days of hospitalization and had fewer complications like arrhythmia, Pulmonary Edema, shock) than the NP group. Accordingly prayer helped! Of course, this study cannot say how it helped, but believers concluded that the one to whom prayer was directed was somehow helped in recovery.

This is the first, albeit indirect, "Godometer" to be used to test scientifically for God's intervention. Conceivably, other ingenious methods may make God reveal Herself, a notion which struck awe into the hearts of the students discussing these studies. As I understand their fear, it was like that of Indiana Jones at the conclusion of <u>Raiders of the Lost Arc</u> when the Arc of the Covenant was opened. Jones, tied up to a post next to Miriam, screamed at her with eyes shut "Don't look at the Arc!" while all surrounding Nazis and high priests who did look melted. Among other concerns, they raised the possibility that this may not really be an appropriately blinded study, for the patients, prayers, and physician investigators are blinded but the one who may be effecting the recovery is not.

Another approach discussed in a third session on "Near death experience (NDE)" interviewed patients who were resuscitated to enquire what they observed. A list of 15 highly scientific observations were reported by all patients with NDE, causing the author to conclude this was a real phenomenon which included a warm welcome from a bright light enshrouded Jesus–like personage. Not surprisingly this description brought a group of neurologists explaining how all these observations could be explained by sudden and reversible brain ischemia. It seems that believers have all the evidence they need to confirm God's existence in his still small voice, while skeptical scientists point out that those observations are anecdotal, non-repeatable, and non-reproducible. Of course, the latter are correct, but they also can't exclude God's existence for lack of a "Godometer". Still there exists a cadre of unknown size of appropriately skeptical scientists who are believers. Like me! For that still small voice of loving affirmation and surprising message is enough for me. I know that I know He talks to me, but I don't expect my belief to convince others. Only their own experience will do that.

24

Now It Begins!

For several years beginning about 2000, Elaine kept noticing that I dragged my right foot when we walked. About the same time, my writing was becoming smaller, especially in the Progress Notes I wrote in my patient's charts. On several occasions, it got so small that the pen stopped—froze up as it were. Reluctantly, I took these new complaints to my physician, who listened, examined and watched me walk down the long corridor in the clinic. Then we sat to review and discuss his findings.

"You don't move your right arm when you walk, you drag your right foot, you display progressive micrographia, the tone in your right arm and leg is increased, you have an intermittent tremor in your right thumb and forefinger, and the rest of your neurological examination is normal. It seems you have acquired a motion disorder, most likely Parkinson's Disease (PD). I recommend you see one of our Neurologists, have an MRI of your brain, and then we will discuss drug management and changes in life-style you might encounter."

Dazed but not surprised, I knew something was wrong. In a perverse way, having a name to the problem helped. I read about PD in my Harrison's Principles of Internal Medicine. Motor disorder—PD—tremor, increased tone, paucity of movement. It didn't say much about the associated autonomic dysfunction that was already present and got worse—constipation, sleep fragmentation, urinary urgency, erectile dysfunction, depression. All new information, and I don't think I absorbed much.

I can't remember whether I started reading _Lucky Man_[1] before or after I saw the Neurologist. Whenever, that book described his response to the diagnosis of PD and his upbeat behaviors that I wanted to emulate. The Neurologist confirmed my physician's findings, adding that the MRI of the brain was normal, typical of PD but excluding other motion disorders. "Parkinson's Disease", he said softly, "we know a lot about it, and we have effective medications"—I didn't take it in—"which help the motor disorder. You don't have much tremor, just increased tone and paucity of movement, so I think your motor disorder will respond favorably to Sinemet."

Now, I was trying to remember something, anything about my disability insurance, so I heard even less. "We will start you on a low dose of Sinemet—and save the higher doses for when you need it more. In the meantime, we will search for a dopamine agonist, and start you on Comtan. It has no direct effect on PD, but prolongs the action of whatever Sinemet you are taking."

Need it more—did he say need it more? and I brought to mind the vision of all the older patients I saw but didn't treat who shuffled down the hallways with characteristic PD gait. I wonder how fast the PD progresses. "The rate of progression varies considerably among patients", he said as if he heard my silent question, "we hope for the slower progress. Any questions about drug therapy?"

No, but regarding the life-style—what should I expect for work, golf, diet, complications? "Good questions, all", said he. "It will take awhile for you to digest all the information that is available, but we can start with these brochures"—he handed me several—"describing PD support groups and what they say about the topics. How is your work going now?" I paused to scan my work scene, then I replied "There is a lot going on. I need to reconsider it in the light of this diagnosis."

PARKINSON'S DISEASE AND MY CAREER PROGRESSION

And reconsider I did. First, I needed to recall what transpired after the 1997 LCME site visit. The School was re-accredited for 7 years, and the LCME had several concerns they wanted addressed in a Progress Report in early 2000. Glenn Steele responded with a letter I wrote with Norma Wagoner, the Dean of Students at Pritzker. Shortly thereafter, Glenn and Norma had a falling out. Glenn asked me to expand my job description to include the title and responsibilities of Dean of Students under the title Dean of Medical Education. And he made Norma a special assistant to him. Then he resigned and went to Pennsylvania.

Bryce Weir became interim Dean, and among other challenges, responded to the LCME's next request for a Progress Report by 2002. Again I crafted the reply, which LCME accepted, announcing that these concerns will be revisited on their next site visit in 2004.

By the time my diagnosis of PD was made, James Madera was the new Dean of the Biological Sciences Division and the Pritzker School of Medicine. Having interacted with him for several months, I was impressed by his careful listening and positive upbeat and affirming demeanor. Already he had asked Holly Humphrey and me to co-chair an institutional self-study for the 18 months preceding the LCME site visit in October 2004. The combination of the self-study, the multiple curriculum changes, the implementation of the Clinical Performance Centre, and the new tasks of Dean of Students (Promotions Committee, Dean's Council, Student Mistreatment issues) made my job description and work activities full. That was my answer to my Neurologist's question "How is your work going?", and it caused Elaine and me to begin a conversation about whether cutting back would help me feel better and perhaps slow the course of the PD.

An issue in this discussion was how we would live now and transition into retirement if I quit. In this regard, review of my disability insurance with my Benefits Officer revealed the good news—if my illness caused me to stop working, my disability insurance would match my salary at the time, and continue it for the 5 years until I became 65 years old. This took awhile to sink in, but as it did I began seriously to envision my life without work and then to consider the effect of my retirement on the Pritzker School of Medicine. Slowly over several weeks, it became clear that I would be less stressed if I were relieved of my Dean's responsibilities, especially that feeling of having too many balls in the air, and the worry of dropping something important. I gave equal time to the question—who could/should replace me as Dean for Medical Education. I had no doubt it should be Holly Humphrey for the continuity of Pritzker, but whether it was good for Holly needed her input.

I made an appointment with Jim Madera to resign. Caught off-guard by the topic, he listened carefully and extended his condolences for my illness. He then sought clarification of my intent, wanting to be reassured by me that if I quit and he acted on that, I would not change my mind later. So reassured, he asked me to suggest who should replace me. I told him that there was no doubt that Holly was the best anywhere—her knowledge of Pritzker and the university, her experience with the Housestaff, her intelligence and her personality placed her head and shoulders above all comers. If she did not want the position, Halina Brukner or a search for outside candidates would be appropriate. Jim thanked me, then asked me to keep my decision between him and me until he had time to ponder the consequences and talk to Holly.

In due course, Jim told me he had spoken with Holly and asked me to do the same. Holly and I had several meetings when she heard my view of the job and was able to question me on aspects I had not mentioned. It became clear that if she accepted, she would include Graduate Medical Education (GME) in the purview of the Dean of Medical Education, with an Associate Dean from our faculty responsible for GME and reporting to her. Further, Holly thought the OME was light on the infrastructure, by which she meant assistant Dean level Faculty to direct aspects of Medical Education.

Together, we wrote to the Medical Students to prevent their being surprised and to grease the skids for Holly's appointment. We then addressed several gatherings of these students to outline the plan and answer their questions. At Holly's request, I stayed on as Dean of Medical Education until September 2003 when she took over. I also agreed to complete our Institutional Self-Study and to stay through to the LCME site visit in October 2004.

In the meantime, I was completing my application for income from my Disability Insurance policy. This extensive process would provide a monthly income beginning 3 months after I was deemed eligible. The insurance company said this would be about January 1, 2004. And if I were not eligible for disability, I needed to look for another source of income.

L.D.H. Wood, MD PhD

A BEACH HOUSE IN THE MOUNTAINS

Equipped with these sources of uncertainty, Elaine and I did the adventurous thing—we traveled to Furry Creek, British Columbia—a small community of about 200 inhabitants, to look at a home and property that had caught our eye on a previous trip. With the help of a Real Estate Agent and the company of our eldest daughter, Catherine, we tried on this gorgeous home with a spectacular view of Howe Sound, sitting on a hillside overlooking the Furry Creek Golf Course. The owners had left soft music on the sound system, and two blue armchairs were placed in front of the middle level's window with the best view. After being enthralled with the elegance and convenience of the layout of the home, Elaine and I sat in the blue chairs to rest, and take in the view. I looked over at Elaine who had a tear running down her cheek, and noticed a tear running down mine. Together we could not get over the beauty of this remote exotic place, nor could we imagine not buying it to live here.

There were financial challenges. Having never owned a home, we had limited equity and a substantial down payment was required for non-Canadians to purchase in Canada. We worked at collecting diverse investments, coming up short of the requisite down payment. A call to our Financial Planner revealed a pleasant surprise—it was possible, indeed common, to borrow against our T1AA-Cref Pension for purposes of buying a home. So we signed the offer sheet dependent on the fixing of several subjects and went home to Chicago. Several days later, on the sidewalk leading to Iasha Sznajder's party, the realization descended on us like a lead balloon. Down payment or not, the principal, interest and taxes on our mortgage were substantial, and I had no income unless the disability insurance came through. For several agonizing minutes searching yet again for a way out went fruitless, so we called our agent and withdrew the offer. Disappointment all around, the party itself was heavy for us.

And then came the light of a new day, when Elaine looked at me and said with new conviction "of course the disability insurance will be approved! Then we will have a monthly income which can handle the mortgage.' I was persuaded, so disregarding the risks, we went back to the phone, requesting reinstatement of the offer, hoping the home hadn't been bought by others. Another glitch—we can't reinstate an offer withdrawn, but must make a new offer, which will take a day to draw up. We did it and waited to hear the outcome. Our offer was accepted!! We now owed more money and had less income than ever before.

On the day of the closing of the sale, Elaine and I were walking at dusk toward our bank to get a large check for the down payment. As we walked along, Elaine picked up a beautiful feather, a First Nation's sign for "you are going in the right direction". When we got to the bank to draw the cheque, we learned for the first time that the value of the US dollar had peaked that afternoon at $1.38 Canadian, so our paltry savings and our T1AA-Cref loan had become a substantial down payment, reducing our mortgage payment accordingly. And then we heard that the disability insurance was approved, providing enough income to maintain our life style and pay the mortgage.

Jumping ahead 5 years to November 2008, when my disability insurance was over, a major economic downturn cost many retirees their nest egg. We saw our retirement fund shrivel considerably, so that we were threatened often with insufficient cash flow to meet our living expenses including our mortgage. In casual conversation with the venders/builders of our home who had become good friends, they mentioned the potential value of taking equity out of our home using refinancing and a line of credit (LOC). Pursuing this possibility revealed that the value of our home had appreciated considerably since we bought it, in large part due to the improvements in the area due to the approaching 2010 Winter Olympic games. Accordingly, the refinancing gave us a helpful LOC and reduced our monthly mortgage payment. We never stop thanking the Lord for the gift of our home in Furry Creek.

RETIREMENT

So there I was in September 2003, out of my work as a Dean of Medical Education and an intensive care physician, anticipating the leisure of retirement 5 years earlier than expected, living in a new home in the remote exotic Pacific Northwest in Canada, salaried by disability income, living on a golf course of immense beauty able to play as often as I wanted. And, oh, did I say with 4 of our 5 adult children living within 25 miles of us.

Now it begins! Life as I had hoped for it was handed to me on a platter. They gave me a retirement reception, and I listened to the glowing testimonials from faculty, friends, fellows, residents and students. They gave me over 100 collated letters from individuals from each of these groups. They announced a Teaching Award in my name—the L.D.H. Wood Pre-Clinical Teaching Award—for outstanding teaching in the first and second years of Medical School. And they asked me to speak about my response to PD in my life.

What could I say but to recite my gratitude for the gifts of life bestowed, and tell them with what anticipation I looked to the future. And I ended my speech:

"Now It Begins!"

EPILOGUE

As a Critical Care physician, I was often consulted to provide advice on a wide range of very sick patients. To get to the bottom of their problems, I used science, belief and intuition to guide my research, teaching and treatment – hence the title of this book. The scientific method provided the most accessible and reliable information. Beliefs were generated in such large numbers that they were not helpful unless they were verified by intuition or the still small voice. So verified, belief becomes a spiritual source of knowing similar to the scientific method. This book talks of living the interface of science and spirituality, and how a person is encouraged to approach life to learn the truth from God to give God glory in awe and gratitude.

RETELLING THE STORY

Sometimes delving deeply into a multi-faceted story stirs the plot, so the essential issues come to the surface. Then it becomes easier to tell the story briefly. Consider this retelling of my living the interface of science and belief:

Once upon a time, a boy was born needing to prove himself worthy. As he grew up, he set his heart on things far beyond him. But with ceaseless striving, he accomplished a lot. He excelled at athletics, he married young against all advice, he graduated from Medical School, he fathered 5 children, he obtained a PhD, and he initiated a career in academic medicine. The trouble was he felt that he alone was responsible and accountable for his successes. In each endeavor, he felt overwhelmed, as if he were alone, trying to solve problems for which he had not acquired sufficient skill. Rather than feeling grateful for gifts received, he developed a whining demeanor, pleading constantly for help to overcome his perception of being overwhelmed. This made his life more difficult than it needed to be had he recognized and acknowledged that he was being looked after. He noticed however, that each time he cried out to the Lord of his life, help came quickly, often accompanied by a still small voice speaking affirmation, encouragement, support, wisdom and scripture.

For example, when he cried out that he had lost his marriage, home and access to his children, he was given a place to live in a gentle, peaceful and spiritually mature community while he grieved his losses and learned how to let go. Sufficiently stabilized, he was given a soul mate who brought the joy that heals. Together, they created a space in their wounded healing hearts to welcome each of the 5 children as they returned to relationship. As he grew accustomed to being looked after, he listened more for the still small voice, and the more he listened, the more he heard. In one sense he now lived happily ever after in their dream home on the mountains by the sea, grateful and amazed at God's answers to his prayer, abundant in providing more than he knew to ask for, pressed down and flowing over.

In another sense, the drama of life persisted in the complexity of acquiring and practicing the scholarship of discovery and teaching, and providing leadership in academic Critical Care. The tension of this drama often arose from living the interface of science and belief, where his search for understanding using the tools of science conflicted with his patiently waiting for revelation from the still small voice providing wisdom, intuition, synchronicity, insight, clairvoyance, and prophecy. In the end he came to accept there was no conflict between his science and his belief—only a need for more time to discover truth through use of the separate and distinct skills needed to get the most out of each. Science was a better method of inquiry than belief, except when the still small voice gave assent to the belief. In a sense, that voice verified the belief and so replaced the attribute of the scientific method which falsified erroneous hypotheses. This made belief a much more useful method to navigate the vagaries of life. But most of all, he learned to be grateful for his living both approaches which each separately enhanced his life, but together magnified his understanding of the other. And so he does live happily ever after, spending his days in joyful anticipation of the next good things the Lord of his life will provide in looking after him.

In writing this story I hoped to integrate the diverse events and realizations of my life so as to become more aware of what transpired. My synthesis at the end of the process looked like this, with the highlights rank-ordered as my Top 9 according to their contributions under the themes of science and spirituality:

1. A critical cross-road occurred on October 12, 1979 when Elaine came into my life, bringing the joy that heals. There was the initial blessing of being loved, accepted and sought by one so attractive to me. Then came the blessing of her commitment in life-long fidelity with the warmth of her loving heart, the delight she shared with me, providing a home and an oasis—a place of refuge for my needy soul. For completion, there were her wisdom and her grace, providing through companionship a stable place to define and address our challenges. In this regard, Elaine was instrumental in building my conversational relationship with the Lord of my life, and with my adult children, just by being herself.

2. Looking forward from the other crossroad in my life only a year earlier, my separation from my 5 children in December of 1978, I took a faith-filled step to imagine that the Lord of my life would hear our prayers and keep the children safe and healthy to mature and be fully alive. I could not have imagined how wonderfully they turned out. And now in our later years, I have the joy of interacting with them as educated adults, intelligent, articulate, interested—and they want to spend time with us! A spin-off of processing the grief of losing the upbringing of my children was the changed heart I acquired, one willing to discern the needs of people and be their supply.

3. Through these relationships I have been blessed with a conversational relationship with the Lord of my life. His still small voice has conferred an intimacy on our relationship, one so essential to my living and learning, loving and laughing, insofar as I was enabled. He walked with me

and He talked with me and He healed me as His own—patiently, kindly, gently.

4. The joy of my work abounds. Notwithstanding my chronic whining, which for me was an aggravating habit, I was blessed with teaching a lot and mostly well, to students who appreciated the learning; with researching new ideas, and having trainees who grew to their potential as the bright stars they became; with the opportunity to provide excellent and compassionate Critical Care for patients and their families who chose to tell me so; and with opportunities to build infrastructure for a wonderful group of Pulmonary and Critical Care colleagues, for an Office of Medical Education, and for a research program, each with competent and humane colleagues who joined me in appreciating their roles in building and sharing the fruits of our friendship.

5. The opportunity to retire early and live in the home of our dreams on a golf course overlooking sea and mountains with Elaine, without the need to work, and with our adult children nearby and liberated from the distractions of noise, hurry and crowds to focus on the joys of my life.

6. The excitement of travel to take in the wonders of the natural world; Europe, Israel, New Zealand, Australia, Hawai'i, Mallorca, Mexico, Uruguay and Punta del Este, Brazil and the Iguaçu Falls, Argentina, San Diego, Pecos, Banff, Lake Louise, it goes on.

7. Understanding the amazing intricacies of how some components of the human body are made, ie: actin–myosin, components of the cardiac myocite and how a fistful of myocites are enabled to contract synchronously to establish systolic ejection of a stroke volume from the heart; how factors controlling venous return control the cardiac output; the metabolic and neural control of the distribution of blood flow; how oxygen is transported to meet the varying needs of organ metabolism; the mechanics of breathing; pulmonary

gas exchange; the control of the internal environment, it also goes on.

8. The most difficult times were triggered by humiliation, abandonment and jealousy. A lifetime of psychological and spiritual counseling leaves me with confidence that I detect these triggers earlier than I used to so I can get on with the antidotes: for humiliation, work on humility; for abandonment, work on reaching out; and for jealousy, let go. Another 70 years, and I'll have them licked!

9. The process of inner work and psycho-spiritual growth was aided by consistently choosing to seek help in looking at my negative feelings, my shadow side, to learn from my mistakes and become more whole; a habit of psycho-spiritual counseling and spiritual retreats helped.

SCIENCE AND SPIRITUALITY

Two popular worldviews which lead proponents to differing ideas about reality are science and spirituality[1]. Science looks out to describe how the world works, while spirituality looks inward for meaning and purpose. Given these different goals, it is not surprising that these worldviews are different, but not necessarily antagonistic. Many of the topics for discussion between science and spirituality seem to miss the point of the other, like two parallel paths which never seem to cross. One such topic is the method of inquiry used by each. The scientific method is designed to avoid bias and preconceived ideas, because people tend to observe what they expect. So science seeks to test hypotheses about phenomena to generate evidence-based knowledge. Belief is a habit or state of mind which places trust in an idea or person without convincing evidence. Belief seems to arise from a function of the brain to cope with its surroundings by providing explanations for its observations—a story or myth. The brain is a great myth-maker, so it generates many stories for each encountered phenomena; but unlike the scientific method, it has no way to reject or falsify erroneous beliefs. Instead, belief adds to knowing when intuition or the still small voice verifies the most likely story so to create a spiritual source of knowledge akin to the scientific method.

Examining the limitations of science and belief reveals the possibility that these two methods of inquiry are complementary. When followed rigorously, the scientific method is slow and tedious because there are so many erroneous hypotheses to falsify and it provides little useful information about interior phenomena of great importance. By contrast, belief provides understanding of interior phenomena through introspection and gets help to sort and choose among too many beliefs by asking questions about the belief and hearing the answer from the still small voice or intuition. Even when the chosen belief is wrong, the process of communication builds relationship between the still small voice and the believer, so belief also serves to build relationship with God.

To the extent that science and belief are complimentary methods of inquiry, it becomes possible to imagine how they might interact in other spheres of human activity. One such which comes up often is daily navigation through the vagaries of our complex surroundings. To be effective, one must make innumerable decisions or choices among very many different courses of action. Critical thinking and testing and rejecting many possible courses of action is effective, if slow and tedious. On the other hand, imagining innumerable myths about how to behave, then picking one or more and asking God to verify our choices can save a lot of time. This complementary approach gives the decision maker more tools with which to choose, and this complex process becomes a shared endeavor by God and Her children. One outcome offering support for this explanation is the frequent response of gratitude, awe and joy when diverse challenges are faced with doubt and fear until help is requested to solve the problem. An explanation of the surprising outcome is that the still small voice or other manifestations of God's communication anticipates our needs, sorts through the excessive number of solutions, and puts the most benevolent course in our intuitive mind.

A CONVERSATION WITH GOD

To complete this Epilogue, it seems reasonable to ask the Lord of my life His opinion about science and belief. The following conversation is an example of what I mean. I initiated this inquiring conversation to hear God's thoughts about His contribution to our beliefs through intuition or conversation with us. It began at 11am on June 7, 2010.

Hi Lord,

Well, here we are again, just you and me, on a quiet Monday morning in Furry Creek. Elaine is in Chicago and will be there 2 more weeks. I am in the blue chair conversing with you as the right start to a full day. Let's talk about something Lord. Let's discuss something. On my mind is the book—a few uncertainties—I fell into this theme of science and belief in my life because I did a lot of science and I believe a lot. There is a feel about conflict between them that I don't espouse because our conversations guide me and teach me through intuition and your still small voice that feels real.

Every day, or as often as I make myself available, you, my Lord, listen and speak to me. Why me, Lord? And if me, is it really so common for the Lord of the Cosmos to be talking to the likes of me—nothing special that I can see—so why? And what is Your advice about how Your children should navigate life—science or belief?

Dear Larry,

You just won't get it, will you? It is like the Nelson Mandela prayer by Marianne Williamson[F]. You are mine. I have begotten you. Not 1 of millions—you! I have carved you in the palm of my hand. And if there is any specialness about you in all my creation, it is your openness and willingness to converse with me, believing it is true because it feels real.

How do you think that makes me feel? I set in motion evolution billions of years ago, giving it the chance to generate a listening creature to converse with. And after all this time, here you are, sitting in the blue chair, asking me good questions and listening for my reply.

Belief and spiritual experience are not subject to scientific analysis because you have no measure—no transducer which detects belief or spirituality—unless it is the soul or part of it—which is attuned to my frequency, and rings when I am near. When it rings, it feels real because it is as responded by Newberg's spiritual pathway. Likewise your conversation with me occurs on a spiritual frequency that you now know, so you can dial me up whenever you want. It works the other way too—so be ready to answer.

[F] Our deepest fear is not that we are inadequate.| Our deepest fear is that we are powerful beyond measure. It is our light, not our darkness that most frightens us. We ask ourselves "who am I to be brilliant, gorgeous, talented, fabulous? Actually, who are you not to be? You are a child of God. Your playing small does not serve you. There is nothing enlightened about shrinking so that other people won't feel insecure around you. We are all meant to shine, as children do. We were borne to make manifest the glory of God that is within us. It is not just in some of us; it's in every one. And as we let our own light shine, we unconsciously give other people permission to do the same. As we liberated from our own fear, our presence automatically liberates others." In: _A Return to Love_ by Marianne Williamson.

You come to the right place, for this is where the truth resides. And you do well to tap into it. If only my people would ASK I would tell them The Truth About anything. Yet I made them as they are—mythmaking and believing machines are good functional definitions. It would be better for God's children if they sought to believe what I tell them. Then they would be seated at the banquet of discourse learning and giving feedback to Me regarding My magnificent plan to allow evolution to develop God's children with an open line of communication to Me. It would sure save a lot of time and effort. Your story tells how a person is made to approach life to learn the truth from God and give God glory. Amen. Alleluiah.

This conversation with God affirms the role of the still small voice of God in providing verification of beliefs. This happens when a soul is equipped with God's frequency and uses this gift to listen to Her. And this works best when the listener asks questions and feels and expresses gratitude and awe. Although all human reasoning concludes that the Scientific Method is a far better method of inquiry than belief, God's participation in providing direction and support of belief more than evens the score because belief is a much more prevalent tool for navigating the vagaries of life. This is the "Godometer", that detecting instrument giving the listener faith-filled permission to hear and obey the answers to his questions. What exciting access this provides for belief to explore creation! And if there is a glitch in the believers' access or listening, this interaction builds relationship with the Lord of Life.

To my surprise and delight, I conclude that belief—supported by the still small voice—complements Science as the preferred way to guide oneself through the vagaries of life. Other forms of communication from God also support, such as intuition, critical thinking, clairvoyance and the voice of Nature. Then the Scientist in me can use whatever luxury of time saved to use the scientific method to pursue my inquisitiveness and curiosity and to explore creation as an avocation, as slow and tedious as that process is.

ABOUT THE AUTHOR

Lawrence Wood received his MD from the University of Manitoba in 1966 and his PhD from McGill University in 1974. He worked for 7 years at the University of Manitoba Department of Medicine establishing a Research Program while serving as an attending Physician in the Intensive Care Unit at the Health Sciences Centre in Winnipeg. Dr. Wood moved to the University of Chicago in 1982 as Professor of Medicine and Founding Chief of the Section of Pulmonary and Critical Care Medicine. He published 167 peer-reviewed articles addressing the link between pathophysiology and treatment of Cardiopulmonary disorders in the critically ill. He authored and edited a 2000 page textbook *The Principles of Critical Care*. For 23 consecutive years he was selected by the Graduating Medical School Class as one of their Favorite Teachers, and on four of these years was named the Outstanding Basic Science Teacher at Pritzker. Two awards in his name are available for Outstanding Teaching at Pritzker. During the last decade of his time at Chicago, he served as Dean of Medical Education, responsible and accountable for the Medical School Curriculum. He is the recipient of a National Teaching Award from the AOA Honors Medical Society and he received both a Distinguished Achievement Award from the American Thoracic Society (ATS) and a Lifetime Achievement Award from the ATS Assembly on Critical Care. Dr. Wood is retired and lives with his wife Elaine in Furry Creek, BC, Canada.

APPENDIX

REFERENCES

PREFACE

1. Newberg, A.B., Waldman, M.R. *How God Changes Your Brain: Breakthrough Findings from a Leading Neuroscientist.* Ballantyne Books, NY, 2009.
2. Hybels, D. *The Power of a Whisper.* Zondervan, Grand Rapids, MI. 2010.
3. Chopra, D., Mlodinow L. *War of The Worldviews: Science vs Spirituality.* Harmony Books, NY, 2011.
4. Newberg, A.B., *Principles of Neurotheology.* Ashgate Publishing Company, Burlington, VT, 2010.

CHAPTER 1

1. Wood, L.D.H., and A.C. Bryan. Effect of increased ambient pressure on flow-volume curve of the lung. *J. Appl. Physiol.* 27: 4-9, 1969.
2. Wood, L.D.H., and A.C. Bryan. Exercise ventilatory mechanics at increased ambient pressure. *J. Appl. Physiol.* 44: 231-237, 1978.

CHAPTER 2

1. Wood, L.D.H., Engel, L, et al. The effect of gas physical properties and flow on lower pulmonary resistance. *J. Appl. Physiol.* 41: 234-244, 1976.

2. Bake, B., Wood, L.D.H., et al. The effect of inspiratory flow rate on the regional distribution of inspired gas. *J. Appl. Physiol.* 37: 8-17, 1974.

CHAPTER 3

1. Nouwen, H. *The Wounded Healer.* Image Books/Doubleday Publishers. 1979.
2. Nouwen, H. *Reaching Out*. Doubleday Publishers, 1975.
3. VanBreeman, P. *As Bread That Is Broken.* Dimension Books, 1981.
4. Breen, P.H., P.T. Schumacker, J. Hedenstiema, J. Ali, P.D. Wagner and L.D.H. Wood. How does increased cardiac output increase shunt in pulmonary edema? *J. Appl. Physiol.* 53(5): 1273-80, 1982.
5. Breen, P.H., P.T. Schumacker, J. Sandoval, I. Mayers, L. Oppenheimer and L.D.H. Wood. Increased cardiac output increases shunt: Role of pulmonary edema and perfusion. *J. Appl. Physiol.* 59: 1313-1321, 1985.
6. Malo, J., J. Ali and L.D.H. Wood. How does positive end-expiratory pressure reduce intrapulmonary shunt in canine pulmonary edema? *J. Appl. Physiol.* 57(4): 1002-1010, 1984.

CHAPTER 5

1. Wood, L.D.H. *The Pathophysiology of Critical Illness (p1-25).* *In* Hall, J.B. Schmidt, G.A, Wood, L.D.H. eds; *Principles of Critical Care*, 1/e. McGraw-Hill, New York, NY, 1992.

CHAPTER 6

1. Popper, Karl. *The Logic of Scientific Discovery*. Routledge, 1992.
2. Fuller, S. *Kuhn vs Popper: The Struggle for the Soul of Science.* Columbia Press, 2003.
3. *Scientific Method*, Wikipedia, updated September 7, 2011.

4. Newberg, A.B., Waldman, M.R. *How God Changes Your Brain: Breakthrough Findings from a Leading Neuroscientist*. Ballantyne Books, NY, 2009.

5. Braden, G. *Deep Truth*. Hay House Incorporated, NY. 2011

6. Lipton, B.H., *The Biology of Belief: Unleashing the Power of Consciousness, Matter and Miracles*. Hay House, USA, 2008.

7. Chopra, D. and Mlodinow L. *War of The Worldviews: Science vs Spirituality*. Harmony Books, NY, 2011.

8. Manthous, C.A., P.T. Schumacker, A. Pohlman, G.A. Schmidt, J.B. Hall, R. W. Samsel, and L.D.H. Wood. Absence of supply dependence of oxygen consumption in patients with septic shock. *J Crit Care*. 8: 203-211, 1993.

9. Ronco, J.J., Fenwick, J.C., Wiggs, B.R., et al. Oxygen consumption is independent of changes in oxygen delivery by dopamine in septic patients who have normal or increased plasma lactate. *Am Rev Resp Dis*. 147: 25-31, 1993.

10. The National Heart Lung Blood Institute Acute Respiratory Distress Syndrome (ARDS) Clinical Trials Network. Comparison of two fluid management strategies in acute lung injury. *N. Engl. J. Med*: 354: 2564-2575, 2006. *(Please have a careful look at Figure 1 for an explanation of the delay discussed in Chapter 6)*

11. Prewitt, R.M., McCarthy, J.M. and Wood, L.D.H. Treatment of Acute Low Pressure Pulmonary Edema in Dogs: Relative effects of hydrostatic and oncotic pressure, nitroprusside, and positive end-expiratory pressure. *J. Clin Invest*. 67: 409-419, 1981.

12. Long, R., Breen, P.H., Mayers, I. and Wood, L.D.H. Treatment of canine aspiration pneumonitis: fluid volume reduction vs. fluid volume expansion. *J. Appl. Physiol*. 65: 1736-1744, 1988.

13. Hall, J.B. and L.D.H. Wood. Acute Hypoxemic Respiratory Failure. *Med. Grand Rounds 3*: 183-196, 1984.

14. Hall, J.B. and L.D.H. Wood. Acute Hypoxemic Respiratory Failure. In *Principles of Critical Care*. Eds J.B. Hall, G.A.

Schmidt, and L.D.H. Wood. McGraw-Hill, New York 1992: pp 1646-8.

15. Malo, J., J. Ali and L.D.H. Wood. How does positive end-expiratory pressure reduce intrapulmonary shunt in canine pulmonary edema? *J. Appl. Physiol.* 57(4): 1002-1010, 1984.

16. Corbridge, T., L.D.H. Wood, G. Crawford, M.J. Chudoba, J. Yanos, and J.I. Sznajder. Adverse effects of large tidal volumes and low peep in canine acid aspiration. *Am Rev Resp Dis,* 141:311-315, 1990.

17. ARDS Network. Ventilation with lower tidal volumes as compared with traditional tidal volumes for acute lung injury and ARDS. *N. Engl. J. Med:* 342: 1301-1308, 2000.

18. Brower, R.G., Lowken, P.N., MacIntyre, N., Manthous, C.A., et al. Higher versus lower positive end-expiratory pressures in patients with acute respiratory distress syndrome. *N. Engl. J. Med*: 351: 327-336, 2004.

19. Humphrey, H., J. Hall, J.I. Sznajder, M. Silverstein, and L.D.H. Wood. Improved survival following pulmonary capillary wedge pressure reduction in patients with ARDS. *Chest*, 97: 1176-1180, 1990.

20. Breen, P.H., P.T. Schumacker, J. Hedenstiema, J. Ali, P.D. Wagner and L.D.H. Wood. How does increased cardiac output increase shunt in pulmonary edema? *J. Appl. Physiol.* 53(5): 1273-80, 1982.

21. Breen, P.H., P.T. Schumacker, J. Sandoval, I. Mayers, L. Oppenheimer and L.D.H. Wood. Increased cardiac output increases shunt: Role of pulmonary edema and perfusion. *J. Appl. Physiol.* 59: 1313-1321, 1985.

22. Sandoval, J., G.R. Long, C. Skog, L.D.H. Wood and L. Oppenheimer. Independent influence of blood flow rate and mixed venous PO2 on shunt function. *J Appl. Physiol.* 55: 1128-1133, 1983.

23. Linn M., Linn D, Fabricant S. *A Prayer Course for Healing Life's Hurts*. Paulist Press, New York, 1974.

24. Russell A.J. ed., *God Calling.* Jove Books, 1978.

25. Russell A.J ed., *God At Eventide*. Barbour Publishing Incorporated, 1992.
26. Walsch N.D., *Conversations With God; An Uncommon Dialogue.* Penguin Putnam Inc, New York, 1995.
27. Hybels, B., *The Power of a Whisper; Hearing God, Having the Guts to Respond*. Zondervan, 2010.
28. Newberg, Andrew. *God and the Brain: The Physiology of Spiritual Experience*. Sounds True, 2007.
29. Benvenuti AC, Davenport EJL. *The New Archaic: Neurophenomenological Approaches to Religious Ways of Knowing.* In Stafford M, ed. *A Field Guide to a New Meta-Field: Bridging the Humanities-Neurosciences Divide*. University of Chicago Press, 2011.
30. Newberg, A.B., *Principles of Neurotheology*. Ashgate Publishing Company, Burlington, VT, 2010.
31. Cannato, J., *Field of Compassion: How the New Cosmology Is Transforming Spiritual Life*. Sorin Books, Notre Dame, 2010.
32. James, W., *The Varieties of Religious Experience: A Study in Human Nature* (first published in 1902). Modern Library, Random House, 2002.
33. Myss, Caroline. *Anatomy of the Spirit*. Three Rivers Press, New York, NY. 1996.
34. Campbell, J., Moyers, B. *The Power of Myth*. 2–DVD. Athena, 2010.

CHAPTER 14

1. Hall, J.B., Schmidt, G.A., Wood, L.D.H., eds; *Principles of Critical Care*, 1/e. McGraw-Hill, New York, NY, 1992.

CHAPTER 15

1. Wood, L.D.H., and A.C. Bryan. Effect of increased ambient pressure on flow-volume curve of the lung. *J. Appl. Physiol.* 27: 4-9, 1969.

2. Wood, L.D.H., and A.C. Bryan. Exercise ventilatory mechanics at increased ambient pressure. *J. Appl. Physiol.* 44: 231-237, 1978.

3. Manthous, C.A., J.B. Hall, M.A. Caputo, G. Walter, J. Klocksieben, G.A. Schmidt, and L.D.H. Wood. The effect of heliox on Pulsus Paradoxus and peak flow in non-intubated patients with severe asthma. Am J. Respir. *Crit. Care Med.* 151: 300-308, 1995.

4. Prewitt, R.M., McCarthy, J.M. and Wood, L.D.H. Treatment of Acute Low Pressure Pulmonary Edema in Dogs: Relative effects of hydrostatic and oncotic pressure, nitroprusside, and positive end-expiratory pressure. *J. Clin Invest.* 67: 409-419, 1981.

5. Long, R., Breen, P.H., Mayers, I. and Wood, L.D.H. Treatment of canine aspiration pneumonitis: fluid volume reduction vs. fluid volume expansion. *J. Appl. Physiol.* 65: 1736-1744, 1988.

6. Zucker A.R., C.J. Becker, S. Berger, J.I. Sznajder, and L.D.H. Wood. Pathophysiology and treatment of canine kerosene pulmonary Injury: The effects of plasmapheresis and positive end-expiratory pressure on canine kerosene pulmonary injury. *J. Crit. Care.* 4:184-193, 1989.

7. Wood, L.D.H., and R.M. Prewitt. Cardiovascular management in Acute Hypoxemic Respiratory Failure. *Am J. Cardiol.* 47: 963-972, 1981

8. Hall, J.B. and L.D.H. Wood. Acute Hypoxemic Respiratory Failure. *Med. Grand Rounds 3*: 183-196, 1984

9. Wood, L.D.H. and J.B. Hall, A Mechanistic Approach to provide adequate oxygenation in acute hypoxic respiratory failure. *Resp Care*: 38: 784-799, 1993.

10. Brower, R.G., et al. Higher versus lower positive end-expiratory pressures in patients with acute respiratory distress syndrome. *N. Engl. J. Med*: 351: 327-336, 2004.

11. ARDS Network. Ventilation with lower tidal volumes as compared with traditional tidal volumes for acute lung injury and ARDS. *N. Engl. J. Med:* 342: 1301-1308, 2000.

12. Weidemann H.P., et al. Comparison of two fluid management strategies in Acute Lung Injury. *N. Engl. J. Med:* 354: 2564-2575, 2006.

13. Prewitt, R.M., L. Oppenheimer, J.B. Sutherland and L.D.H. Wood. The effects of positive end-expiratory pressure on left ventricular mechanics in patients with acute hypoxemic respiratory failure. *Anesthesiology* 55: 409-415, 1981

14. Walley, K.R., C.J. Becker, R.A. Hogan, K. Teplinsky, and L.D.H. Wood. Progressive hypoxemia limits left ventricular oxygen consumption and contractility. *Cir. Res.,* 63:849-859, 1988.

15. Walley, K.R., T.H. Lewis and L.D.H. Wood. Acute respiratory acidosis depresses left ventricular contractility but increases cardiac output. *Circ. Res.* 67:628-635, 1990.

16. Teplinsky, K., M. O'Toole, M. Olman, K.R. Walley, and L.D.H. Wood. Effect of lactic acidosis on canine hemodynamics and left ventricular function. *Am. J. Physiol.* H1193-H1199, 1990.

17. Oppenheimer, L, L.D.H. Wood and R.M. Prewitt. Acute effects of nitroprusside in patients with AHRF. *Surg Forum* 32: 306-308, 1981

18. Sznajder, J.I., A.R. Zucker, L.D.H. Wood and G.R. Long. Effects of plasmapherisis and hemofiltration on acid aspiration pulmonary edema. *Am Rev Respir Dis* 134: 222-228, 1986.

19. Samsel, R.W, D.P. Nelson, W. M. Sanders, L.D.H. Wood and P.T. Schumacker. The effect of endotoxin on systemic and skeletal muscle oxygen extractions. *J. Appl. Physiol.* 85: 1377-1382, 1988.

20. Manthous, C.A., P.T. Schumacker, A. Pohlman, G.A. Schmidt, J.B. Hall, R. W. Samsel, and L.D.H. Wood. Absence of supply dependence of oxygen consumption in patients with septic shock. *J Crit Care.* 8: 203-211, 1993.

21. Prewitt, R.M. and L.D.H. Wood. The effect of positive end-expiratory pressure on ventricular function in dogs. *Am. J. Physiol.* 236: H534-H544, 1979.

22. Prewitt, R.M. and L.D.H. Wood. Effect of sodium nitroprusside on cardiovascular function and pulmonary shunt in canine oleic acid pulmonary edema. *Anesthesiology*, 55: 537-541, 1981.

23. Prewitt, R.M. and L.D.H. Wood. Effects of altered resistive load on ventricular systolic mechanics in dogs. *Anesthesiology*, 56: 195-202, 1982.

24. Mink, S., M. Ziesmann and L.D.H. Wood. Mechanisms of increased maximum expiratory flow during HeO_2 breathing in dogs. *J. Appl. Physiol.* 47(3): 490-502, 1979.

25. Mink, S.N. and L.D.H. Wood. How does HeO_2 increase maximum expiratory flow in human lungs? *J. Clin. Invest.* 66:720-729, 1980.

26. Mink, S.N., B. Light and L.D.H. Wood. The effect of pneumococcal lobar pneumonia on canine lung mechanics. *J. Appl. Physiol.* 50: 283-291, 1981.

27. Mink, S.N., B. Light, T. Cooligan and L.D.H. Wood. The effect of PEEP on gas exchange and pulmonary perfusion in canine lobar pneumonia. *J. Appl. Physiol.* 50: 517-523, 1981.

28. Light, R.B., S.N. Mink and L.D.H. Wood. The pathophysiology of gas exchange and pulmonary perfusion in pneumococcal lobar pneumonia in dogs. *J. Appl. Physiol.* 50: 524-530, 1981.

29. Light, R.B., S.N. Mink and L.D.H. Wood. The effect of unilateral PEEP on gas exchange and pulmonary perfusion in canine lobar pneumonia. *Anesthesiology*, 55: 252-255, 1981.

30. Cooligan, T.G., R.B. Light, S.N. Mink and L.D.H. Wood. Plasma volume expansion in canine pneumococcal pneumonia. *Am. Rev. Resp. Dis.* 126: 86-91, 1982.

31. Light, R.B., T. Cooligan, S.N. Mink and L.D.H. Wood. The pathophysiology of recovery in experimental lobar pneumonia. *Clin. Invest. Med.* 6: 147-151, 1983.

32. Breen, P., J. Ali and L.D.H. Wood. High frequency ventilation in lung edema: Effects on gas exchange and perfusion. *J. Appl. Physiol.* 56(1): 187-195, 1984.

33. Breen, P.H., P.T. Schumacker, J. Hedenstiema, J. Ali, P.D. Wagner and L.D.H. Wood. How does increased cardiac output increase shunt in pulmonary edema? *J. Appl. Physiol.* 53(5): 1273-80, 1982.

34. Breen, P.H., P.T. Schumacker, J. Sandoval, I. Mayers, L. Oppenheimer and L.D.H. Wood. Increased cardiac output increases shunt: Role of pulmonary edema and perfusion. *J. Appl. Physiol.* 59: 1313-1321, 1985.

35. Breen, P.H., J.I. Sznajder, P. Morrison, D. Hatch, L.D.H. Wood and D.B. Craig. Constant flow ventilation in anesthetized patients: efficacy and safety. *Anesthes. Analges.,* 65: 1161-1169, 1986.

36. Breen, P.H., L.J. Becker, P. Ruygrok, I. Mayers, G.R. Long, A. Leff and L.D.H. Wood. Canine bronchoconstriction, gas trapping, and hypoxia with methacholine. *J. Appl. Physiol.* 63(1): 262-269, 1987.

37. Mayers, I., P.H. Breen, S. Gottlieb, R. Long and L.D.H. Wood. The effects of indomethacin on edema and gas exchange in canine acid aspiration. *Respir. Physiol.* 69: 149-160, 1987.

38. Light, R.B., J. Ali, P. Breen and L.D.H. Wood. Pulmonary vascular effects of dopamine, dobutamine and isoproterenol in unilobar pulmonary edema in dogs. *J. Surg. Res.* 44: 26-35, 1988.

39. Mayers, I., R. Long, P.H. Breen and L.D.H. Wood. Artificial ventilation of a canine model of bronchopleural fistula. *Anesthesiology.* 64: 739-746, 1986.

40. Yanos, J., M.F. Keamy III, L. Leisk, J.B. Hall, K.R. Walley and L.D.H. Wood. The mechanisms of respiratory arrest in inspiratory loading and hypoxemia. *Am. Rev. Resp. Disease.* 141: 933-937, 1990.

41. Walley, K.R., L.E. Ford and L.D.H. Wood. Effects of hypoxia and hypercapnia on the force-velocity relationship

of rabbit myocardial muscle. *Circ. Res.* 69(6): 1616-1625, 1991.

42. Manthous, C., G. Schmidt, R. Kemp and L.D.H. Wood. Fulminant hepatic failure treated with anti–endotoxin antibody. *Critical Care Medicine.* 20: 1617-1619, 1992.

43. Manthous, C.A., J.B. Hall, G.A. Schmidt and L.D.H. Wood. Metered–dose inhaler versus nebulized albuteral for treatment of bronchospasm in mechanically ventilated patients. *Am. Rev. Resp. Dis.* 148: 1567-1570, 1993.

44. Manthous, C.A., J.B. Hall, D. Olson, M. Singh, W. Chatile, A. Pohlman, R. Kushner, G. Schmidt and L.D.H. Wood. Effect of cooling on oxygen consumption in febrile critically ill patients. *Am J Respir Crit Care Med.* 151: 10-14, 1995.

45. Manthous, C.A., J.B. Hall, R. Kushner, G.A. Schmidt, G. Russo and L.D.H. Wood. The effect of mechanical ventilation on oxygen consumption in critically ill patients. *Am J Respir Crit Care Med.* 151: 210-214, 1995.

46. Ali, J., W. Chernicki and L.D.H. Wood. The effect of furosemide in canine low pressure pulmonary edema. *J. Clin. Invest.* 64(5): 1494-1504, 1979.

47. Ali, J. and L.D.H. Wood. Does increased blood flow redistribute toward edematous lung units? *J. Surg. Res.* 35: 188-194, 1983.

48. Ali, J., C. Serrette and L.D.H. Wood. The effect of postoperative intermittent positive pressure breathing on lung function. *Chest.* 55:192-196, 1984.

49. Ali, J. and L.D.H. Wood. Pulmonary vascular effect of furosemide on gas exchange in pulmonary edema. *J. Appl. Physiol.* 57(1): 160-167, 1984.

50. Malo, J., J. Ali and L.D.H. Wood. How does positive end-expiratory pressure reduce intrapulmonary shunt in canine pulmonary edema? *J. Appl. Physiol.* 57(4): 1002-1010, 1984.

51. Ali, J. and L.D.H. Wood. The acute effects of intralipid on lung function. *J. Surg. Res.* 38: 599-605, 1985.

52. Ali, J. and L.D.H. Wood. Factors affecting perfusion distribution in canine oleic acid pulmonary edema. *J. Appl. Physiol.* 60(5): 1498-1503, 1986.

53. Yanos, J., L.D.H. Wood, K. Davis and M.F. Keamy III. The effects of respiratory and lactic acidosis on diaphragm function. *Am. Rev. Respir. Dis.* 147: 616-619, 1993.

54. Corbridge, T., L.D.H. Wood, G. Crawford, M.J. Chudoba, J. Yanos and J.I. Sznajder. Adverse effects of large tidal volumes and low PEEP in canine acid aspiration. *Am. Rev. Resp. Dis.* 141: 311-315, 1990.

55. Yanos, J., K. Presberg, G. Crawford, J. Melier, L.D.H. Wood and J.I. Sznajder. Effect of hypopnea in low pressure pulmonary edema. *Am. Rev. Resp. Dis.* 141: 316-320, 1990.

56. Zucker, A.R., S. Berger, L.D.H. Wood. Management of Kerosene-Induced Pulmonary Injury. *Critical Care Medicine* 14: 303-4, 1968.

57. Zucker, A.R., L.D.H. Wood, M. Curet-Scott, G.F Crawford and I. Sznajder. Partial lung bypass reduces pulmonary edema induced by kerosene aspiration in dogs. *J Crit Care.* 6: 29-35, 1991.

58. Zucker, A.R., Bruce A. Holm, G.F Crawford, K. Ridge, L.D.H. Wood and I. Sznajder. PEEP is necessary for exogenous surfactant to reduce pulmonary edema in canine aspirations pneumonitis. *J Appl. Physiol.* 73: 679-686, 1992.

59. Hall, J.B., Schmidt, G.A., Wood, L.D.H., eds; *Principles of Critical Care*, 1-3/e. McGraw-Hill, New York, NY: 1992, 1998, 2005.

CHAPTER 16

1. Hall, J.B., Schmidt, G.A., Wood, L.D.H., eds; *Principles of Critical Care*, 1-3/e. McGraw-Hill, New York, NY: 1992, 1998, 2005.

2. Hall, J.B., Schmidt, G.A., Wood, L.D.H., eds; _Principles of Critical Care: Companion Handbook_. McGraw-Hill, New York, NY: 1993, 1999.
3. Hall, J.B., Schmidt, G.A., Wood, L.D.H., eds; _Principles of Critical Care: Pre-Test Self Assessment and Review._ McGraw-Hill, New York, NY: 1991, 1998.

CHAPTER 17

1. Hall, J.B., Schmidt, G.A., Wood, L.D.H., eds; _Principles of Critical Care_, 1/e. McGraw-Hill, New York, NY, 1992.

CHAPTER 18

1. Roy, R., et al. The Structure of Liquid Water; Novel Insights from Materials Research. _Mat Res Innovat._ 4:93-124, 2005.
2. Avanti, S.K. et al. A Randomized Controlled Trial of Auricular Acupuncture for Cocaine Dependency. _Arch. Int. Med._ 150: 2306-2312, 2000.
3. Yuan, C.S., Bieber, E.J. _Textbook of Complementary and Alternative Medicine._ Parthenon Publishing, New York, NY, 2003.

CHAPTER 19

1. Hall, J.B., Schmidt, G.A., Wood, L.D.H., eds; _Principles of Critical Care_, 1/e. McGraw-Hill, New York, NY, 1992.

CHAPTER 20

1. Walsch N.D., _Conversations With God; An Uncommon Dialogue._ Penguin Putnam Inc, New York, 1995.

CHAPTER 22

1. Vaillant, G.E., _Spiritual Evolution._ Broadway Books, New York, NY, 2008. _(see Chapter 11, p 188-206)_

CHAPTER 23

1. Manning, G and Curtis, K. *The Art of Discussion Leadership.* McGraw-Hill, New York, NY, 2002.
2. Fadiman, Anna. *The Spirit Catches You and You Fall Down.* Noonday Press, New York, NY, 1992. *(see p. 261)*

CHAPTER 24

1. Fox, Michael J. *Lucky Man.* Hyperion, 2003.

EPILOGUE

1. Chopra, D. and Mlodinow L. *War of The Worldviews: Science vs Spirituality.* Harmony Books, NY, 2011.
2. Koestler, A. *The Act of Creation.* Viking Penguin Inc. New York, 1964.

RECENT BOOKS AND CDS DISCUSSING SCIENCE AND BELIEF

Anatomy of the Spirit: The Seven Stages of Power and Healing, by Carolynn Myss, PhD. Three Rivers Press, 1996.

Awe Filled Wonder: The Interface of Science and Spirituality, by Barbara Fiand, Paulist Press, NJ, 2008

Belief Works; The Art of Living Your Dream, by Ray Dodd, Hampton Roads, Charlottesville, VA, 2006

Consilience: The Unity of Knowledge, by E.O. Wilson, Village Park Press NY, 1999.

Deep Truth: Igniting the Memory of Our Origin, History, Destiny and Fate, by Gregg Braden. Hay House Incorporated, NY, 2011.

Field of Compassion: How the New Cosmology Is Transforming Spiritual Life, by Judy Cannato, Sorin Books, Notre Dame, 2010

God and the Brain: The Physiology of Spiritual Experience, by Andrew Newberg, Sounds True, 2007

God After Darwin: A Theology of Evolution, by John F. Haught, Westview Press, Boulder, CO, 2008

How God Changes Your Brain: Breakthrough Findings from a Leading Neuroscientist, by Andrew B. Newberg and Mark Robert Waldman, Ballantyne Books, NY, 2009

The Moral Landscape: How Science Can Determine Human Values, by Sam Harris, Simon & Schuster, 2010

The Power of a Whisper; Hearing God, Having the Guts to Respond, by Bill Hybels, Zondervan, 2010

Principles of Neurotheology, by Andrew B. Newberg, Ashgate Publishing Company, Burlington, VT, 2010.

Radical Amazement: Contemplative Lessons from Black Holes, Supernovas, And Other Wonders of the Universe, by Judy Cannato, Sorin Books, NotreDame, 2006

Spiritual Evolution: How We Are Wired for Faith, Hope, and Love, by George E. Vaillant, Broadway Books, New York, 2008

The Biology of Belief: Unleashing the Power of Consciousness, Matter and Miracles, by Bruce H. Lipton, Ph.D. Hay House, USA, 2008.

The Universe in a Single Atom; The Convergence of Science and Spirituality, by Dalai Lama, Morgan Road Books, Random House, 2005

The Varieties of Religious Experience: A Study in Human Nature, by William James (first published in 1902). Modern Library, Random House, 2002.

The Varieties of Scientific Experience; A Personal View of the Search for God, by Carl Sagan, Penguin Press, New York, NY, 2007.

War of The Worldviews: Science vs Spirituality, by Deepak Chopra and Leonid Mlodinow. Harmony Books, NY, 2011.